Praise for
iPad in the Enterprise

"This is a must read for those that are considering or are in the process of figuring out how to manage tablet technology and specifically iPads in their IT environments. There is something for everyone in this book, beginning with foundational topics regarding mobile devices, the application store, consumerization of IT, and building a mobile device strategy."

— Robin Bell
Chief Technology Officer
Long View Systems

"Nathan Clevenger gets it. The consumer technology revolution is sweeping through the enterprise and becoming adopted faster than any change before it. Read this book, or risk getting left behind."

— Marc Benioff
Chairman and Chief Executive Officer, salesforce.com
Best-selling author of Behind the Cloud

"A great resource for those struggling to come to terms with why this time it's 'different.' Clevenger first explores and explains the iOS-led trends affecting enterprise IT and then lays out a coherent road map to guide sane investment while always keeping a weather eye on the realities of restricted budgets and capacity."

— Dan Bennett
Senior Director, Technology
Thomson Reuters

"Nathan has done an excellent job of not only defining the impacts and opportunities of this disruptive technology, but also providing the in-depth details on how best to embrace and leverage it."

— Steven Birgfeld
Chief Information Officer
Hostess Brands

iPad® in the Enterprise

iPad® in the Enterprise

Developing and Deploying Business Applications

Nathan Clevenger

Wiley Publishing, Inc.

iPad® in the Enterprise: Developing and Deploying Business Applications

Published by
Wiley Publishing, Inc.
10475 Crosspoint Boulevard
Indianapolis, IN 46256
www.wiley.com

Copyright © 2011 by Wiley Publishing, Inc., Indianapolis, Indiana

Published simultaneously in Canada

ISBN: 978-1-118-02235-1
ISBN: 978-1-118-14745-0 (ebk)
ISBN: 978-1-118-14747-4 (ebk)
ISBN: 978-1-118-14746-7 (ebk)

Manufactured in the United States of America

10 9 8 7 6 5 4 3 2 1

For general information on our other products and services please contact our Customer Care Department within the United States at (877) 762-2974, outside the United States at (317) 572-3993 or fax (317) 572-4002.

Wiley also publishes its books in a variety of electronic formats. Some content that appears in print may not be available in electronic books.

Library of Congress Control Number: 20119330284

To my wife, Francine.
Thank you for your love and support through the
long nights and weekends as I wrote this book.

About the Author

 **Nathan Clevenger** has been developing mobile software for over 12 years. In addition to his role as enterprise editor for *iPhone Life* magazine, he is the chief software architect at ITR Mobility, a management and IT consulting firm, where he works with FORTUNE 500 companies to develop mobile strategies and enterprise architectures for mobile line-of-business solutions. He has consulted with clients including 3M, Ameriprise Financial, Best Buy, Boston Scientific, Ecolab, General Mills, Medtronic, St. Jude Medical, Target, Thomson Reuters, UnitedHealth Group, and Wells Fargo. He regularly speaks at industry events around the country, and is extremely passionate about the unrealized potential for mobile technology like the iPad within the enterprise.

Nathan lives in Minneapolis with his wife, Francine, and kids, Jonathan, Justin, with another on the way.

Nathan can be reached at nc@nathanclevenger.com.

About the Technical Editors

Scott Olson has spent the past 18 years building software and advising clients on the potential of software and mobility. He's an active blogger, and a contributing writer for *iPhone Life* magazine. Throughout his career he has worked with many Fortune 500 companies. He lives in Hudson, Wisconsin, with his wife, Michelle, and their three children, Samantha, Trevor, and Soren.

Peter Ericksen has designed and developed enterprise systems in the education, communications, and health-care industries for over 16 years. When not developing mobile systems for Fortune 500 firms, he is a contributing writer for *iPhone Life* magazine and a consulting iOS game developer. He lives in Saint Paul, Minnesota, with his wife and two children.

Credits

Acquisitions Editor
Mary James

Project Editor
William Bridges

Technical Editors
Peter Ericksen, Scott Olson

Production Editor
Rebecca Anderson

Copy Editor
Lisa Sheridan

Editorial Director
Robyn B. Siesky

Editorial Manager
Mary Beth Wakefield

Freelancer Editorial Manager
Rosemarie Graham

Associate Director of Marketing
David Mayhew

Production Manager
Tim Tate

**Vice President and Executive
Group Publisher**
Richard Swadley

**Vice President and Executive
Publisher**
Barry Pruett

Associate Publisher
Jim Minatel

Project Coordinator, Cover
Katie Crocker

Proofreader
Louise Watson, Word One
New York

Indexer
Robert Swanson

Cover Designer
Ryan Sneed

Cover Image
Wiley Inhouse Design

Acknowledgments

I want to thank everyone who gave me access to their precious time and words of wisdom throughout the writing of this book:

Chris Anderson, the editor-in-chief of *Wired* and author of *The Long Tail*; Kate Bass, CIO, Valspar; Sanju Bansal, chief operating officer, MicroStrategy; Marc Benioff, chairman and CEO, salesforce.com; Dan Bennett, senior director, technology, Thomson Reuters; Allen Benson, VP business technology, Spectrum Brands; Steven Birgfeld, CIO, Hostess Brands; Mike Blake, CIO, Hyatt Hotels; Lisa Caplan, VP and business information officer, Kaiser Permanente; Brian Carlson, editor-in-chief, *CIO.com*; Mike Cohn, author of *Succeeding with Agile*; Josh Clark, author of *Tapworthy*; Raul Cruz, CIO, AECOM; Miguel de Icaza, CTO, Xamarin; John Dix, editor-in-chief, *Network World*; Ken Dulaney, VP and distinguished analyst, Gartner; Louie Ehrlich, CIO, Chevron; Scott Ellison, VP mobile and consumer-connected platforms, IDC; Rick Fabrizio, CIO, AmeriGas; Alan Farnsworth, CIO, Bausch & Lomb; Eileen Feretic, editor-in-chief, *Baseline* magazine; Dr. Donald F. Ferguson, CTO, Computer Associates; Scot Finnie, editor-in-chief, *Computerworld*; Bud Flagstad, VP strategic initiatives, UnitedHealth Group; Art Glasgow, CIO, Ingenix; Suzanne Ginsberg, author of *Designing the iPhone User Experience*; Hal Goldstein, editor-in-chief, *iPhone Life* magazine; Vishy Gopalakrishnan, author of *Work Goes Mobile* and director at AT&T Mobility; Michael Hedges, CIO, Medtronic; David Hemendinger, VP and chief technology officer, Lifespan; Vishal Jain, analyst, Mobile Services, The 451 Group; Art Kleiner, editor-in-chief of *strategy+business*; Bill Martin, CIO, Royal Caribbean Cruises; Craig J. Mathias, principal, Farpoint Group; David McCue, VP and CIO, CSC; Paul Melchiorre, global VP, Ariba; Frank Modruson, CIO, Accenture; Geoffrey Moore, author of *Crossing the Chasm*; Eric Openshaw, VP, Deloitte; Daniel Pink, author of *A Whole New Mind* and *Drive*; Jim Prevo, CIO, Green Mountain Coffee Roasters;

Joseph Puglisi, CIO, EMCOR; Scott Robertson, VP of technology, Transcend Services; Al Sacco, mobile and wireless editor, *CIO* magazine; Kevin Shearer, CIO, Weyerhaeuser Company; Clay Shirky, author of *Here Comes Everybody* and *Cognitive Surplus*; Frank Slootman, executive chairman, BRS Division, EMC; Joseph Spagnoletti, CIO, Campbell Soup; Robert Stephens, founder of the Geek Squad and CTO, Best Buy; Patric Thomas, corporate VP and CIO, Scripps Health Information Services; Rich Williams, VP and CIO, AstraZeneca; Philippe Winthrop, managing director, Enterprise Mobility Foundation.

I also want to give a big thank you to everyone on the mStar team at Medtronic and the Mobile Forward team at Target for all the great mobile strategy and architecture discussions and debates (and yes, even those that occasionally stretched into the late hours of the evening).

For all your help with graphics and design, thank you very much to Brian Porter. And for all those long hours working through code samples, Kenny Goers, I'm very appreciative.

I also need to give a very big thank you to my technical editors, Scott Olson and Peter Ericksen. I know you both put a lot of time in above and beyond, and I'm very grateful for all your efforts.

I must also give my father, Doug Clevenger, kudos for pushing me to make this book much better than it would have been otherwise. Thanks again, Dad, for challenging me and my writing — the book is what it is because of it.

Last, but certainly not least, I want to give a huge thank you to my wife, Francine, and sons Jonathan and Justin for putting up with all my late nights, early mornings, and long weekends through the writing of this book.

Contents at a Glance

Continued

Contents

Introduction

The iPad has revolutionized the mobile computing landscape, and the impact that this device is having on corporate IT is no less significant. The mobile revolution is all about the apps, but using iPad apps in the enterprise is more complex than simply clicking an icon from the App Store. The challenges around software development, system integration, information security, application deployment, and device management are very real, but the rewards can be significant to the organizations that are able to successfully navigate those obstacles.

Having taken the enterprise by storm, iPads are now in the hands of workers on virtually every level of company in almost every industry, and users are beginning to demand line-of-business applications to help them be more productive and efficient from wherever they are. From business intelligence and executive dashboards to customer relationship management and order capture solutions, the iPad has incredible potential to leverage existing investments in information systems and enterprise applications. Even many paper-driven processes today, from sales presentations to survey data capture, can be dramatically enhanced through the introduction of the iPad.

This book is a guide for how business and IT must collaborate to develop a mobile strategy to properly take advantage of this transformative technology. Readers will also learn about the high-level software architectural options, the importance of design and user experience, application development tools and techniques, and best practices for deploying and managing iPads in the enterprise.

While dozens of books cover iPad app development, most have focused on consumer application development, and there was nothing that covered the unique needs and special considerations for developing applications within an enterprise environment.

How This Book Is Structured

This book is broken into five parts: Strategy, Architecture, Design, Development, and Deployment. Each of these parts was written to more or less stand on its own, so feel free to skip around and read the parts of the book that are most applicable to you and your situation.

Part 1 on Strategy covers the landscape of mobility, approaches to embracing the consumerization of IT, and how to develop an enterprise mobility strategy and application road map.

Part 2 on Architecture discusses the multiple dimensions of mobile application architecture, and how to select the best architecture for any given application, including thin-client vs. web vs. native vs. hybrid, as well as platform-specific vs. cross-platform approaches.

Part 3 on Design focuses on the creative and artistic aspects of iPad application development, which, as it turns out, is actually quite important to creating successful mobile apps.

Part 4 on Development provides an introduction to mobile development approaches and techniques for several architectures, raises common security issues, demonstrates best practices, and shows sample code for both client-side app and server-side web service development.

Finally, Part 5 on Deployment describes how iPad deployments can vary significantly from traditional kinds of technology deployments, and describes best practices for security, provisioning, configuration, app deployment, and device management.

Whom This Book Is For

This book is for anyone involved in iPads within the enterprise, including those in IT and business leadership, enterprise architecture, and application development, as well as infrastructure, security, and support.

If you are an IT executive (CIO, CTO, VP of IT, VP/Director of Application Development), Part 1 on Strategy is for you, and you may also find Part 2 on Architecture and Part 5 on Deployment applicable to your situation.

Additionally, if you are a non-IT business executive and would like to learn how your organization could benefit from deploying iPad applications to your workforce, Part 1 on Strategy will be interesting to you.

If you are involved in enterprise architecture, it is likely that you will find all five parts of the book applicable to your needs.

If you are an application developer, you may be interested in Part 1 on Strategy, but if not, feel free to skip directly to Part 2 on Architecture, Part 3 on Design, and Part 4 on Development.

If you have infrastructure-related responsibilities, Part 5 on Deployment is for you, but you may also find Part 1 on Strategy and Part 2 on Architecture valuable.

If you are a business analyst, Part 1 on Strategy and Part 3 on Design are likely the most applicable for you.

Otherwise, if you are an executive or developer at an enterprise software company, you will find value throughout this book in understanding how to develop iPad versions of your company's software, or companions to this software, and provide solutions to your customers.

Conventions

To help you get the most from the text and keep track of what's happening, we've used a number of conventions throughout the book.

WARNING   **Boxes with a warning icon like this one hold important, not-to-be-forgotten information that is directly relevant to the surrounding text.**

NOTE   **The pencil icon indicates notes, tips, hints, tricks, or asides to the current discussion.**

As for styles in the text:

- We *highlight* new terms and important words when we introduce them.
- We show filenames, URLs, and code within the text like so: `persistence.properties`.
- Illustrative code is presented as follows:

```
We use a monofont type for most code examples.
```

iPad® in the Enterprise

Part

I

Strategy

In This Part

Understanding the Mobile Industry Landscape

The iPad is transforming the way businesses use technology. More than just a consumer phenomenon, the iPad is disrupting business models and power structures within corporate information technology (IT) departments. Within 90 days of being released, the device was already adopted by 50 percent of Fortune 100 companies. This unprecedented rate of market penetration represents a fundamental shift in the way technology enters the enterprise.

IT departments have traditionally had complete control over the selection and management of technology, but that iron-clad grip is being threatened. Corporate employees, who are consumers themselves, are bringing their own personal devices into the workplace. While many IT departments have moved quickly to ban this, such a ban is very difficult to enforce, especially when executive leaders are among the offenders. Even when it can be enforced, the ban puts significant pressure on IT departments to support the popularized consumer technologies demanded by the employee base.

Many industry leaders have begun to recognize that it can be in the company's best interest to support this trend instead of fighting it. Gartner, Inc., the market-moving analyst and technology advisory firm, issued an advisory recommending that businesses embrace the iPad. Gartner went so far as to say that, because the iPad is such a disruptive technology, there will be significant obstacles to its adoption, and that top executive management should get involved to clear barriers to the iPad within the enterprise.

"It is not usually the role of the CEO to get directly involved in specific technology device decisions, but Apple's iPad is an exception," said Stephen Prentice, Gartner Fellow and vice president. "It is more than just the latest consumer gadget, and CEOs and business leaders should initiate a dialogue with their CIOs about it if they have not already done so."

Disruptive technologies can be both powerful and dangerous to companies that employ them, and the iPad is no exception. But according to Prentice, "Even if you think it is just a passing fad, the cost of early action is low, while the price of delay may well be extremely high."

Apple as the Catalyst

To fully understand the potential for the iPad in the enterprise, it is important to take a step back and look at the big picture. The iPad's explosive growth is not set in a vacuum. Multiple factors and trends have contributed to create the current environment.

Smartphones were around for years before Apple released the iPhone, and tablet-based computers were on the market for more than a decade before the launch of the iPad. Although Apple did not invent these technologies, it simplified the user experience and brought these technologies to the mainstream consumer with mass appeal.

When Apple launched the iPhone in June of 2007, it sparked unprecedented sales of smartphones. Building on Apple's momentum with the iPod, the iPhone had instant appeal to a large user base, whose members carried both their cell phones and iPods and could now replace both devices with a single piece of hardware.

Exchange ActiveSync Standardization

The first generation iPhone was undoubtedly a consumer phenomenon, but it was not at all enterprise-friendly. IT organizations were quick to announce policies specifically stating that iPhones were not supported devices and were not allowed to access corporate networks or data. Many users were not happy, but there wasn't really anything they could do, since the iPhone really wasn't ready for the enterprise.

With the launch of iPhone OS 2.0 in June 2008, Apple made a subtle yet brilliantly strategic move that shifted the power within the industry. And by early 2008, Microsoft's Windows Mobile platform was just beginning to gather momentum in taking significant market share from the Research in Motion (RIM) BlackBerry. While RIM was selling the BlackBerry Enterprise Server (BES), Microsoft had decided to compete by integrating push e-mail as well as calendar and contact sync into Exchange Server 2003. BES is a server-based product that provides BlackBerry smartphones with wireless mobile access to messaging servers like Microsoft Exchange or IBM Lotus Notes. When Microsoft decided to build mobile synchronization capability directly into Exchange Server with the Exchange ActiveSync, it eliminated the need for a separate server product like RIM's BES. This created an opportunity for Apple to come into the enterprise through the back door by licensing Exchange ActiveSync from Microsoft and allowed iPhones and iPod touches using the iPhone OS 2.0 to connect to corporate networks and access business information.

All of a sudden, personally owned iPhones were coming into the enterprise through the same Microsoft Exchange ActiveSync infrastructure that the IT department had set up to support corporate-owned deployments of Windows Mobile devices. Even though Microsoft Exchange allowed for the ability to block iPhones from connecting, many organizations did not take advantage of this feature. Since the iPhone enforced most of the basic security and device management policies offered by Exchange ActiveSync, organizations could, for instance, require that users configure a power-on passcode for their devices, as well as remotely wipe their iPhones if these were lost or stolen.

In order to provide enterprise-friendly support for the iPhone, Google licensed Exchange ActiveSync for its cloud-based Google Apps. Even IBM licensed Exchange ActiveSync from Microsoft so that Lotus Notes could support the iPhone. The product, released in late 2009, was called Lotus Notes Traveler. Up to that point, the only way for organizations with Lotus Notes to get mobile e-mail was through the BlackBerry Enterprise Server, which could sit on top of either Microsoft Exchange or Lotus Notes.

Except for RIM's BlackBerry, the major mobile platforms were also standardizing on Exchange ActiveSync. In addition to Microsoft's mobile platforms and the iPhone, Palm/HP Web OS, Android, and even Nokia smartphones could now access enterprise e-mail, contacts, and calendar on almost any messaging environment: Microsoft Exchange, Lotus Notes, or Google Apps. Virtually overnight, RIM went from being the dominant messaging platform to a proprietary solution struggling to stay relevant.

iPhone OS 3.0 arrived in June 2009 with additional security and device management Exchange ActiveSync policies. The iPhone 3GS also brought hardware-based data encryption to the platform along with the ability to enforce the rule that only hardware-encryption-capable iPhone devices were allowed to connect. These events contributed to setting the stage for the iPad's success.

Tablets Go Mainstream

When the rumors of an Apple tablet finally turned out to be true, the product turned out to be more successful than almost anyone had expected. Apple's CEO, Steve Jobs, unveiled the iPad on Jan. 27, 2010, as a "magical and revolutionary device at an unbelievable price." Many pundits predicted that it would be a niche device like so many of the tablets that came before it.

Nearly a decade earlier in 2001, Bill Gates, the founder of Microsoft, unveiled the Windows-based Tablet PC. He made some very strong predictions, saying, "It's a PC that is virtually without limits and within five years I predict it will be the most popular form of PC sold in America." Five years later, in 2006, the Tablet PC had achieved only 1.2 percent of the PC market. Bill Gates saw the opportunity, but Microsoft was unable to take the tablet mainstream.

Apple launched the iPad on April 3, 2010, and sold 300,000 devices on the first day. Sales grew quickly with one million units sold in the first month, and three million by June 22, 2010. In the first full quarter of selling the iPad, Apple shipped 4.19 million devices, bringing the total to 7.5 million in less than six months. By the end of 2010, nearly 15 million iPads had been sold, capturing more than 95 percent of the tablet market. If sales of the iPad are included as part of the entire Mobile PC market, the iPad has claimed more than 10 percent market share in less than a year.

Consumers loved the iPad and embraced it with open arms. In September 2010, CNBC reported that the iPad scored higher on the American Consumer Satisfaction Index than any product had ever scored before on that leading index, which is affiliated with the University of Michigan. By the time Oprah Winfrey anointed the iPad to be her "No 1. favorite thing ever," the device had truly captured the hearts and minds of the mainstream consumer. "From our very first moment together, I knew it had stolen my heart," the television personality proclaimed to her audience. "Words cannot describe what I feel for this magnificent, magnificent device," Winfrey said, holding an iPad in her hand. "I really think it's the best invention of the century so far."

Apple unified the iOS line of devices in late 2010 with iOS 4.2, which supported the iPad in addition to the iPhone and iPod touch. The update brought significant enterprise-friendly improvements like mobile device management (MDM) and over-the-air (OTA) deployments of in-house apps. As multiple third-party MDM vendors scrambled to support the iPad, adoption of the iPad into the enterprise accelerated through the end of 2010 and into 2011. By the end of the first year on the market, the tablet had not only achieved mainstream acceptance by consumers, it was reaching mass acceptance with businesses as well.

Consumer Choice

Just as Apple was bringing the iPhone up to par for enterprise use, the ingredients were swirling to create the perfect storm that would change the mobile and wireless landscape forever. The global economic downturn of 2008 put pressure on corporate spending and left companies looking for ways to cut spending any way possible. As many employees with corporate-owned mobile devices started buying their own personal iPhones out of their own pockets, companies realized that they could reduce their wireless spending while simultaneously increasing worker satisfaction. It turns out that lots of employees are more than willing to cover all or part of their own wireless expenses if they can carry the phones they want. As the IRS decided to start cracking down on personal use of corporate mobile phones, it only put more fuel on the flames. The result was a fairly dramatic and rapid shift within the industry from corporate-liable to individual-liable wireless plans, a shift illustrated in Figure 1-1.

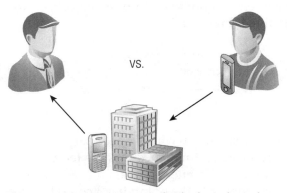

Figure 1-1: Corporate vs. individual wireless plans

By June of 2010, the iPhone had achieved 80 percent adoption within the Fortune 100. At first glance this might sound quite impressive, considering the traditional purchasing cycle within the enterprise, but it's important to understand that most of these enterprises were not purchasing the devices for the users. They were giving their users the option of using an iPhone.

Genentech is an example of a forward-thinking organization that was quick to embrace consumer choice. The San Francisco-based biotech firm, now part of the Roche Group, previously had more than 5,000 BlackBerry devices. Even though most Genentech users loved their BlackBerrys, as the company began letting users choose the phones they wanted, these users switched en masse to the iPhone. By late 2009, Genentech had more than 5,000 employees using iPhones and only 1,500 with BlackBerrys.

While the iPhone was brought into the enterprise mostly by individual users, the iPad is taking a different path. The first few devices brought into the enterprise environment in many cases were personally owned devices, but companies very quickly saw the benefits of the iPad and began purchasing the devices in bulk.

For example, the medical device industry has demonstrated widespread corporate adoption and deployment. By the end of 2010, less than nine months after the release of the iPad, Medtronic had deployed 4,500 iPads, Boston Scientific had rolled out 2,000, and St. Jude Medical, Abbott Labs, Zimmer Holdings, and Stryker had all rolled out units as well. Within many of these same companies, mobile phones were transitioning to individual-liable deployment models and away from the centralized corporate-liable deployments of years past.

This seems to represent a very interesting trend in consumerization, where even corporate-driven centralized deployments seem to be migrating to consumer-oriented technologies. In the context of the history of the computing industry, this appears to be a reversal of a trend in which technological innovations were driven by the government, then moved into the private sector, and finally were brought to consumers (Figure 1-2).

Figure 1-2: The old trend in innovation

This trend developed when the only organization with the necessary resources to finance development of new computing technologies was the federal government. Once the heavy research and development costs had been covered, the cost of the technology would come down to the point that it could be used by private sector businesses. Over time, the costs would continue to fall until eventually the technology would even hit a price point that would make it acceptable to consumers.

Through the internet and personal computing revolutions, not to mention the ongoing march of Moore's law (simply stated, computing power will double every 18 months), the historical trend of technology going from government to the private sector and then to the consumer has been flipped on its head. In many ways today, the consumer has the most advanced technology, which is then working its way into the business world and then finally the government.

Figure 1-3: The new trend in innovation

Not only is the consumer technology itself (like the iPhone or iPad) making its way from the consumer's hands into the corporation, but the consumer's desires are now able to impact purchasing decisions within the enterprise. This trend is only beginning to emerge, and it's unknown how far it will go. One thing is clear though: today's enterprise employee is also a consumer, and those users will continue to have significant influence over the technology decisions of their corporations.

It's All About the Apps

It's easy to forget that when Apple first launched the iPhone there was no App Store, no iPhone SDK, and no developer ecosystem. People thought their phones were great for making voice calls, checking their e-mail, and maybe even browsing the Web. The average user had no idea that the phones could run a blizzard of "apps" (Figure 1-4).

Figure 1-4: The proliferation of "apps."

Even though the first generation iPhone did not support native apps, when Apple did introduce the iPhone SDK and the App Store it really was nothing new. Windows Mobile had what many viewed at the time to be a thriving developer ecosystem with more than 20,000 mobile applications available. What Apple did with the App Store, though, was simplify the user experience. It made the act of installing an app onto your phone into a clean and straightforward process. Then it ran primetime TV commercials about all the apps available in the App Store and how easy it was to install them on your device. Apple took a geeky, complicated process of installing software onto your mobile phone and transformed it into an incredibly simple experience.

Apple was able to build the App Store on top of its already successful iTunes platform, and as a result it already had nearly 100 million credit card numbers on file. As an owner of an iPhone or iPod touch, you didn't have to give Apple a credit card number for its file, but you couldn't download free apps until you did. The result was a thriving ecosystem built around the impulse purchase.

The vast majority of downloads from the App Store are of free apps, but this hasn't prevented the gold rush in which tens of thousands of developers quickly developed apps for just about anything. The App Store launched with just 500 apps, but quickly grew to 5,000, then 25,000, then 100,000. It will likely hit the half-million mark in mid-2011.

First with the iPhone

There's an app for that. And that. And that, too.

As the App Store exploded with growth, the average consumer discovered there was an app for almost anything. As Apple's TV commercials stated, whether you "want to read a restaurant review, read an MRI, or just read a regular old book" there was an app for anything. Want to play a game? Recognize a song on the radio? Pay your bills? Order a pizza? Start your car? Unlock your front door? iPhone users quickly realized that there really was an app for almost anything they could imagine.

The auto insurance industry provides an excellent case study for how Fortune 1000 organizations first began to embrace consumer-facing mobile applications. In April 2009, Nationwide Insurance launched Nationwide Mobile in the iPhone App Store. The app provided Nationwide's customers with an "Accident Toolkit." In addition to calling emergency services, the app could file an accident report that used GPS to pinpoint the user's exact location and captured pictures of the damage with the camera. It even provided a flashlight feature. The company then ran an extensive primetime TV advertising campaign that showcased the iPhone app. In addition to providing a great marketing message, the app offered a huge value proposition to customers by replacing manual labor-intensive processes with self-service functionality that they could use right from their phones.

By December 2009, Geico Insurance had launched its own Geico GloveBox app in the App Store, and shortly thereafter began featuring the app in television commercials along with its trademark cavemen.

By the spring of 2010, almost all the major auto insurance companies, including Allstate, American Family, esurance, Farmers Insurance, Progressive, and State Farm, had all released iPhone apps. State Farm continued in the tradition of running primetime TV commercials to announce its iPhone app. Nationwide took this trend to the next level, and ran a second television campaign around another iPhone app it developed called Cartopia. This app not only was marketed to existing Nationwide customers, but was also designed as a lead-generation engine where users could comparison car shop and even run free vehicle identification number (VIN) checks on used vehicles. The app could then instantly provide auto insurance quotes to car shoppers on the go, who already had taken the time to enter the vehicle information into the app.

Take a moment to imagine that you work for one of these auto insurance companies as a claims adjuster. How would you feel about the fact that your employer is giving better technology to consumers than to you, the employee? How would it make you feel that, in the time it takes to boot up your company-provided laptop, you could pull an iPhone out of your pocket, install an app from the App Store, log in, start a claim, capture GPS coordinates to get your precise location, and take several pictures of the damage with the built-in camera?

For another example, let's look to the retail industry. Most major brick-and-mortar retailers, like Barnes & Noble, Best Buy, Home Depot, Macy's, Target, Toys "R" Us, and Walmart, have consumer-facing apps. Several of these apps, including those from Best Buy and Target, have the ability to use the camera in the iPhone to scan a barcode on a physical product and pull up additional information about the product, including detailed technical specs and product reviews.

Now take a moment to imagine that you work on the sales floor of a retail store. How would you feel if a customer came up to you to ask a question but already had more detailed information about the product on his or her own mobile phone than you have access to on the rugged handheld scanner provided to employees by the store?

These thought exercises are not just imagined scenarios; rather, they are real-life situations faced by thousands of corporate employees every day. As a consumer, you have grown to expect an app for everything, and to expect that all your favorite brands will provide you with apps to complete your consumer-oriented branded experience. But as an employee, you can't access the same information from your phone that you can from your desktop or laptop. Sure, your IT department now finally allows you to synchronize your mail, calendar, and contacts with your phone, but why do you still have to boot up your computer when you want to run some reports? Why do you have to be at your desk to "approve" workflow requests? Why can't you run the apps you need to do your job from wherever you're doing your job? Why can't you access the information you need, when you need it, where you need it?

As a result, it's not a matter of whether enterprises are going to embrace employee-facing iPhone apps, it's a matter of when. In the same way that consumerization trends brought support for mobile platforms into the workplace, enterprises must also recognize the demand and even outright expectations of employees to have apps for business purposes. The release of iOS 4.0 with the over-the-air deployment capabilities of in-house enterprise apps has accelerated the rate of adoption within many enterprise IT departments.

By the end of 2009, Genentech had developed over 30 in-house apps for the iPhone and had deployed its own Genentech App Store for employee use. An example of these apps is shown in Figure 1-5. In an interview, Todd Pierce, Genentech's CIO, said, "I spent $10 million making my purchasing system usable on SAP. I spent $10,000 making it usable on my iPhone. You do the math."

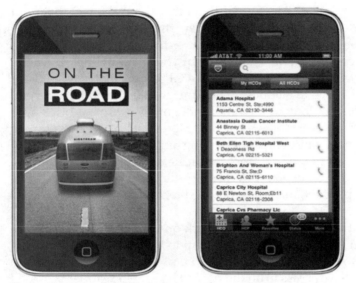

Figure 1-5: Genentech's in-house sales applications give reps access to customer information "on the road."

Now with the iPad

The iPad launched with the ability to run around 200,000 apps that were originally designed for the iPhone and iPod touch. While the user experience wasn't necessarily the greatest, this helped kickstart the iPad's explosive adoption. Even though the web-browsing experience on the iPad is quite good, many major websites have provided iPad-optimized apps that take the browsing experience to the next level. Think about the typical user who spends extensive time on a computer browsing the Web on sites like Bloomberg, *USA Today*, the *Wall Street Journal*, the *New York Times*, or Weather.com. The iPad apps for those sites provide an extremely rich and engaging user experience that in many cases is significantly better than the websites themselves consumed on a traditional computer.

From day 1, the iPad was viewed as more than just a consumer device. With apps like Apple's Keynote to give presentations, the device was quickly embraced by professionals to show a slide deck to a colleague. Whether in a conference room or at a restaurant table, the iPad is simply more convenient than a laptop ever was, and as a result it was quickly grabbed by professionals to use for business purposes. After that, it didn't take long for companies to see the potential for the iPad.

As one of the first organizations to embrace the iPad, Mercedes-Benz developed a custom application that it rolled out to 40 pilot dealerships in June 2010. The application, called MB Advantage, gives dealership employees access to the point-of-sale system right from the iPad (Figure 1-6).

Figure 1-6: Mercedes-Benz salespeople can access their point-of-sale system from the sales floor on their iPads.

Mercedes-Benz salespeople can use the iPad to take credit applications and look up marketing programs with the prospective customer right next to the vehicle on the sales floor. The iPad has also been used to replace paper-based forms for the lease-vehicle turn-in process in which the dealership employees needed to fill out an inspection checklist for the automobile.

Andreas Hinrichs, the VP of Marketing for Mercedes-Benz Financial, has been quoted in a press release as saying, "MB Advantage on iPad allows Mercedes-Benz dealers to increase their mobility and efficiency, from the initial finance and lease process through the lease turn-in process." By the end of 2010, Mercedes-Benz had also added the ability to capture customer signatures for certain documents right on the iPad (Figure 1-7).

But Mercedes-Benz isn't the only automaker to embrace the iPad. BMW developed a custom iPad application to display interactive vehicle info and pricing at trade shows. The app includes many photographs and videos, and features a digital configurator to allow consumers to design their own vehicles. GM also launched a "Chevrolet Dealer" app for iPads, which gives salespeople access to available vehicle colors, options, and pricing along with dealership inventory.

Figure 1-7: Customers can also use the Mercedes-Benz iPad app to sign certain documents.

In the context of apps, let's revisit the example mentioned earlier of the medical device industry. Medtronic is the world's largest medical device manufacturer and was one of the first large corporations to purchase significant quantities of the device. With the rollout of 4,500 iPads, Medtronic may have had the largest iPad deployment of 2010. Within weeks of the device's coming to market, the company ramped up a team to begin developing internal applications for the iPad. According to Mike Hedges, Medtronic's CIO, quoted in the *Wall Street Journal*, "The iPad enables our sales employees to do a much better job of engaging in a really different way than we've done before."

Boston Scientific, another Fortune 500 medical device manufacturer that deployed more than 2,000 iPads within months of the device's launch, is in the process of developing many employee-facing applications for the iPad. At a conference in late 2010, Ray Elliott, the CEO of Boston Scientific, talked about why the company is investing significant money into the iPad platform even while it's in a cost-cutting mode. He said, "We're beginning the process for our sales force of downloading more than 20 specific product apps and [will give them the] opportunity to get into pricing, time efficiency, expense reports, filling out requests, and all the other things that we manage to do to take time away from the sales force."

It might seem surprising that a Fortune 500 CEO would spend time during a company conference to talk about IT strategy relative to deploying iPads, but it's becoming increasingly common for business executives to talk about IT, especially as it relates to the iPad. As noted before, in November 2010, the Gartner analyst firm issued an advisory to CEOs, recommending that they clear any obstacles that IT might have in the support of the iPad.

This represents a radical and disruptive shift in business-as-usual for corporate IT. The iPad is shaking things up, and organizations have an opportunity to take advantage of the potential of the technology to improve mobile worker productivity and efficiency.

The Innovator's Dilemma

In 1997, a Harvard Business School professor, Clayton Christensen, wrote a book titled *The Innovator's Dilemma* in which he described the tendency of new technologies to be quite disruptive in the market. While market leaders are focused on meeting the needs of their existing customers through incremental improvements in existing technologies, they leave the door open for new market entrants to leverage disruptive technologies. The disruptive technologies might initially be attractive only to a small, niche, or low-end section of the market, but once they begin to mature and gain traction in the market they can overtake existing technologies, and the previous market leader will be unable to do anything about it. The effect of such disruptive technologies is illustrated in Figure 1-8.

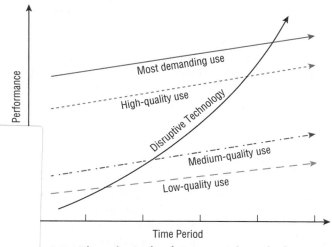

e 1-8: Disruptive technology moves from the low
ena to the high end of the market over time.

In the steel industry, for example, when mini-mill technology was developed in the 1960s, the mini-mills did not threaten the larger established integrated mills. The integrated mills, as their name suggests, are vertically integrated production facilities that have all the functions necessary for steel production, including the blast furnaces for the conversion of iron ore, coke, and limestone into the liquid iron, which is then converted into liquid steel before being cast and rolled into the finished product.

The mini-mills used scrap steel, which was often recycled from old equipment or automobiles, and at first the quality of the steel produced was acceptable only for the low end of the market in products like rebar. The mini-mills used an electric-arc furnace, which could be easily started and stopped, unlike the blast furnaces used by the integrated mills. As a result, the mini-mills were able to scale up production when demand was high and lower it when demand was lower.

This allowed the mini-mills to align their supply more closely to the market's demand and therefore achieve higher levels of profitability than the integrated mills. The integrated mills were more than happy to give up the low end of the market to the mini-mills, but the capture of that market share gave the mini-mills the runway they needed to allow their technology to evolve and mature. The quality of the steel produced could move up the value chain from rebar into other bars and rods. The market share that was captured thus fueled growth, and the mini-mill technology continued to mature. By the 1980s the mini-mills could produce structural and sheet steel that was of comparable quality to that of the integrated mills but at lower cost. This allowed up-start mini-mill steel companies like NuCor, now one of the largest steel companies in the world, to take market share from the previously dominant integrated-mill steel producers like US Steel and the now-defunct Bethlehem Steel.

Another example is the history of the disk drive industry, in which 14-inch disks gave way to 8-inch ones and in turn to 5.25-inch and ultimately 3.5-inch disks. During each phase of the disk drive industry's evolution, the established market leaders focused on the incremental improvements demanded by the high end of the market, while smaller disruptive innovators targeted the low end of the market and eventually leveraged their market share to move upstream.

Apple's Disruptive Evolution

In this context, it's quite striking how Apple has leveraged this phenomenon of disruptive technologies to successfully move up the value chain multiple times in multiple industries. While it competed solely in the personal computer space, Apple Computer was unable to break out of being viewed as just a niche player. While the Mac had a religious following of almost cult-like dedication, it was unable to grow much beyond 5 percent market share.

Instead of targeting IBM or Microsoft directly, Apple Computer chose rather to compete with Sony. In the 1980s Sony had created the personal music player industry with the Walkman, and it held a majority of the market share. Even as the industry transitioned from cassette tapes to compact discs in the 1990s, Sony was able to maintain its market-leading position. As digital music, or MP3, players began to enter the personal music player industry in the late 1990s, Sony was focused on incremental improvements to its existing technologies as opposed to embracing the new disruptive technology of digital music.

Steve Jobs saw the opportunity in digital music players, but observed that the products on the market were clunky, held only a few dozen songs, and had "unbelievably awful" user interfaces. That was the opening Apple Computer needed, and in October 2001 it launched the iPod that put "1,000 songs in your pocket." The product was designed to have a very simple user experience and to have enough capacity to carry an entire music library. The iPod achieved incredible success and by 2004 had achieved the majority market share not just in the digital music player space, but in the personal music player industry as well.

To support the momentum of the iPod as well as to provide a more unified user experience, Apple Computer launched the iTunes Store in the spring of 2003. Within several years, the iTunes Store had grown to be the largest music vendor in the United States and to command more than 70 percent of digital music sales world-wide. Figure 1-9, reprinted here with permission of the copyright holder, Alex Kleinschmidt (www.Alex-K-Art.com), illustrates this evolution.

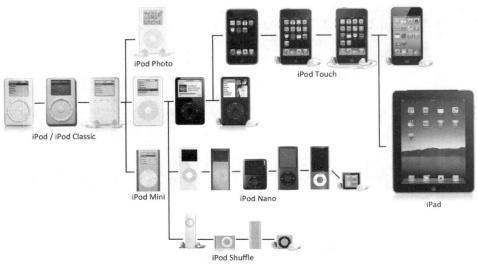

iPod Photo

iPod Touch

iPod / iPod Classic

iPod Mini

iPod Nano

iPad

iPod Shuffle

Figure 1-9: The evolution of the iPod, 2001–2010

By January 2007, the iPod was dominating the market with more than 70 percent market share. This represented a turning point for the company, and Apple Computer dropped the word "Computer" from its name to signify that computers were no longer the focus of the organization. At the same time, it also announced both the Apple TV and the iPhone, which was essentially an iPod with a built-in phone. The iPhone launched in June 2007. Shortly thereafter, in September 2007, Apple launched the iPod touch, which was also powered by iPhone OS but didn't have cellular telephone capabilities.

The iPhone SDK and the App Store launched in July 2008 and sparked what many have come to call the "App Revolution" as developers raced to create hundreds of thousands of apps. The App Store created an ecosystem that for the first time simplified software sales and distribution to a point that made them accessible to the typical consumer. With its current momentum and growth, the App Store will reach 500,000 apps by mid-2011.

When the iPad was launched in April 2010, it targeted a use case that was somewhere between a mobile phone and a laptop. For many users, the iPad did not replace either the smartphone or the laptop, but it displaced much of the use. Apple had taken the iPod and used that foothold to break into the phone market, which it then used to create the runaway success that is the iPad. Shortly after the launch of the iPad, Apple renamed iPhone OS to be simply iOS, signaling that the future of the platform was less about any specific device and more about supporting an entire spectrum of devices.

Continuing the Innovation

In its continued march up the value chain (Figure 1-10), Apple launched the Mac App Store in January 2011. This brought the extremely simple user experience of iTunes and the iPhone/iPad App Store to a desktop and laptop computing platform. In the same way that the typical consumer could easily install an app onto an iPhone and iPad, apps can now be installed onto a desktop or laptop Mac.

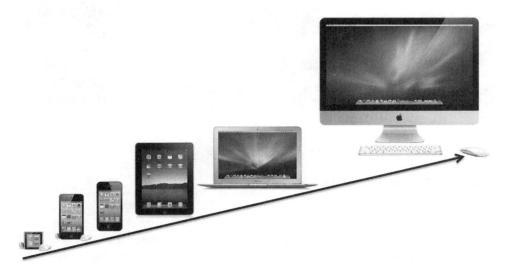

Figure 1-10: Apple has gathered momentum up the value chain from the iPod to the iPhone to the iPad. Can it leverage this to increase market share for the Mac?

It will be very interesting to watch and see if Apple is able not only to hold its leadership position in personal music players, mobile phones, and tablet computers, but also to continue working its way up the value chain to gain significant market share in the laptop and desktop personal computer space.

Summary

The iPad is a disruptive innovation not just in the marketplace, but also within corporate IT. These types of technological transformations are often painful, but they can be very valuable for the companies that take advantage of them strategically. This chapter has set the stage by outlining the industry landscape. Now let's take a deeper look at the overall trend of consumerization and its impact on the development of a company's strategy to maximize its returns relative to the iPad.

CHAPTER 2

Embracing the Consumerization of IT

Now that we've set the stage in the context of the greater mobility landscape, it's important to understand in greater detail the overall trends that are driving the adoption of the iPad within the enterprise.

As I wrote this book, I spoke to, interviewed, and received feedback from dozens of technology authors, industry analysts, enterprise software executives, Fortune 1000 CIOs, and other visionaries of enterprise IT. Perhaps the best way to explore this concept is to hear from those industry leaders. While the iPad is an extremely polarizing topic on its own, the concept of the "consumerization of IT" is even more controversial. I spoke to nearly as many people who were unwilling to go on the record as to those who allowed me to quote them here.

In this chapter, we'll define what we mean by the consumerization of IT, how this overall trend has accelerated the adoption of the iPad within the enterprise, and thoughts and commentaries from "thought leaders" on this subject.

What Is Consumerization?

The term *consumerization* first gained popularity in 2001 when it was used by Douglas Neal and John Taylor as a description for how information technology innovation was emerging in consumer-based technology, with the expectation that it would eventually migrate into the enterprise.

In many ways, the idea of consumerization seems to be fairly simple and straightforward. At first glance, it might appear to be interesting, but unlikely to have a big impact on the industry landscape and power structure of enterprise IT.

Does consumerization really challenge the status quo of enterprise IT?

In 2005, Gartner, Inc., released a report saying, "The growing practice of introducing new technologies into consumer markets prior to industrial markets will be the most significant trend affecting information technology during the next 10 years."

In late 2010, Stephen Prentice, Gartner Fellow and vice president, wrote a Gartner CEO advisory titled "Seize the iPad Opportunity Now." But as early as 2005 he had written: "As perceptive CIOs seek to transform their rigid, legacy-ridden infrastructures into agile, efficient, service-driven delivery mechanisms, they must adopt a pragmatic approach to managing the risks of consumer IT while embracing the benefits. Otherwise, the CIOs risk being sidelined as the 'enemy' by their constituencies."

In 2005, the idea promoted by Gartner that consumerization is the most important trend of the next 10 years might have been controversial. But the traction found by the iPhone, which went from 0 percent to 80 percent of the companies in the Fortune 100 between June 2008 and June 2010, demonstrates undeniably the powerful impact of this trend.

Even so, Philippe Winthrop, founder and managing director of the Enterprise Mobility Foundation, believes that the mobile consumerization trend demonstrated by the iPhone and now the iPad has some subtle differences from the general trend of consumerization. According to Winthrop, "The consumerization of enterprise mobility is slightly nuanced from the consumerization of general IT. First and foremost, the price points make mobile devices far more accessible than other computing devices. Second, the massive diversity of applications, and the ease of purchase and installation of these applications is very different from what IT departments are typically used to. Forward-thinking companies have recognized the opportunity to embrace, as opposed to fight, this change and use it to their advantage. True ROI [return on investment] is still elusive in many cases, but there is no question that the future of the workplace is predicated on the use of mobile devices and applications."

But what does the "consumerization of IT" actually mean to a corporate leader of information technology?

In my search for a clear definition of this concept, one of the best explanations I've heard was from Mike Blake, the CIO of Hyatt Hotels. He shared with me the journey that Hyatt went through to both recognize and then ultimately embrace this trend of consumerization with the iPad. In Blake's words:

> When iPad came out it was the latest "shiny object" introduced by one of the most innovative companies in the world. Everyone had to have one, yet no one really knew what it was for. The power in the product, aside from its beautiful design and solid operating system, was found in the spark that it created in the imagination of its users. Users were defining ways of leveraging the tool to prove that it is more than just flash, that it could offer true utility. In our case, IT embraced the iPad from day one, helping to get the product out into as many people's hands as possible. From that grass roots trial we have found ways of serving our customers in new ways, and providing powerful tools to our employees that they truly enjoy using. That's where consumerization of IT really comes into play. It is IT recognizing the power of a consumer product, cultivating it, and giving it a fair chance to succeed. We have shed our arrogance, but we keep a little bit of our skepticism and our conservative approach to make sure the enterprise systems are still secure and our help desks are not overwhelmed.
>
> IT's acceptance of consumerized technologies in the enterprise has led us to enable a more agile organization with users empowered with choice in selecting their computing platform preference. In fact, IT's embracing of these technologies has helped to propel a more positive view of IT. Where IT was previously considered to be rigid and dictatorial, it is now viewed as a true partner who proactively works with the business and uses consumer technologies to help solve critical business issues.
>
> The end result is that employees are able to get the data and information they need to better inform decisions. These consumerized tools enable people to better use and interpret information: they are easier to maintain, and have a higher satisfaction level with the user base than any previous generation of tools.

I believe that Blake has demonstrated that the "consumerization of IT" is ultimately a positive trend for corporations. It may involve some painful changes in the status quo of corporate IT, including, as Blake said, how IT groups have to "shed our arrogance" in order to give the underlying technology a chance to succeed. But this trend provides the business, the entire company, and even the whole economy with an improvement in efficiency, productivity, and ultimately profit.

So how long has this consumerization trend been going on? Is the iPad acting as a catalyst, or has the trend been going on for a while?

Scot Finnie, the editor-in-chief of *Computerworld*, believes that consumerization has been happening for a long time. He said, "The rise of consumerization of IT has become highly visible over the past several years. The immediate causes of the trend include the prevalence of powerful and versatile smartphones and tablets, the popularity of simple and useful mobile apps, and the recession, which has driven the need for greater levels of productivity and effectively longer workdays."

"Even so," Finnie continued, "the consumerization of IT has been evident for 20 years, beginning with the advent of the personal computer. Microsoft, for example, rose to dominance in the early '90s in part on its intense focus on the end-user usability of its operating systems and applications. Apple, of course, has been a consumer electronics company for some time. The key for IT organizations is to recognize and embrace massive consumer trends, because they almost always manifest themselves in business environments, as well. Enterprises ignore or attempt to thwart the consumerization of IT at their own peril."

There is a big up side to the business if IT embraces consumerization. The up side is that the users themselves are bringing the latest technology into the company sooner than would otherwise happen. That can mean better integration, better communication, better tools, and ultimately a competitive advantage for the company.

Finnie offered hope to discouraged leaders: "At its core, the consumerization of IT is about employee freedom and employee productivity. At some point you have to just trust your employees and not only let them do their jobs better, but support them in doing so. The ROI will follow."

Donald Ferguson, the CTO at CA Technologies, agrees with Finnie, saying, "The consumerization of IT has been gradually occurring for years. The iPhone followed by the iPad has made 'consumerized' IT the new normal. Enterprises can either enable and support iPhone, iPad, and new consumer devices, or their employees will go around IT."

Frank Slootman, the former CEO at Data Domain and executive chairman of the BRS Division at EMC, shared similar sentiments: "Consumerization of IT is not a new phenomenon with the emergence of the iPad or even the smartphone. As far back as the mid-1980s, the very first Macs and LaserWriters were ushered into departments of the enterprise completely against the tightly locked-down policies of the IT department who refused to support them. It is an unstoppable grass roots dynamic many decades under way now. I am sure we ain't seen nothing yet."

Consumer technology is walking in the front door of the corporation, and Eric Openshaw, principal and vice chairman at Deloitte, says this trend is just as prevalent in the executive suite as it is on the front lines of the enterprise. He observed, "The seemingly insatiable appetite for corporate adoption of tablets — and the iPad as a proxy for that broader adoption — reflects a fundamental shift from IT driving the how, when, what and where of technology use toward the user dictating those parameters. It's fascinating that this is being driven both from the bottom-up and the top-down. In this case, people fresh out of school and CEOs alike have embraced an unobtrusive device that supports many if not all of their personal and professional computing needs."

According to Robert Stephens, founder of the Geek Squad and CTO at electronics retailer Best Buy, the iPad is facilitating an even more fundamental shift within the enterprise: user-driven design, which is driving improvements in business processes. "Up until recently," Stephens said, "most business executives didn't have any confidence to know what to ask IT for. But now they see that they can track a FedEx package right from the iPad, and see exactly where it is or who signed for it. You can customize and order a pizza from Papa John's right from your iPhone. IT no longer has the unique set of knowledge about what is possible. The user now knows what they want, and now they can and will demand it from IT."

Crossing the Chasm

Ever since best-selling author Geoffrey Moore wrote *Crossing the Chasm* in 1991, this book has served as a strategic guide for technology product entrepreneurs and marketers everywhere. In the book, Moore describes the Technology Adoption Lifecycle, where new technology products are adopted according to a bell curve pattern, as shown in Figure 2-1. In this pattern, the initial purchases of a product are Innovators, after which come the Early Adopters, the Early Majority, the Late Majority, and finally the Laggards. Rather than a smooth curve, though, there is a "chasm" in the Technology Adoption Lifecycle within the segment of the Early Adopters. This is because customers tend to look for references from other companies in the same segment. Since Innovators buy products simply to have the latest and greatest technology, they do not serve as very good references to Early Adopters, who are focused on the benefits provided by the technology, not the technology itself. This makes it very challenging for the marketers of innovative new products to "cross the chasm" as they pursue mainstream customers.

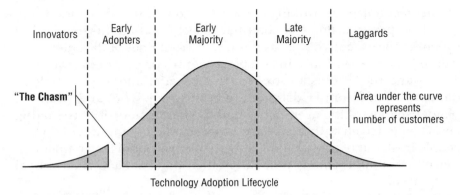

Figure 2-1: How did the iPad seem to leapfrog the Technology Adoption Lifecycle?

With the launch of the iPad, though, it seemed that this technology was able to defy the pattern of adoption that has held fast within enterprise IT for decades. How was Apple able to pull this off?

I asked Moore how the iPad was able to jump over the entire Technology Adoption Lifecycle, and he shared with me his thoughts regarding the iPad and the consumerization of IT. His response was, "The key thing about the iPad and iPhone, and the consumerization movement in general, is that there is no Technology Adoption Lifecycle for the end users — no training even — so there is no adoption lifecycle for enterprise when the technology is being brought in by the end user. Indeed there is a pent-up demand based on decades of retro user interfaces and user experiences. There is some adoption shock for IT, but this time around it is not so bad because there is more flexible infrastructure to absorb it."

But Moore also believes that this provides a dramatic opportunity for enterprises. He continued, "All that is really left is for executive teams to understand the ROI for these deployments. I believe this will come from empowering the legions of middle managers responsible for negotiating actions across a distributed global value chain. These people have intense need for communication, coordination, and collaboration facilities of the sort that the consumer market has already embraced, but the enterprise has never had the opportunity to deploy before now."

But again, how did the iPad achieve such rapid adoption within the enterprise? How did Apple penetrate 50 percent of the Fortune 100 in less than 90 days?

Of everyone that I talked to, I think Frank Modruson, the CIO of Accenture, had the most vivid explanation of how the iPad penetrated that organization:

The day the iPad was introduced we had some discussions about adding them into our environment; 24 hours later, we had 500 devices accessing e-mails.

People expect their personal devices — iPads, iPhones, and the like — to be usable at work. They want to be more productive, they want do a better job, and there's an expectation that they'll be able to integrate their consumer devices with enterprise applications at the office. It's a sensible and reasonable expectation, and we feel it's imperative to oblige them. Indeed, we see it as an opportunity. We're always plowing ahead, moving toward the next generation of technology because the next generation is almost always better, faster, and cheaper.

CIOs who resist will eventually be forced to change. Consider, for example, when the personal computer arrived on the scene. Its initial target market was the home. And then people started to recognize that PCs were very powerful tools that could be used at work. Many CIOs and procurement departments declined to authorize their purchase. So people circumvented the restrictions by saying they were purchasing a calculator. CIOs should not be asking if they should be taking advantage of the devices. They should be asking how they can take advantage.

Zero to 500 devices overnight! That represents an incredibly rapid rate of change for CIOs who have traditionally embraced stability. Is Modruson correct in not only allowing this rapid rate of change, but also believing that CIOs don't even have a choice?

Ken Dulaney, a vice president and Distinguished Analyst at Gartner, agrees with Modruson. According to Dulaney, "These devices have become inexpensive enough that end users can overwhelm IT through widespread consumer-fueled adoption. It's kind of a parallel with the Egyptian Revolution of 2011, a relatively peaceful protest that the government cannot ignore. The IT dictatorships of the past do not work any longer; the end user is more than equipped to adopt compelling technology and to work around IT when necessary. Either IT helps the end user with new technologies or risks widespread criticism."

Many IT leaders believe that while the iPad adoption rate was rapid, it was also superficial. This is a widespread view among quite a few of the IT leaders I talked to, but the only executive who was willing to go on the record with that point of view was Kate Bass, the CIO at Valspar, who said, "Personally, I think that the fact that 50 percent of Fortune 100 have adopted the iPad is a gross overstatement. Yes, we have iPads in the organization but that does not mean widespread adoption nor that iPads are being used for daily processes. They work great for 'consuming' information that is available to the 'consumer.'

They do not work well for creating information. I do think that they introduce an imperative, however, for the ERP [Enterprise Resource Planning] vendors to make it easier to 'consume' data that we have spent years locking up in Fort Knox databases and storage systems."

Bass's imperative is felt in the exponentially growing demand for high-quality apps that can consume and add value to data.

So what does this mean for the enterprise software industry?

The founder and CEO of salesforce.com, Marc Benioff, agrees that this is a transformative shift that is just as much about the software as it is the hardware. He says, "Our industry has gone through many shifts, but ultimately, the big ones have always been about software, not hardware. Now, we are seeing a simultaneous software and hardware revolution. Sales of mobile devices and tablets have far outpaced PCs. The key apps we use will all be rewritten to take advantage of this fundamental transformation. That transformation even extends to where we use these apps. Because devices like the iPad are so easy to carry and can be used anywhere, it creates a truly mobile workforce. That's why I plan to put an iPad in the hands of all my salespeople."

MicroStrategy, the enterprise software firm focused on business intelligence, has also recognized how consumerization is creating a highly productive mobile workforce. According to Executive Vice President and Chief Operating Officer Sanju Bansal, "People expect to be able to access any information they need at any time of the day from a mobile device, whether at home or at work. More and more companies are recognizing the value of mobile devices for their businesses and are building mobile apps for employees, executives, suppliers, and business partners. The phrase 'I'll get back to you' will eventually disappear as every conversation will be infused with information and every decision will be fact-based. The ability to access business information 24/7 shortens decision-making time, streamlines business processes, enhances collaboration, and makes every location an office."

The Long Tail

In 2006, the editor-in-chief of *Wired* magazine, Chris Anderson, wrote the *New York Times* bestseller *The Long Tail*, in which he describes the economic phenomenon of abundance. As virtual inventory and digital products are no longer constrained by physical capacity restrictions, the number of available products for sale can approach infinity. The result is a reduction of sales for "mega-hit" products as buyers are able to fulfill their desires through more personal or niche selections, and total sales are distributed from the spike and move farther down the distribution of the curve, like the one shown in Figure 2-2.

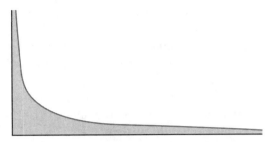

Figure 2-2: Digital marketplaces like the App Store create an environment where the Long Tail offers products for every desire and niche.

So what is the impact of the explosive growth of the App Store on enterprise IT?

I posed that question to Anderson, and his response was that "the App Store just keeps growing. And growing. And growing. Consumers now expect that there's really an app for anything, and then when that consumer goes into work, he's beginning to expect that there should be 'apps' for that, too. The Long Tail of mobile apps has altered the mindsets of corporate employees, and IT is having trouble coming to grips with all this."

The economic impact of the Long Tail may seem clear to many in enterprise IT; however, many may think it will affect the business of companies like Amazon .com or Apple's App Store and iTunes, but not them, at least directly. I tend to agree with Anderson that this does have a direct and significant impact on corporate IT.

Ultimately, this idea represents a fundamental shift for IT that is shared by Donald Ferguson, the CTO at CA Technologies, who says, "Traditional IT has provided a modest number of applications to customers and employees. IT will evolve to provide data and API calls to an unknown galaxy of applications that employees and end users download from app stores. IT will evolve from building web interfaces and pages to delivering new apps and updates each day."

"As we move forward into a world where cloud enabled networks are the norm," says Art Glasgow, the CTO at Ingenix, "CIOs have to accept the fact that the world has changed. Any device at any time on the network will be the norm and it will have to be done without sacrificing security and manageability. Cool matters and usability rules the day so devices like the iPad have to be not just accounted for, but designed for. The good news is that devices like the iPad aren't just cool. They are flexible, multifunction tools that are changing the way we work and create and in that sense may very well be not just an innovation themselves, but a catalyst to innovations."

Bill Martin, the CIO at Royal Caribbean Cruises, in response to the assessment that enterprise IT is "having trouble coming to grips with all this," shared with me the dozens of ways that his cruise line is using the iPad to strategically transform both internal processes and guest experiences. He concluded by saying, "So I would disagree that enterprise IT is having trouble coming to grips with the onslaught of mobile technology now available. On the contrary, we're embracing it and trying to apply unconstrained thinking to find new ways to leverage it. From our perspective we say, 'Bring it on.'"

Martin is certainly among the IT visionaries who are choosing to embrace the iPad, but not all IT leaders are as positive about this transformation.

Allen Benson, the vice president of business technology at Spectrum Brands, is actually quite excited about the potential for the iPad in the enterprise but is not entirely bullish on this explosive growth of apps. He says, "The runaway train called the App Store is bound to derail. Just like your closet, there is only so much room for individual apps before you won't be able to find what you are looking for in an efficient manner. The 'cool' factor will subside and the 'cost' factor will take over, forcing companies to take another look at their portfolio of applications. The iPad, while being considered a consumer device, actually filled a larger void in the executive wing as executives [use it] for ERP. Touch one button, enter one password, and access all the corporate information necessary to feed the board of directors or any other senior executive. The iPad may have started in the consumer's hands, but it will finish as the business device of choice for some time to come without a dependency on apps."

A Whole New Mind

In the 2005 *New York Times* bestseller *A Whole New Mind*, author Daniel Pink writes about how "we are moving from an economy and a society built on the logical, linear, computerlike capabilities of the Information Age to an economy and society built on the inventive, empathic, big-picture capabilities of what's rising in its place, the Conceptual Age."

He goes on to talk about how, in the Conceptual Age, "Commingling work and play has become both more common and more necessary. At times, it is even an explicit corporate strategy." The resulting implications around the blurring of personal and professional aspects of enterprise mobility only raise users' expectations of corporate IT.

I asked Pink about his view on this trend of consumerization, and he shared with me his perspective, saying, "What's amazing about the iPad ought to be alarming to established organizations. An entire, gargantuan, and lucrative ecosystem of apps emerged without the creators needing a training and development department to teach them what to do or an IT department to help them distribute their creations."

As we enter the Conceptual Age, it's clear that technologies like the iPad will have a dramatic impact on the day-to-day operations of corporate IT.

So how can IT leaders strategically harness this trend for positive impact on their businesses?

Some IT leaders see the potential for higher user satisfaction and flexibility. Alan Farnsworth, CIO at Bausch and Lomb, explains the benefits his company has achieved from embracing consumerization and the blurring of personal and professional activities. He says, "We're a big believer in the power of the iPad and Apple technology in general to increase employee engagement and satisfaction. For too many years enterprises have forced employees to communicate and collaborate much differently at work than they do in their personal lives. Why? There's no need or good reason for that, particularly with the power of devices like the iPhone and iPad."

At Thomson Reuters, Mobile Technology Director Dan Bennett shared with me the impact the iPad is having on that business, saying, "Clearly, the iPad is becoming the must-have business accessory: execs finally have something they can take into the boardroom, sales folks can ditch the laptop. Many are buying their own devices and demanding connectivity."

"The challenge," Bennett continued, "seems two-fold: immediately, IT must determine how to provide secure access to enterprise resources — this is distinctly non-trivial. Longer term, the mediocre user experience of the typical enterprise app must be improved if one is to translate the gains of consumerization to business value."

Vishal Jain, an analyst focused on mobile services at the 451 Group, also believes that technologies like the iPad are elevating user expectations of corporate IT. He said, "Form factors for information consumption and dissemination have changed, partly led by the explosion of consumer-centric technologies that are finding ways into enterprise. Always-on smartphones and tablets with their excellent UI [user interface], processing power, and contextual capabilities serve all the computing needs of the discerning consumer. As real-time communication, social media, and search gets embedded within the application stack or device, the user expectation moves a notch higher. Today's office of the CIO is itself a business organization and the availability of such devices presents an opportunity to have a fresh look at systems, processes and presentation."

IT will have to respond to increased expectations, which you should see as an opportunity to differentiate your business from the inside out.

Many CIOs are taking that challenge seriously, but recognizing that real problems, like those around security, must be both acknowledged and addressed by an effective post-consumerization IT organization. Joseph Spagnoletti, senior vice president and CIO at Campbell Soup, said, "The personally owned iPads walking in the front door created awareness for the need of mobility to consolidate personal and professional information. Security was the biggest barrier up until now, and our R&D [research and development] effort began right away to address the security issues."

At Chevron, CIO Louie Ehrlich recognizes that devices like the iPad are bringing challenges but also significant opportunities, saying, "Consumer devices such as smartphones and tablets can be game changers for an enterprise. They provide an opportunity for steep change in the speed of business decisions and increased individual productivity, but come with a distinct requirement for IT to rethink old paradigms around application development, delivery, and support."

Brian Flynn, senior vice president and global CIO at Crawford & Company, said, "In general, the iPad is unavoidable for the enterprise. They made such a big splash by understanding the customer, and through the marketing hype, that they made it difficult for the CIO who had been standardizing on other platforms to discount iOS as a platform."

Here Comes Everybody

Clay Shirky, best-selling author of *Here Comes Everybody* and *Cognitive Surplus*, is a consultant and teacher at New York University on the social and economic impacts of technology. One of my own favorite quotes of Shirky's is, "It's when a technology becomes normal, then ubiquitous, and finally so pervasive as to be invisible, that the really profound changes happen."

Shirky shared with me a personal story:

> *Just this morning, when I took my kids to the dentist, he handed me an iPad to check them in and update my information. The usual, horrible "We know we've seen you 20 times, but here's a clipboard" experience was transformed. Any data they already had was filled in, so I only had to add or alter new things. Even more interesting, the "app" for this was the web browser — this was a web interface to a cloud-hosted application, running via the office's local Wi-Fi.*

> *The iPad's adoption has been like a cork popping out of a champagne bottle in part because of the pent-up demand it unleashes in other areas as well. The dental app wouldn't have worked without good web design, cloud-hosted apps, local Wi-Fi, [and] a whole host of technologies that were worth less than the sum of their parts before there was a working tablet you could hand someone and have it just work. And the real kicker for businesses is that these kinds of uses don't just act as replacements for PCs and laptops, they replace clipboards, paper, [and] local databases, and all kinds of inefficient practices get smoother and better.*

I am personally quite excited by Shirky's own first-hand observation of how the iPad is taking advantage of so many of the macroeconomic trends that he so articulately documents in his own books. Additionally, I find it extremely interesting that his observations revolve around the health-care industry. While much of my own time has recently been spent consulting with companies in the health-care, medical device, and pharmaceutical industries, I believe that the iPad has disproportionately impacted those industries. In the last chapter, I discussed how the iPad is already in the process of transforming the medical sales industry, with the adoption by virtually every major corporation in that industry, but in many ways this is just scratching the surface of how the iPad will impact the overall health-care industry.

According to David Hemendinger, the CTO at Lifespan, a healthcare delivery system, "We are at the tipping point in health care, and I believe the iPad has the potential to radically enhance the way health care is delivered and consumed. Instant access to clinical information at the point of care using a kinesthetically pleasing, easy-to-use, app-enabled device is just what the doctor ordered. I believe the iPad will become as important to health care as the invention and everyday use of the stethoscope."

Michael Hedges, the CIO of the medical device giant Medtronic, concurs: "In the health-care industry, tablets like the iPad may soon replace laptops for salespeople and other employees who deal with customers. If a clinician only has five minutes to talk, a salesperson can use it to quickly display valuable data or do a demo. These devices have a huge gain on speed, clarity, and ease of use."

"Through mobile technologies like the iPad and iPhone," continued Hedges, "patients will be able to order their supplies from companies from anywhere/anytime and physicians will be able to review patient information and make necessary therapy changes. In the future, we foresee a highly connected world where patients, care-givers, and physicians interact through their mobile devices and take timely actions to better manage their own health. The fact that the iPad has a fast start-up time, [is] easy to use, [and has] long battery life, great screen size and clarity makes its use in this space very valuable."

Rich Williams, vice president and group CIO of the pharmaceutical manufacturer AstraZeneca, agrees, saying, "Devices like the iPad and the consumerization of IT really have fundamentally shifted the corporate network model toward truly ubiquitous and uniform information access. Corporate IT cannot stick their head in the sand and hope it goes away. Employees want access to information at a time and place convenient for them — now — just like they get at home. While this will create challenges for security and network capacity, leading organizations will get in front of these new ways of working and encourage on-demand computing. The results will be higher collaboration, engagement, and information sharing leading to better business decisions and higher business performance."

The iPad is also directly hitting the medical point of care. Lisa Caplan, the vice president and business information officer of Care Delivery, part of health-care giant Kaiser Permanente, said, "Simple and innovative consumer technology products have changed the trajectory of enterprise expectations. Every corporate citizen wants what launched Tuesday at their local electronics store to support them in the office, too. This drives great advances aimed at enterprise markets as well, but in a highly regulated industry like health care, where technology is life-critical, consumerization also means enterprise-level security, priced to scale, and stable enough to support decision-making at the point of care. These are table stakes, before the ROI discussion can really even begin."

The iPad is impacting every aspect of the health-care industry, including the payers. At a major health insurer, UnitedHealth Group, Bud Flagstad, vice president of strategic initiatives, commented, "The iPad has the potential to significantly change and enhance how we interact with our members, customers, and partners. You turn it on and it works. The need for extensive training is gone. The similarity of the UI from app to app makes user support calls a thing of the past!"

Embracing Consumerization

In many ways, to embrace this trend is make a complete reversal in many positions that IT has traditionally taken. Once IT led users to new technology; now the reverse is true. Over the last 50 years, the focus of IT has progressed from the back end to the front end; now the mobile experience, led by the iPad, is creating new demand for intuitive UI, ubiquitous connectivity, and greater access and control of the back end. The direction is reversed.

John Dix, the editor-in-chief of *Network World*, put it quite well: "IT has often prided themselves on control. Control of the devices used, regulation of who has access to what, the programs that are permitted. And over the years IT has struggled as that control has slipped away. Employees started using their own instant messaging tools, then arrived with their own social network/collaboration options, their own smartphones, their own computers and netbooks and tablets, and with the advent of Google Voice, even their own phone number and voice mail. While there are risks involved, there is little question that this consumerization of IT will slow down anytime soon, and smart companies realize it is better to try to channel the tide than fight it."

Eileen Feretic, the editor-in-chief of *Baseline* magazine, agrees with that position, saying, "For years, IT managers resisted the incursion of PDAs and smartphones into the enterprise, primarily because of the security risks involved in letting employees access corporate data over their mobile devices. But that was a losing battle. Once employees enjoyed the benefits of using these devices in their personal lives, they were determined to bring them to work as well. The consumerization of IT forced technology managers to figure out how best to manage, monitor, and secure mobile technologies — the latest of which is the iPad and other tablet devices. Smartphones paved the way for enterprise acceptance of mobile devices, and tablet users are reaping the benefits: legitimacy and support."

So are IT leaders ready to let go of control and fully embrace consumerization?

David J. McCue, the CIO at CSC, believes so. He says, "The iPad is a transformational platform for the delivery of services and applications. Enterprises have been criticized for not adapting the iPad quickly enough, and IT departments have been castigated for being obstructionists. The reality is that every CIO I know has already bought into the value of the device and is deploying it."

Rick Fabrizio, the CIO of propane giant AmeriGas, sees this disruptive transformation as an opportunity for positive change. Fabrizio said, "Companies that embrace 'New Tech' will have a competitive advantage over those that don't. Adoption of technology by the internal business customers of IT has always been a challenge for IT, so here's an opportunity for IT to adopt and leverage technology that the business community is already using. The iPad and iPhone are perfect examples of this."

Steven Birgfeld, senior vice president and CIO of Hostess Brands, also sees this as an opportunity: "I believe the consumerism impact on the enterprise is not a matter of if, but when, and IT needs to be certain they are proactive in addressing this new dynamic. In our case, it was actually the CEO that pushed the iPad into our environment, so it helped to force the issue for addressing the need. It is now a matter of staying on top of ways to further leverage, and hence manage, the iPad technology as new enterprise capabilities start to present themselves."

At paper giant Weyerhaeuser, CIO Kevin Shearer views the iPad as a positive opportunity for IT. According to Shearer, "The lightning-fast speed of adoption of the iPad into the business world caught everyone by surprise. Now business execs are showing up with their own iPads, bought with their own money, expecting full and seamless connectivity and integration between personal and business applications. It's what every CIO dreamed of, but we all thought we would have more time to prepare for these customer expectations."

The Evolution of Corporate IT

From the many points made in this chapter about the consumerization of IT, I believe it's clear that corporate IT has an imperative to leverage this trend for the benefit of the business and the corporation as a whole. This undoubtedly represents a significant and dramatic challenge to the status quo, and to enterprise IT as a whole, but even though change be painful, it's often necessary to realize the full benefits of this ultimately evolutionary macroeconomic trend.

While the topic of consumerization remains a controversial subject, Brian Carlson, the editor-in-chief of *CIO.com*, believes that strategically embracing enterprise mobility is an imperative for those in IT leadership positions. According to Carlson, "The convergence of consumer electronics and the enterprise IT organization is in full swing now, and nowhere is this more evident than in the exploding mobile enterprise market. Enterprise mobility is set to eclipse cloud computing as the biggest trend in the technology industry in 2011, with businesses expanding the use of smartphones, tablets, and mobile apps for all levels of employees. Expect to see enterprises mobilizing all their core applications from CRM [customer relationship management], ERP, expense management, inventory management, and time tracking. An effective enterprise mobile strategy is no longer a nice-to-have, but a necessity for business growth."

Scott Ellison, vice president for mobile and consumer-connected platforms at IDC, advises IT leaders that "The combination of tablets, smartphones, and apps is where reality is regularly outpacing hyperbole. The challenge for the enterprise is to better leverage the 'appaholic' behavior that their employees bring into the workplace in ways that benefit the enterprise. Three keys to doing so are solutions that allow employees to use their state-of-the art personal tablets and smartphones for core work functions, converting overly complex software programs into more user-friendly, app-like experiences, and fully leveraging touch as the best way to interact with most information."

Vishy Gopalakrishnan, author of *Work Goes Mobile* and director of industry solutions at AT&T Mobility, believes that embracing personally owned devices is a requirement of an effective enterprise mobile strategy. "As enterprise IT organizations try to meet the needs of an increasingly mobile driven business," says Gopalakrishnan, "they look to a 'Bring Your Own Device' (BYOD) approach as a critical element of their mobility strategy. While this approach frees the IT organization from the typically cumbersome process of certifying and procuring mobile devices, it puts the onus on IT to put in place a sustainable framework to develop the mobile applications across multiple device platforms, paying particular attention to the device lifecycle; and instituting the processes, infrastructure, and tools like mobile device management to get the desired level of visibility and control."

Summary

The iPad is an incredibly disruptive technology; there is no debate about that. But exactly what impact the iPad and the overall trend of consumerization will ultimately have on enterprise IT is yet to be seen.

How are you responding to the consumerization of IT within your organization? Is your company ready to embrace the disruptive change necessary to realize the full benefits of this trend?

In the next chapter, we'll discuss how these concepts can be applied in the development of an enterprise mobility strategy for your organization.

Developing an Enterprise Mobility Strategy

- Information technology as a strategic business enabler
- Understanding the elements of a mobile strategy
- How to ensure that mobility delivers business results
- Managing the often conflicting demands of mobility
- Taking advantage of enterprise-wide economies of scale
- Developing and maintaining enterprise best practices

In the first two chapters, you were introduced to the overall mobile landscape and the impact that the iPad is having on corporate IT. We also discussed the trends around the "consumerization of IT" and how the iPad is acting as a catalyst and encouraging greater and more rapid enterprise adoption as a result of those trends.

This chapter explores the concept of information technology as a strategy, and how mobile technology, including the iPad specifically, should fit into an enterprise's mobile strategy. There are seven key components of a mobile strategy that will be discussed in this chapter.

After digging into the specific components of a mobile strategy, you'll learn how to make sure the iPad is driving the results and benefits desired by the business.

Then you'll cover the process of managing all the conflicting demands for mobility across the business. There are many different roles that view mobility from widely differing perspectives, from the users themselves to the business operation, the marketing department, and of course the IT department.

In developing a mobile strategy, it's important to understand and acknowledge all these perspectives.

We'll also examine how organizations can take advantage of economies of scale across the enterprise to establish strategic mobile platforms for innovation that foster and accelerate the development of innovative mobile applications.

Finally, you'll look at how best practices concerning mobility can be established and shared across the enterprise. Whether information is informally distributed or best practices are established through a formal structure like a Mobile COE (Center of Excellence), there are many benefits to identifying and fostering best practices.

Strategic IT

In most companies, the vast majority of IT-related spending is focused on "keeping the lights on," while only a small percentage is used for new projects and innovation. As a result, resources are always squeezed when it comes to leveraging new technologies like the iPad. When IT is focused entirely on managing costs, the tendency is to ignore a device like the iPad since it doesn't really change the cost equation, at least from the perspective of the status quo. The value of the iPad, though, is the transformational nature of the technology, which enables functionality and behavior in the work force that's never before been possible.

Although in some respects, the arrival of the iPad at the door of the enterprise represents a loss of control, it also presents IT with a chance to embrace what users are asking for and simultaneously to help the business discover the ultimate value of the technology.

In *The Transformational CIO*, author Hunter Muller says, "In today's environment — in the Age of Immediacy — the CIO can't afford to be seen as a naysayer. If you don't find a way to work with the business, the business just might find a way to work without you. At many companies, you will hear stories of business units that went ahead and purchased technology after losing patience with the IT department."

And that is exactly the type of situation that the iPad is creating within many organizations. This also creates an opportunity for IT to develop a strategy that can enable and empower the business to be more efficient and productive. By aligning IT strategy with the overall business strategy, corporate IT can take advantage of the disruptive change caused by the iPad to empower workers and to help create a more effective organization.

Developing an IT strategy should never be done in a vacuum, as the purpose of IT should be to provide the business with technology that enables the business to achieve its overall goals. Those goals may revolve around enabling business growth, improving profitability, enhancing competitiveness, increasing work-force utilization, or raising employee satisfaction. Whatever the goals of the business, the IT strategy should directly align with them.

In the book *World Class IT*, author Peter A. High discusses the ideal process of strategic planning for IT:

> *There needs to be a bottom-up aspect to strategic planning. This does not suggest that all of IT should be engaged at the point at which there is a blank slate. On the contrary, that would be a risky formula, as ideas would be offered with little structure, and the initial excitement of being engaged in an important process for the company would yield to feelings of disappointment as most people's ideas would not be considered. Instead, the creation of the highest-level objectives is still probably the domain of IT leadership. The tactics on how to accomplish each should be the domain of the larger organization. The objectives provide the structure, and the tactics provide a list of ideas to which the organization can turn when a new round of project ideas is needed.*

While the development of a complete IT strategy is outside the scope of this book, it's important to recognize that a mobile strategy should be a component of the overall IT strategy. Therefore the mobile strategy should also directly align with the overall goals of the business. Since mobile technology like the iPad is often forced upon IT, the IT organization often views mobility in a reactive sense as opposed to proactively seeking out and developing the optimal mobile strategy as a part of the entire IT strategy.

Components of a Mobile Strategy

Discussions on mobile strategy over the previous decade have focused on the control and management of mobile devices, and the governance of the corresponding business processes. Those topics are still critically important, but the "consumerization of IT," proliferation of mobile platforms, the widespread introduction of personally owned mobile devices, and the mainstream expectation of mobile applications for everything are driving the need for a more robust and sophisticated mobile strategy that takes all those components into consideration.

Although many companies have developed and managed mobility strategies for quite a few years now, the widespread disruptive change introduced by the iPhone and the iPad, combined with the mainstream adoption of mobile applications beyond e-mail, has left most of the traditional enterprise mobile strategies obsolete and irrelevant.

As mentioned in the previous chapter, Brian Carlson, the editor-in-chief of *CIO.com*, said, "Expect to see enterprises mobilizing all their core applications from CRM, ERP, expense management, inventory management, and time tracking.

An effective enterprise mobile strategy is no longer a nice-to-have, but a necessity for business growth."

While the mobility of the past may have revolved around e-mail, calendar, and contacts, today's mobile revolution is about complete and total worker empowerment. The successful delivery of those applications beyond e-mail requires much more of a strategic focus than IT has typically given to mobility.

Additionally, the rapid and accelerating pace of change in the mobile industry necessitates that a mobile strategy not try to predict the future. Rather, it should be developed and maintained in such a way that it expects and even plans for dramatic change. The iPad came bursting into the enterprise virtually overnight, and while it may have been the first to accomplish that feat in such a dramatic manner, it will certainly not be the last.

The process of developing and defining a mobility strategy will be different for every company, but an effective mobile strategy should consist of these core components:

- The business drivers
- Hardware ownership and support
- Deployment, provisioning, and management
- Enterprise services platform for innovation
- Application portfolio and road map
- Corporate governance and processes
- Security standards and audit processes

If you are developing a strategy for a division or department, as opposed to an enterprise-wide one, some of the components may not be applicable to your strategy. For instance, a division-level strategy may focus on the business drivers and application portfolio and road map specific to that business unit, while the issues involving hardware ownership, support, deployment, provisioning, management, corporate governance, security standards, and audit processes may be handled on the enterprise level.

On the other hand, your enterprise-wide strategy may choose to focus more on the underlying infrastructure issues and leave the application portfolios and road maps to the various business units based on the shared foundation.

In any case, whether the responsibility for any of these given strategic components falls under your purview or not, you should ensure that all these components are ultimately addressed.

The Business Drivers

What results are desired by the business that can be delivered by the strategic application of mobile technology? Like all good IT strategies, the foundation of any mobile strategy should be the business drivers, goals, and objectives. Technology should never be used simply for technology's sake, but rather to drive the results desired by the business.

These business drivers should come directly from the overall company strategy, business plan, goals, and objectives. These goals could be anything, but may focus on topics like growth, profitability, innovation, customer satisfaction, worker productivity, or employee empowerment.

It can also be very helpful to engage in a dialogue with the business's leaders about their overarching strategy. When dealing with a transformational technology like the iPad, it's important to keep an open mind. As business processes and even entire business models are designed to be as efficient as possible within a set of constraints, technology innovation can fundamentally alter those constraints. The result can be a force imposing dramatic change upon the status quo.

Hardware Ownership and Support

There are two important dimensions to the discussion of hardware ownership and support. First, there's the decision between corporate vs. individually owned hardware. In many organizations, there will be a combination of the two, but what are the criteria for determining the appropriate ownership structure for a given enterprise? While the industry is trending overall toward individually owned devices, there will always be situations where corporate-owned devices are preferred or even necessary. For instance, many organizations do not want salespeople to be able to take their mobile phone numbers with them if they leave to go with a competitor. Organizations that allow personally owned devices to be managed by the company should also ensure that they have the appropriate legal agreements and liability waivers in place so that employees can acknowledge that the company has the right to remotely wipe the device, including any personal information or data, if the employee leaves the company or if the device is lost or stolen.

Secondly, there is the topic of platform support. While traditionally IT has been able to maintain full centralized control through standardization on a single platform, the trend of consumerization is making that difficult, if not impossible. There is a growing trend toward embracing consumer choice with respect to mobile phones, but standardizing on the iPad as a tablet form factor device. It will be interesting to see if that trend holds up over time, or if tablet form factors will also go the way of mobile phones.

Finally, it is important to note that the mobile strategy should cover both internal- and external-facing mobility. Generally speaking, the external-facing mobility toward customers and business partners will involve devices that are owned by the individuals or organizations (and so there is no control over platform support). However, I am aware of several organizations that have purchased iPads for business partners and also have temporarily provided iPads to customers to assist with specific workflows and activities.

Some of these topics are discussed in greater detail in Chapter 17.

Deployment, Provisioning, and Management

The topics of mobile device deployment, provisioning, and management are heavily dependent on the previously discussed strategic components of hardware ownership and platform support.

Device deployment is generally only applicable in the context of a homogeneous deployment of corporate-owned hardware. As mentioned earlier, centralized iPad deployments are growing in popularity even as smartphones are moving to a "bring your own device" paradigm.

Provisioning and management, though, are important for both a homogeneous deployment and the heterogeneous result of "bring your own device." In a centralized deployment, the devices may be already provisioned and pre-configured before being distributed to users, or the brand-new hardware could be provided directly to the users and they could provision the devices themselves in a self-service manner. In the "bring your own device" paradigm, self-service is generally preferred to full-service device configuration.

In either case, once the devices are provisioned, configured, and enrolled, the organization should have the ability to manage the devices. In a homogeneous corporate-owned deployment, it may not be appropriate to provide users with the ability to opt out of device management policies, but this may very well be appropriate and even advisable in a "bring your own device" paradigm where a carrot-and-stick approach is used to give users the incentive to opt in to corporate security policies and device management.

The process of deployment will be discussed in greater detail in the following chapters: Chapter 17 discusses many of the issues related to facilitating a mobile deployment; Chapter 18 covers the details of configuration and security policy enforcement; Chapter 19 outlines the process of application deployment and update management; and Chapter 20 includes details of mobile device management solutions and vendor selection.

Enterprise Services Platform for Innovation

As mobile technology continues to change and evolve so rapidly, the business should have the ability to rapidly and inexpensively innovate on the iPad. While most traditional enterprise mobility revolved entirely around mobile e-mail, calendar, and contacts, the current explosion of mobile innovation is building upon the availability of a mobile platform to enable entirely new types of applications that extend far beyond those basic apps.

The vast majority of the cost of mobile development within the enterprise is usually the integration with back-end data. By exposing access to those systems and functionality through a standardized mobile-friendly enterprise services layer, the cost of innovation can be dramatically reduced.

Additionally, by providing out-of-the-box access to shared functionality in enterprise libraries for things like application authentication, authorization, analytics, logging, and other utilities, developers can focus on creating apps that drive business value without having to reinvent the wheel.

We will also cover these topics quite a bit in later chapters. Chapter 14 discusses how data, functionality, and utilities can be shared across applications. Chapter 7 discusses the development of enterprise-friendly solutions, including some of these aspects of reuse. You will learn more about the process of creating mobile-friendly web services in Chapter 8. While Service-Oriented Architecture (SOA) has grown in popularity, enterprise services have been established, but those services are usually designed to be consumed and interacted with from applications residing in a data center on a private network, not a mobile device potentially coming in from an external public network.

Application Portfolio and Road Map

With the iPad in the enterprise, value does not come just from putting the device into the hands of users. The business value will come from empowering those workers and enabling them to do their jobs more effectively. Realizing the full return on investment for iPads requires the deployment of applications that enable the functionality and capabilities that your users require.

It's important to recognize, though, that the iPad is a fundamentally new and revolutionary category of computing technology. I don't believe that even Apple fully understood what the iPad was going to become when it released the device. As a result, not every existing enterprise application is appropriate for the iPad. And many of the apps that would provide significant value if delivered on the iPad will not be identical mirrors of existing applications. The iPad version will ideally be a subset of the existing functionality with a newly introduced superset of functionality made possible through the unique capabilities and attributes of the iPad. Those unique capabilities and attributes can also enable the iPad to deliver entirely new types of applications that were not previously possible.

The development of a strategic iPad application portfolio requires both the business and IT to work together to innovate and discover what's possible. This is where IT has the opportunity to step up to the challenge and deliver unprecedented levels of value to the business.

The next chapter (Chapter 4) will cover the process of identifying and prioritizing applications as part of a mobile road map, as well as the management of the portfolio of those applications. Chapter 5 discusses the decision-making process in deciding whether to build or buy your applications. Chapter 6 outlines the implications of the various application architectures available to the iPad, and Chapter 7 describes how these applications can be delivered as enterprise-friendly solutions.

Corporate Governance and Processes

The topic of establishing and maintaining IT governance is well outside the scope of this book, but I personally believe it is important to recognize that certain long-standing processes and policies may stand in the way of the iPad in the enterprise. Given the radical changes in the industry, with the iPad and the general consumerization of IT, it might be appropriate to consider how some of the governance processes and policies may need to evolve to recognize the rapidly changing technological landscape.

The emphasis of IT governance is often placed on ensuring compliance with enterprise standards and managing risk, but in my opinion the ultimate purpose of good IT governance is maximizing the value delivered for each dollar spent. When it comes to disruptive technologies like the iPad, even the best-intentioned IT governance function may initially be viewed as standing in the way of delivering maximum value. In today's environment of consumerized IT, enterprise standards and IT governance must be able to respond to the rapidly changing needs of the business and the individual user, whether on the front lines or in the C-suite. As necessary and appropriate for your own organization, these topics should be included in the development of your mobile strategy.

Security Standards and Audit Processes

Both iOS and the general consumerization trends are requiring that the enterprise adopt a new paradigm for mobile technology security. While traditional mobile security focused on the device level, the commingling of personal and business data and functionality requires additional attention to application sandbox-level security. Also, as applications are delivered to customers and business partners on non-managed devices, all security must of course be managed on the application level, as there is no ability to apply any security on the device level.

The good and the bad of the sandbox security model is that it is as secure as you build it to be. If you follow industry best practices and establish enterprise standards, then your applications can be extremely secure, but if security is left up to ad hoc development teams with no enterprise standards for iOS or sandbox-level security, then your applications may not be so secure.

This is just as important when you choose to buy applications instead of building them in-house. It is important to audit all your mobile applications, whether bought or built, to ensure consistent compliance with enterprise security standards. As the iPad is new to most organizations, the IT security group may not be familiar with all the potential attack vectors on iOS or the best practices for securing those applications. Additionally, these best practices and enterprise standards, as well as consistent iOS application security assessment and audit processes, should ultimately be integrated into the methodologies and processes of the organization's Software Development Lifecycle (SDLC).

Some of these security topics related to architecture are covered in Chapter 7. Security issues and best practices related to iOS enterprise applications are covered in Chapter 16. Security policies and enforcement are discussed in Chapter 18, and the management of those security policies in Chapter 20.

Ensuring the Value Proposition

The iPad in the enterprise is all about driving value. As discussed by many of the Fortune 1000 CIOs quoted in the previous chapter, the value of the iPad is not inherent in the device itself, but in how IT and the business can collaborate on discovering specific uses and applications that drive the ultimate value to the business.

Just as with the PC, the iPad is only as valuable as the results it can deliver from the applications it runs. IT today has the rare ability to leverage a brand-new transformational technology to help deliver the outcomes that the business so desperately desires.

In the book *Real Business of IT*, authors Richard Hunter and George Westerman write, "What executives ultimately want from IT is not alignment, nor being treated like a customer. Executives want outcomes. Increased sales, increased margins, and increased market share are examples of the outcomes that executives want. If the IT team is talking about and helping to deliver those outcomes, then 'alignment with the business' is a non-issue."

Talk about a double whammy of value creation! Take a device the business desperately wants to use, and use it to help them achieve the outcomes they are focused on. IT should not look at the iPad with fear, but rather with excitement about all the value they can create with the proper use of the device.

Managing the Conflicting Demands for Mobility

With disruptive technology like the iPad, there are often many conflicting demands of interested parties within the organization. It is usually IT that ends up in the middle to resolve these varied perspectives. While not necessarily explicitly included as part of a mobile strategy, it is important to recognize these different voices to ensure that their needs are addressed within the mobile strategy.

Users

Whether they're front-line employees or C-suite executives, users want to be able to use their mobile technology to accomplish their jobs. And whether they bring their own personal hardware into the workplace or are provided with a device by the organization, they want to use that technology to be more productive and effective.

Mobile technology has evolved into an extremely personal extension of the individual within today's culture. Devices like the iPad blend the boundaries of the personal and professional lives of a user. Rather than fighting that, embrace it. Empower your users and they will not only be more productive, but they will have higher levels of employee satisfaction.

Operations

The raw potential of mobile technology like the iPad to transform business processes is quite significant. Many organizations have numerous internal business processes that can achieve vastly higher efficiency through the introduction and transformation of mobile technology to streamline the capture of, distribution of, and access to information and functionality.

If the business sees an opportunity to take advantage of the iPad to optimize an operational process, they should be encouraged to experiment and innovate in the delivery of results that align with the overall business goals and strategy.

They should not be bogged down with trying to establish the iPad as an enterprise standard for the sake of IT governance.

Marketing

As the popularity of mobile technology increases, and as apps for devices like the iPod touch, iPhone, and iPad have achieved mainstream adoption, these devices have become an enviable platform and channel for marketing to and connecting with the customer.

Mobility has become an integral component of most marketing strategies and campaigns. In fact, the term "mobile strategy" is commonly used within the advertising and marketing arenas to describe a consumer-focused marketing or advertising strategy specific to mobile devices and channels. As external agencies or in-house marketing teams seek to develop the iPad and other mobile applications, they should be encouraged to follow architectural best practices and be provided with enterprise standards for things like security and access to shared mobile web services layers, which ultimately will provide the organization with a lot of value, since services and data required by external-facing applications can often be widely reused for internal applications.

IT

Of course, it is IT that is at the center of these conflicting perspectives. Since IT is ultimately responsible for ensuring security and managing support, the knee-jerk reaction is to push back on these demands for mobility. If a data security breach occurs, or a business operation shuts down because of a technical system malfunction, or if the call center is overwhelmed with support requests, IT is the throat to choke.

As discussed extensively, though, if IT chooses to ignore these demands for mobility, then other parties will just go around IT. This does force IT into a corner to some extent, but the flip side is that it gives IT a chance to create significant amounts of new value for the business.

Internal vs. External Mobility

The relationship between marketing and IT is a very interesting one in the context of mobility within the enterprise. For most companies, the first iPhone or iPad developed within the organization was driven by marketing. In many cases, this put IT in a defensive position, since these apps were often dropped into IT's lap to maintain and support long-term. It further complicates the situation that, through the development of these apps, the marketing department is filling a need for apps expressed not just by external customers and business partners, but by internal employees as well.

In the first chapter, a number of examples of this trend were discussed in detail, citing industries as varied as insurance and retail, where the companies often provide better data and functionality to customers through public-facing applications than they do to internal employees. Additionally, it's important to recognize that the functionality required for external consumption is often quite similar to the functionality needed for internal use.

For instance, a customer-facing marketing app distributed through the App Store, which contains product details, pictures, videos, and pricing, may also provide a significant amount of value to the direct or channel-based sales force. Another example might be an external application to provide customers with self-service types of functionality. Internal employees may have just as significant a need for that functionality as the customer.

There's an additional layer of complexity because, while the marketing group is often out in front of IT in the push to develop these applications, the customer-facing version is usually a subset of the functionality that would be required for an internal-facing application to be used by employees. As with the previous example, the internal sales team may want a version of the marketing app with product information and interactive media to also contain confidential competitive product analysis or specific talking points that should not be made freely available to the public. And with self-service applications, while customers are only acting on behalf of themselves, an internal-facing version would require employees to act on behalf of customers. In both situations, the internal versions of the applications would require greater levels of security and application authentication and authorization than are necessary for the customer-facing versions of those applications.

If IT is not involved in the architecture, design, and development of these external-facing applications, then unfortunately these external apps driven by marketing must often be entirely rewritten to be appropriate for internal use and consumption.

As a result, it is important for IT and marketing to collaborate and consider both external-facing as well as internal-facing apps in the development of mobile strategy and the application road map. When the enterprise mobile strategy takes into consideration the needs of both marketing and IT for internal and external applications (Figure 3-1), significant value and cost savings can be realized.

Since marketing groups tend to want to move faster to embrace the latest technologies than IT, marketing groups often decide to move forward with those new technologies without the support of IT. In the long term, this creates many problems for the management of the technology.

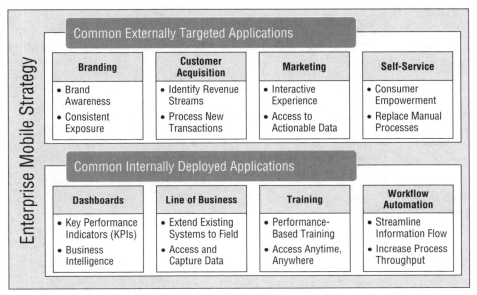

Figure 3-1: An enterprise mobility strategy should encompass both internal-facing and external-facing user profiles and applications.

Because a lot of marketing activities require moving quickly, it's ultimately the responsibility of IT to move as fast as marketing with regard to new technologies if IT wants to be involved in the discussions. As discussed earlier in this chapter, the creation of a standardized, external-facing, mobile-friendly web services layer as part of the enterprise services platform for innovation can dramatically increase the speed to market and reduce the cost to deliver incremental mobile applications, which is in fact exactly what marketing really wants. It's important to take all these internal- vs. external-facing requirements into consideration when developing a mobile strategy.

Defining the Mobile User Profiles

As the iPhone and now the iPad have entered the corporate environment, many of the cleanly defined boundaries and approaches to mobility have changed. Most organizations have multiple mobile user profiles, each with its own unique set of attributes. Through the process of developing an enterprise mobile strategy, the proper identification of these profiles is a prerequisite for the creation of an application road map. In fact, each mobile profile may even have an independent application portfolio and road map, although there is usually some element of overlap.

To understand what these mobile profiles are and the implications they represent, examine the chart in Figure 3-2, which describes four mobile user profiles for a sample enterprise.

	Company Owned	Company Influenced	Employee Owned	Customer Owned
Network Access	Local Network	Global Network	Global Network	Global Network
Device Management	Uses MDM	Uses MDM	MDM N/A	MDM N/A
Communication (PIM)	EAS N/A	Uses EAS	EAS N/A	EAS N/A
Connectivity	Always Connected	Usually Connected	Usually Connected	Usually Connected
Availability	Connected-Only	Disconnected	Connected-Only	Disconnected
Authentication	Shared or Individual	Individual	Individual	None or Individual
Authorization	Role-Specific	User-Specific	User-Specific	Customer-Specific
Focus	Task Oriented	Information Oriented	Information Oriented	Information Oriented
Automation	Extensive	Moderate	Minimal	Moderate
Interface	Efficiency Focused	Productivity Focused	Simplicity Focused	Experience Focused
Graphics	Minimal	Moderate	Moderate	Extensive
Architectures	Hybrid	Native/Hybrid/Web	Native/Hybrid/Web	Native/Hybrid/Web
Platforms (Bias)	Multi-Platform	Cross-Platform	Cross-Platform	Cross-Platform
Device Hardware	Full Control	Moderate Control	No Control	No Control
Device Lifecycle	3+ years	2 years	1 year	6 months

Figure 3-2: This chart compares and contrasts the various mobile user profiles within an example organization.

To set the context, imagine that this company, like most large enterprises, has been using ruggedized mobile computing devices for quite some time. Think of the handheld barcode scanners that are present within most manufacturing facilities and warehouses for applications like product inspection or inventory management. In cases like this, technologies like the iPad will probably not replace existing mobile deployments. The iPad may augment those deployments, though, as the iPad's unique form factor may provide an optimal experience for certain workflows and applications. This profile is referred to as "company-owned" because the devices are assets of the organization and in fact are shared across multiple users. Additionally, because these devices and applications never need to leave the physical premises of the company facility, there are baseline expectations of always-available wireless connectivity, and the network is a private and secure local network.

On the opposite side of the spectrum, the "customer-owned" user profile is quite different from the "company-owned" profile. Since these devices are owned by customers or business partners, the organization does not have the ability to manage the devices and in fact has absolutely no control over them. While this user profile is somewhat new for many organizations, the applications targeting this profile are usually driven by marketing and are therefore moving and evolving at a much quicker pace.

In the middle between those two extremes, this particular example describes two additional mobile user profiles: the company-influenced profile and the employee-owned profile. In many ways, there are significant similarities between these two profiles, but there is an important distinction. In this example, the company-influenced mobile user profile uses Exchange ActiveSync (EAS) for access to corporate e-mail, calendar, and contacts, and is subject to corporate Mobile Device Management (MDM) security policies and restrictions, while the employee-owned profile is not. While both of these profiles may represent personally owned devices, the company is able to exert a certain level of influence and control over the user and the device for one of the profiles but not the other. Many organizations take it for granted that devices used for business purposes will be used for company e-mail, and as such they can have some control over the device. But in some increasingly common scenarios this is not the case. For instance, many large companies have significant numbers of front-line employees who do not use, and often do not even have access to, a corporate e-mail account. As mobility grows more common, a growing number of these workers will use their mobile devices as their primary access to the Internet; any HR or payroll self- portals, time-off request systems, or other types of employee-facing applications should be prepared for mobile access. These applications will be consumed from employee-owned mobile devices that the company has no control over.

Of course, every company will have a unique collection of mobile user profiles that may be similar to the ones described in this example, or the profiles could be quite different. It's important, though, to clearly define these mobile user profiles early in the development of an enterprise mobile strategy, because different people coming from various areas of the organization will have unique perspectives about the "mobile user." So these profiles must be defined up-front and communicated to everyone involved in the mobile strategy.

Leveraging Economies of Scale across the Enterprise

Organizations can realize significant benefits in several ways by taking advantage of the economies of scale available within most large enterprises.

On the infrastructure level, it usually makes sense to standardize across the enterprise on a Mobile Device Management solution, in order to provide consistency in deployment, enrollment, provisioning, management, and security.

On the services level, it can often be valuable to create a mobile-friendly enterprise shared services layer where access to common data and back-end systems can be aggregated centrally. In some situations, it's appropriate to do this on an enterprise-wide basis, but for other situations it's more applicable to the division or business unit.

On the application level, creating standard components, libraries, or frameworks can not only provide significant savings but can also help to provide consistent security through standardization. For instance, centrally developing and maintaining a modularized component for application authentication, authorization, and encryption not only dramatically reduces the effort for a development team to get a new mobile application up and running, but it also ensures a much higher level of consistent security than would be likely if security were left up to individual development groups.

Of course, centralization, especially in application development, can be at odds with agility, so some of these standards are often best developed as part of a specific development effort and then moved into a centralized context.

Developing Organizational Best Practices

Always remember that best practices should not be developed in a vacuum. Of course, organizations can easily and rapidly adopt industry-wide best practices, but they shouldn't stop there.

For instance, as noted in the discussion of enterprise-wide economies of scale, mobile application development best practices will emerge through the actual development of mobile applications. The lessons learned by specific development teams and projects should be captured and shared with the overall organization.

In some cases, it may make sense to establish a Mobile Center of Excellence (COE) to help facilitate the sharing of knowledge and best practices across the organization. As mobility emerges as a critical function of IT, Mobile COEs are becoming more and more common. If that level of formality is not appropriate or desired for your organization, then something as simple as a wiki can and should be used to communicate and share knowledge and organizational best practices.

Summary

The iPad has irreversibly affected the role of corporate IT, and the development of an enterprise mobility strategy is now a critical requirement of any effective overall IT strategy. In this chapter we discussed the components of an effective strategy, including identification of the underlying business drivers, the approach to hardware ownership and platform support, deployment and device management, the establishment of an enterprise services platform to enable mobile innovation, developing an application portfolio and road map, evaluating mobility's impact on the function of IT governance, and the creation of mobile security standards and audit processes.

Of course, there are also the added complexities involved in managing the conflicting demands for mobility, including the importance of incorporating both internal- and external-facing perspectives on mobility into a mobile strategy. The identification and documentation of the mobile user profiles within your organization is an important prerequisite for mobile strategic planning, and it's always a good idea to leverage economies of scale and establish best practices wherever possible.

Are you ready to develop a mobile strategy for your organization?

In the next chapter we'll dig into the process of developing an application road map. And to help jump-start your brainstorming, I'll describe hundreds of potential applications in use by organizations in dozens of vertical industries and horizontal functions.

Creating an Application Road Map

The iPad is a powerful platform, but applications are what give the iPad its full business potential. In order to maximize the return on investment (ROI) of your organization's expenditures on mobility, you must leverage the platform with applications that provide true value to the business.

As you develop and evolve a mobile strategy for your organization, one of the most important aspects of your strategy and plan will center on applications. In previous chapters we discussed developing an enterprise mobile strategy that revolves around specific business drivers, goals, and objectives.

In this chapter, we're going to take a look at the process of developing an application road map in the context of an over-arching mobile strategy. This is done by identifying potential applications, organizing the apps, evaluating them, and prioritizing them by relative cost, benefit, and risk to the business.

Identifying Potential Applications

In identifying potential applications for your enterprise, it's often beneficial to conduct a brainstorming session.

This brainstorming exercise can be performed by an individual or a small team, but my experience has been that cross-sectional teams, consisting of both technical and non-technical individuals from IT as well as different business groups, is often most effective. Those involved will bring their own perspectives into the session, and having a wide variety of perspectives and viewpoints is a good thing.

Start by looking at how companies in your industry are using mobile technology, but then branch out and look at how companies in other industries are using the technology. Then think through the different user profiles and functional groups within your company to see if any ideas resonate from the perspectives of users in those groups.

After taking some time as a group to discuss how other organizations are using the iPad, it's important to set the stage for the brainstorming exercise. Encourage all participants to share any ideas that come to them. Don't shoot down or criticize any ideas at this stage. After the brainstorming generates a long list of potential application ideas, you can evaluate and prioritize the apps, filtering out any inappropriate ideas. The key here is to come up with as many app concepts as possible. The more ideas you have, the higher the likelihood that you will come up with concepts that can drive significant value. Remember, just expressing an idea isn't making the decision to actually implement anything. It's just an idea, and ideas can build on one another.

Vertical Applications

Specific industries, or vertical markets as they are often called, tend to have a lot of potential applications that are similar across companies in that space. Not every application is appropriate for all organizations. Many factors determine applicability; this section will outline some of the more common iPad solutions used by companies in these various vertical markets.

Again, it's often just as valuable to examine how companies in completely unrelated industries are leveraging mobility. Don't just focus on your own vertical markets. Some of the most powerful applications of technology can come from cross-pollination of ideas across completely different domains.

The following is not an exhaustive list of vertical markets, and it doesn't cover every type of potential application. This section will simply outline some of the popular and emerging applications for each of these specific industries (which are arranged here alphabetically).

Consumer Goods

Whether selling consumer goods to distributors through a business-to-business (B2B) channel or direct to the customer in a business-to-consumer (B2C) context, there are many powerful ways to use the iPad to improve and enhance the sales process. Customer relationship management systems can help sales staff keep track of customer interactions and opportunities. Order entry systems can process transactions while in the field and provide data for giving presentations and viewing reports.

For companies that audit retailers or send teams of workers to capture data about their own or competitive product pricing, positioning, or availability, the iPad can provide many time-saving applications. Barcode scanners can also be paired with the iPad to accelerate product information capture.

Many consumer goods companies are also developing customer-facing applications to reinforce their brands, extend the customer experience, find retail outlets, or even order products directly. As overall mobile application adoption continues to trend upwards, marketing and branding apps are becoming a critical must-have channel for major consumer brands.

Financial Services

Financial service organizations were some of the earliest adopters of the iPad, and can use the device for many types of information-driven applications. Business intelligence, executive dashboards, and other types of reporting applications are popular solutions for all kinds of financial service organizations.

Document management and workflow automation are also powerful solutions in this particular industry. Additionally, signatures can be captured electronically to be saved to documents and integrated into workflow. Commercial lending institutions often have additional paperwork, physical inventory examinations, audits, and other processes that can be significantly streamlined with iPad apps.

Most large financial service organizations are also creating many different kinds of external-facing applications for customers. Consumer banks can provide account management, loan applications, and bill-pay solutions. Brokerages can provide portfolio tracking as well as stock trading.

Hospitality

The iPad has the potential to enhance many aspects of the customer experience within hotels and other hospitality organizations. Additionally, some iPad applications can be used by employees and guests alike.

For hotels, iPads can be used by employees to streamline check-in or check-out processes, as well for various maintenance, housekeeping, and room service activities. Applications can also offer guests the ability to order room service, reserve amenities, access account folios, and even check out.

Some high-end restaurants are using the iPad to display extensive wine lists that are accurate with up-to-the-minute inventory. It can also be used by the host or hostess to look up reservations and coordinate table assignments. Quick-service restaurants can also provide menus, along with the ability to place and pay for orders for carry-out or delivery.

Many hospitality organizations are also developing customer-facing applications to reinforce branding, allow bookings or reservations, or otherwise interact with the service provider to enhance the overall customer experience. For larger hospitality companies with strong brands, guest-facing applications and functionality are becoming standard practice.

Insurance

Insurance salespeople can use the iPad to give presentations with interactive and dynamic calculators, including real-time, customizable illustration tools. Policies can be priced and quoted, and proposals can be displayed for viewing or e-mailed to a customer for later review. Contracts can be viewed and signed right on the touchscreen.

Claims adjusters can follow workflow for claims adjustment. Cameras, GPSs, and barcode scanners can also be used to accelerate data collection for many types of insurance claims adjustment. As most types of insurance claims adjustment require significant amounts of paperwork, which subsequently must be re-entered into a computer, there is a lot of potential for mobile apps. These applications usually provide a very compelling return on investment by simplifying data capture, increasing quality by performing data validation in the field, and reducing overhead and errors introduced when information from paper forms is entered into a computer.

For an insurance company that uses independent agents or brokers, it can be valuable to create applications that make it easier for the independent agents to sell the company's own line of insurance policies. Some insurance companies have even gone so far as to reward top-performing sales agents with iPads along with specially-targeted apps to help reinforce their relationships with the insurance company. Additionally, apps that can give independent agents or brokers access to claims status or commissions are growing in popularity.

Insurance companies with consumer products and brands can develop customer-facing apps to provide for policy access, self-service requests, and claims filing. In certain insurance sectors, customer-facing mobile applications can provide a dramatic return on investment for user self-service and have become widely adopted by nearly every large insurance company.

Manufacturing

While iPad adoption among manufacturers has been slower than in other industries, there is a host of applications that can drive a significant return on investment. Organizations that manufacture built-to-order products can extend product configurators to the iPad for use by customers, distributors, dealers, or direct sales teams. Whether selling direct or through distributors, customer relationship management and sales force automation solutions can provide strong value. Product designs can be viewed on the iPad as 2D or 3D computer-aided design (CAD) drawings, and can be used as a reference on the manufacturing floor or to facilitate conversations with customers or partners.

Processes that schedule manufacturing can be viewed, monitored, and even adjusted by management. Alerts and dashboards can provide supervisors with access to real-time performance metrics and let them see manufacturing issues as they are emerging.

Workflow and inspection processes can be streamlined by eliminating paper and digitally capturing data at the point of inspection. Barcode scanners can also be used to track physical assets, look up product inventory status, accelerate inspections, and perform many other data-driven activities. Maintenance personnel can use applications to provide access to equipment reference guides and service manuals, to look up the service history for a specific piece of equipment, and to track work orders or do other maintenance tasks.

If appropriate for the product, it may even be valuable to integrate the product with mobile devices like the iPad to access internal information, provide configuration, or otherwise enhance the usage experience. For manufacturers with strong consumer brands, it is becoming common to develop customer-facing applications for marketing purposes, as well as to provide product guides, references, training videos, and similar functionality.

Medical Devices and Pharmaceuticals

Organizations in the medical device and pharmaceutical industries were among the first large companies to deploy iPads to their field sales forces; the value this gave was incredibly strong. By giving these sales reps access to product information and other sales-oriented functionality on the iPad, the reps could maximize the precious time they have with physicians and dramatically increase overall sales productivity and efficiency. Rather than creating printed material that must be distributed and kept up to date, the sales reps can have constant access to the most up-to-date product brochures, fact sheets, and similar materials, which can then be shown to physicians or e-mailed to them upon request.

Pharmaceutical manufacturers are using the iPad for prescription drug sample management to assist with the process of keeping track of inventory and capturing signatures from physicians when distributing product samples. Medical device manufacturers are also using applications for inventory management as well as sales transaction processing.

Pharmaceutical and medical device manufacturers also use the iPad to develop clinician- and patient-facing applications. Physicians can use applications like these as self-updating electronic brochures, reference guides, product training materials, and calculators. Medical device manufacturers can develop applications for physicians that interact with medical devices to provide status, diagnostic, configuration, and other types of interactive functionality through mobile devices. Pharmaceutical manufacturers can provide drug usage and prescription calculators.

For patient-facing applications, both pharmaceutical and device manufacturers can provide educational content, reference material, and even applications that can give patients the ability to interact with medical devices through the mobile device.

Medical Providers and Practitioners

Physicians have traditionally been among early adopters for mobile technology, and the iPad is no exception. Due to the popularity of the device among medical professionals, an entire application category in the App Store is dedicated to medical applications. As a result, though, there is a lot of fragmentation within providers and institutions, since application usage is being driven by individual users as opposed to the overall organization. This means that most of the applications being used today are relatively stand-alone and aren't integrated with back-end systems and data. The use of stand-alone applications like reference guides and calculators is extremely widespread. Solutions like electronic medical records (EMR) and e-prescribing are gaining traction, but are adopted more slowly because they require integration and management by the provider or institution.

Among the most popular applications used by physicians are medical reference guides. These apps can provide powerful access to general topics, details about specific conditions, and information from the latest articles published in medical journals. Applications with drug databases, prescription calculators, and drug interaction calculators are also extremely powerful and potentially life-saving. The iPad is also popular among nurses and medical students as a powerful platform for training, learning, and reference.

Another popular use of the iPad is as an illustrative tool for patients. The device can be used to display 3D models of anatomy like the heart or spine to help physicians communicate with patients visually and to make it easier for patients to understand hard-to-describe concepts.

For complicated surgical operations, the iPad can be used as an interactive consent form, providing pictures, videos, or 3D renderings of surgical procedures to help medical professionals communicate complex concepts visually with patients, as well as capture on-screen electronic signatures for patient consent.

Applications to automate the capture of diagnosis and procedure codes can streamline the billing process as well as help to catch coding errors at the point of care instead of later during transcription and data entry. Additionally, electronic medical records can be accessed from the iPad, giving practitioners real-time access to information like patient status, radiology reports, and lab tests.

Vital signs can be monitored remotely from the iPad, and physicians can immediately see live patient data and alerts. From fetal heartbeat and the mother's contraction patterns during labor to cardiac rhythm, pulse oximetry, and peak ventilator pressures of patients in intensive care, this type of application gives physicians the ability to closely monitor patients from wherever the physicians are.

Oil and Gas

The oil and gas industry is a longtime user of mobile technology, but much of that use is with the "ruggedized" handheld computers required for extreme environmental conditions. As a result, the iPad is not an appropriate device for some applications in this industry, although for others it may be.

Inspection and maintenance processes can be automated with applications that streamline survey and data collection. Integration with cameras, GPS devices, and barcode scanners can also provide ways to enhance these workflows and processes.

With extensive embedded systems capturing enormous amounts of data and monitoring well- or drilling-equipment status, the ability to access charts, graphics, and alerts right from the iPad can be a powerful way to make use of that mountain of captured data. Executive management can also use the iPad to view the real-time status of various key performance metrics around safety and production. In an industry beset with safety concerns, especially since the Deepwater Horizon disaster, quick access to safety metrics is increasingly important.

Professional Services

Lawyers, accountants, consultants, and many other types of professionals were quick to embrace the iPad. Although independent professionals were free to use the iPad on their own, larger professional services firms also quickly saw the benefit.

Time-tracking applications can be integrated with billing systems, as well as mileage and expense tracking. By making it easier and simpler for professionals to track client interactions, less time is unbilled, which can have significant bottom-line potential for many professional services organizations.

Document management solutions can give professionals access to any document they need from wherever they are. Through sophisticated document search solutions, professionals can quickly pinpoint the exact document they need, saving time and money.

Legal research systems can provide on-the-go access to documents, citations, and case histories. Whether in court or in the boardroom, the ability to gain access to virtually limitless amounts of data is revolutionizing the way legal professionals practice law.

Contract management applications can provide the ability to customize contracts and capture signatures for on-the-go execution. Documents can then be saved to a back-end management system, pushed through a workflow system, or simply printed and/or e-mailed.

Public Service

Even though government agencies have not usually been early iPad adopters, the iPad provides significant opportunities for them. Additionally, government workers have used their own iPads to help them do their jobs more effectively. Government leaders around the world, as well as police officers and health, safety, fire, and transportation workers, are using the iPad to get information from anywhere and ultimately be more productive.

Communications applications can be used to keep field workers in contact with each other and central management. This can also be an extremely powerful application in disaster management.

The iPad can be used for data collection, replacing manual and paper-based processes. Apps can be used to facilitate inspections and streamline the data capture process, as well as refer to historical inspection records. Barcodes and GPS devices can be used to improve the efficiency and accuracy of workflows. Mapping and geographical information systems (GIS) can often provide significant value.

The ability to search for information and access it from anywhere is extremely powerful. Viewing legal regulations and penal codes can help attorneys, law enforcement officers, and others in the legal system. The ability to search for outstanding warrants and do background checks from anywhere can be highly useful to many organizations.

Real Estate

Many functions and roles within the real estate industry can be enhanced with the iPad. Both residential and commercial sales agents can have access to their information and customer data while on the go. Keeping track of appointments, properties, and communications can be challenging; the iPad puts all this information at the agent's fingertips.

Property inspectors and appraisers can use the iPad to replace paper-based forms and capture data more quickly and efficiently than they could with previous manual processes.

Commercial and residential management firms can use the iPad to keep track of service requests and work orders. Maintenance workers can have access to service management systems, and can be dispatched based on location and their skills.

Individual customers can search for property right from their iPads through many consumer-facing applications. Many real estate agents and firms offer their own applications for marketing and branding purposes.

Retail

Retailers are using the iPad for a wide variety of applications. Employees on the sales floor can use the device to interact with customers and to look up product information, availability, and configuration. Credit applications can be captured right on the device. Applications for scheduling can help with appointment management. The iPad can also be used as a kiosk, providing customers with access to product information, interactive functionality, videos, and other features.

Certain types of retailers are using the iPad for point-of-sale applications, and for processing transactions right from the sales floor or in overflow scenarios where checkout lanes are full and there aren't enough fixed point-of-sale terminals in the store. Barcode scanners can also be used for a wide variety of retail applications.

For systems that aren't necessarily customer-facing, apps providing dashboards, reports, alerting, and other critical business information can provide significant value. Applications can be used to aid with "planogramming" — the diagramming of fixtures and products to show how and where retail products should be displayed for highest sales and best use of shelf space. Inspection processes, survey capture, data collection, and similar workflows can easily be moved from paper to the iPad, and barcode scanners can also provide significant value in many of these types of applications.

Customer-facing apps are becoming a norm in the industry. Giving customers access to product information, availability, promotions, store locations, shopping carts, and even checkout capability can provide both a good marketing channel as well as a strong return on investment for customer self-service.

Transportation

Many different types of transportation companies have quickly embraced the iPad. The device is being used for workflow, checklist, and inspection processes by many companies in this industry.

Airline pilots are using iPads to manage their schedules, chart their routes, access airport diagrams, and check airway manuals and terminal procedures. Some airlines are even putting iPads in terminals and lounges for use by travelers.

Courier companies are using the iPad as a platform for proof-of-delivery of packages, as well as to provide real-time location status to customers. They can also dispatch couriers in real time for pick-ups based on the nearest available courier.

Consumer- and business partner-facing apps are also applicable to many aspects of the transportation industry. Package and shipment tracking apps can give customers access to real-time status, as well as functionality in scheduling pick-ups. Apps can also be used by transportation providers to give customers self-service access to information like schedules and to let them book transportation.

Utility

Utilities and other energy-related companies have been using mobile technology for more than a decade, but this industry also has been using ruggedized devices for many applications due to environmental conditions. The iPad can be used for many applications, though, that do not necessarily require extremely ruggedized hardware. Workflow, data collection, inspection, equipment maintenance, and service management are applications that can provide a significant return on investment. Apps that give management access to dashboards, reports, and alerts can also provide a lot of business value.

Utilities can provide their customers with applications to give them access to self-service functionality and usage information, as well as the ability to pay bills.

Horizontal Applications

In addition to vertical, industry-specific solutions, many other solutions are used across businesses in a wide variety of industries. These are called horizontal solutions. Of course, not every horizontal solution is applicable to every industry or company; some solutions are applicable for groups of only a few users while other solutions are applicable across nearly an entire organization.

Again, this list of horizontal markets and applications is not exhaustive, but it is a good representative sample of the most common mobile functionalities.

Business Intelligence

Whether in executive leadership, middle management, or operations supervision, information workers often need access to dashboards, metrics, and key performance indicators. While most business intelligence systems are designed to be used while the user is sitting at a desk, many information workers need access to that data when they are out and about.

The iPad is a powerful platform for interacting with charts and graphs, drilling into data, and viewing alerts. As a result, business intelligence has proven to be one of most rapidly adopted categories of business applications on this platform.

Communications

E-mail is hands down the most popular business communications application, but many additional applications provide value in communications. Online meetings, video conferencing, real-time chat, instant messaging, or online message board collaboration also provide significant value. Many organizations have highly dispersed workforces with deep expertise in specialized topics; mobile communication tools can be used to facilitate collaboration between workers and teams.

Communications systems can simply leverage existing platforms like e-mail via Exchange, message boards via SharePoint, or custom systems designed specifically for mobile workforce communication and collaboration. Communications systems can also be integrated with collaboration, knowledge management, and workflow systems to provide additional value where appropriate.

Consumer Self-Service

Many organizations have external-facing websites or applications that expose self-service functionality to consumers or business partners. Rather than picking up the phone or sending an e-mail, a self-service system can empower these individuals to do what needs to be done without requiring additional human involvement.

For organizations that have potential functionality along these lines, the business case is often very strong, because the alternative is usually a manual process that's extremely labor intensive. By pushing for the adoption of a self-service system, the company will realize significant savings. Mobile applications have proven themselves in many industries to significantly improve the adoption of self-service solutions.

Data Access

Whether data is stored in documents, databases, images, videos, or CAD drawings, the iPad provides a powerful platform for giving users access to whatever data they need from wherever they are.

Think of this type of application as a way for the iPad to become a portal into any source of information, data, or content within the enterprise. Giving information workers access to corporate data is the foundation of virtually unlimited numbers of mobile applications.

Data Analysis

The iPad can offer a unique and powerful user experience for analyzing data from anywhere while the user is on the go. While many mobile computing platforms have not been capable of performing significant calculations and data analysis, the iPad has hardware with a lot of capabilities for advanced processing. Additionally, the platform can provide users with rich interactivity to work with data that has not previously been available. From drilling into data by tapping to navigating around the content with pinch-and-swipe gestures, the iPad provides a one-of-a-kind user experience for many different types of data analysis.

Think of this type of application as a way to maximize the computing power of the mobile device to work with and manipulate data, and make decisions based on any type of corporate data, content, or information.

Data Collection

Even though rugged mobile devices have been used for collecting various sorts of data for more than a decade, the iPad now brings that capability to a new level. The touchscreen can be used to quickly navigate through workflows, fill out forms and checklists, and perform other data collection processes. When combined with geolocation functionality or one of the many iPad-compatible barcode scanners on the market, the data collection abilities can be enhanced even further.

Think of this type of application as a way to streamline and enhance the ability to capture information or content from anywhere and funnel it back to the organization, into whatever back-end system or database it ultimately needs to live in.

Document Management

As many organizations have moved toward a paperless future with electronic document management systems, the ability to extend access to complete document archives from anywhere on an iPad can be a valuable application for companies in many industries. Search apps can help users rapidly locate the exact documents they need.

In addition to the ability to access archived documents, the iPad also provides a powerful platform for completing document-based forms and workflows. Even more, signatures can be captured on the touchscreen for rapid and simplified document authorization and contract execution.

Field Force Automation

For any type of field organization, whether it's capturing data, performing tasks, doing inspections, or simply being on patrol, the iPad can offer a unique form factor for many types of process automation applications. This type of application can optimize the productivity of workers, reduce transcription errors from manual paper-based forms, and increase the overall efficiency of the processes performed in the field.

Field Service Automation

When field service technicians are responsible for managing work orders or other types of dispatch solutions, the iPad can provide an organization with the ability to keep track of these personnel and can communicate in real time with them. From dispatching the right expert technician with the parts on hand, to giving that technician the complete service history for a specific piece of equipment, field service automation solutions can provide dramatic productivity improvements and cost savings.

Geographic Information Systems

Geographic Information Systems (GIS) integrate GPS hardware with maps and other data in order to provide a wide variety of geographically based functionalities in the field; the iPad provides a powerful and user-friendly platform for these types of applications. From searching and querying map metadata, to performing distance or area calculations, to providing layered visual overlays of data, GIS applications are critical in many different business scenarios.

Human Resources

As employees become increasingly mobile, anytime/anywhere access to human resources systems will become a standard expectation. Accessing information like payroll, benefits, and vacation data is important, and so is such employee self-service functionality as vacation requests. Human resource professionals will expect access to the administration, management, and workflow aspects of these systems, while supervisors and managers will also need mobile access to this functionality from a reporting and workflow perspective.

Inventory Management

While the iPad is not necessarily optimal for every kind of inventory management solution, it is suited for many, especially those that need a larger screen for viewing information, or in situations where users are performing only occasional inventory management functions. Utilizing external barcode scanners, the iPad can become an extremely powerful platform that can augment, and in some situations perhaps even replace, existing solutions designed for inventory management.

Knowledge Management

Whether a knowledge management system is used as training or for occasional reference, a company's investment in it can be enhanced by extending that information to the mobile worker. The iPad can provide a very simple user experience to search, browse, and view content from a knowledge management system. For many types of companies, mobilizing the knowledge management system can be relatively simple compared to other types of applications, and can provide an immediate benefit by arming information workers with the knowledge they need to do their jobs most effectively.

Marketing

The iPad is now being used as a discrete marketing platform and channel by many marketing, advertising, and brand management groups. In the same way that iPhone apps provided a powerful mechanism to engage both existing and potential customers, the iPad is taking that trend to the next level. The capability of the iPad to provide interactive functionality and extremely rich user experiences is only limited by how creative one's imagination is.

Mobile Commerce

For both B2B and B2C applications, the ability to perform transactions and capture new customers is a powerful capability of mobile commerce. Mobile commerce applications can give customers self-service access to catalogs with product information and pricing, along with product configuration or customization tools. Transactions can be processed right from within the app, driving revenue in a truly self-service context.

Reporting

Most information workers must run many types of reports in order to stay informed and perform their jobs effectively. Whether reports are static or dynamic with interactive pivoting and drill-down capabilities, the iPad is a powerful form factor for many types of reporting applications. Some companies report that the cost of an iPad can be offset simply by replacing printed paper-based reports with digital reports delivered electronically on the iPad.

Sales Force Automation

One of the most widely deployed iPad solutions addresses sales force automation. Unlike a laptop, the iPad does not interfere with one-on-one conversations and can easily be used as a communications tool and a quick reference to display content or expose information.

Marketing brochures, presentation decks, videos, and other materials can be centrally managed and synchronized with each salesperson's iPad for access anytime and anyplace, rather than having to keep printed materials up to date and distributed throughout the sales organization.

Presentations can either be given on-screen or outputted to an external display or projector. Presentations can be a series of static slides, or they can include animations, audio, video, and other multimedia capabilities. Sales force automation applications can also provide the ability to generate dynamic presentations based on the customer, the audience, or even interactive functionality, as in the case of ROI calculators that update content automatically.

Customer relationship management functionality can give sales professionals access to customer, account, contact, prospect, and lead information. Users can capture customer and prospect interactions, and just as easily pull up historical records of past interactions and conversations.

In what may become their most powerful function, mobile sales force automation systems can also provide the ability to generate price quotes, estimate delivery dates, create proposals, and even capture orders. Those sales transactions can be passed to back-end systems for processing, fulfillment, and billing.

Security

With digital IP video solutions becoming increasingly common, the ability to access real-time or archived security video footage from a mobile device such as the iPad can be a powerful extension of existing security system investments. Systems can also provide alerts to appropriate workers when certain types of events occur. Giving security staff and other management personnel access to this functionality can provide significant benefit in many different use cases.

Training

Many organizations provide e-learning and training systems to employees, and extending those solutions to a mobile platform can often provide significant value. Videos and other forms of animation or interactive content can elevate the learning experience. Quizzing and testing functionality gives users the ability to quickly evaluate their own comprehension, and can also give organizations the ability to ensure that workers are learning the content.

Workflow Automation

In many organizations, workflow automation systems are in place to streamline business processes and give management access to approve or deny various types of requests. These systems can provide significant return on investment, and give organizations the ability to manage their workers from anywhere. With a device like the iPad, overall process efficiency can be improved.

Organizing the Applications

After you have collected a long list of potential applications, it's important to organize the applications into different categories and user groups before prioritizing them. One reason is that it's often difficult to weigh the relative merits of applications targeting completely different user groups. For example, if you were to compare an external-facing branding application (to be used by customers) against an internal-facing application used by executive management, it would be difficult to properly evaluate them. While both applications might target the iPad, provide similar functionality, and be developed using the same technologies, their purpose and value propositions could be completely different. Additionally, each of those applications might be paid for out of completely different budgets and cost centers.

By first organizing the applications into user profiles, applications targeting a specific user profile can be prioritized in the context of that profile. Independently, user profiles can be evaluated, compared, and prioritized by the overall value of applications within that profile. This can help dramatically to provide focus to the overall mobile strategy by prioritizing both user profiles and apps within each profile.

It is also important to recognize that there is often significant overlap between applications in the different user profiles — sometimes even overlap across internal- and external-facing user profiles. Since external-facing applications are often driven by the marketing or branding department, and internal-facing applications are often driven by IT, sales, or other specific operation group, there's often no awareness of what other groups are doing. Because both internal-facing and external-facing applications can be developed using the same tools and technologies, there can be significant benefits to the organization in coordinating these efforts and bringing them under a single mobile strategy, as pictured in Figure 4-1. While this is not possible or appropriate for every organization, it can provide dramatic cost savings for most companies.

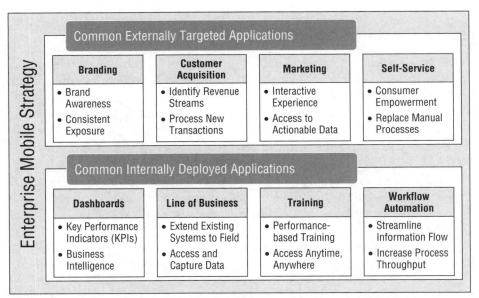

Figure 4-1: The enterprise mobility strategy should encompass both internal-facing and external-facing user profiles and applications.

Internal-Facing Applications

For internal-facing applications, it's important to understand the context and the user profile. The same application can provide significantly more business benefit to one user profile than to another.

You can start by making a list of all the different types of discrete user groups for internal-facing applications. For instance, you might identify executive management, field sales, field sales management, finance, manufacturing operations, and property management. Or you might identify field service technicians, delivery drivers, and distribution management. You might have only a few user profiles, or you might have dozens; it depends entirely on what type of industry your company is in, the size of your company, and whether you're doing this for the whole company or a specific division or operating group.

After you've got your internal user profiles, go through the complete list of potential applications that you've identified, and place each application in one or more internal-facing user profiles. It's likely that an application will be in multiple user profiles, so don't be afraid to duplicate applications. This process can often spark other lines of thought and new ideas for potential applications. Just go with it, and fill out your user profiles with potential applications. Don't worry about prioritizing the applications at this point, though, as that will come later in this process.

External-Facing Applications

As with internal-facing applications, it's important to identify different user profiles within the context of external-facing applications, and segment them so that their needs can be addressed.

For instance, insurance companies may have different types of applications for three distinct user profiles: sales tools for independent agents, policy self-service for existing customers, and interactive marketing apps for prospective customers.

Medical device and pharmaceutical companies might have even more external-facing user profiles, and may develop different application functionality that targets specific user groups like physicians, nurses, medical students, hospital administrators, and patients.

Retailers may have external-facing applications that target customers, as well as an app store distributing applications to suppliers and other business partners.

This segmentation of external-facing user groups independent from internal-facing user groups is important, since some of these applications are driven and controlled by marketing groups while others will be driven by IT or operations.

Again, as with the internal-facing applications, go through the external-facing user profiles and list all the potential applications. Don't be afraid to double up applications across different user profiles, internal or external. There will likely be certain applications that are appropriate for both internal- and external-facing user profiles, and even if the specific functionality differs somewhat between internal and external versions, don't worry about that at this point.

Evaluating and Prioritizing Apps

Once you have worked with your team to identify and organize the many possible ideas for applications, it's important to quickly evaluate the potential costs, benefits, and risks of each application in order to prioritize them effectively.

Cost should include the development, purchase, or acquisition of the application, as well as cost or labor associated with integrating the app with back-end systems.

Benefits should include hard benefits like increased productivity or workforce efficiency and reduced costs, as well as softer benefits like increased employee satisfaction.

In determining risk, one should consider both technical and business risks. On the technical front, it's important to identify any significant technical challenges in either developing the application or integrating it with back-end systems. Sometimes a mobile app might be very simple to develop in a mobile context, but very difficult to integrate with a back-end system in a way that properly exposes data. Business risks should include challenges concerning deployment, training, process change, and user adoption. If a mobile app requires users to change the way they work, adoption will always be more expensive, painful, and time-consuming than with a similar system that doesn't require a user to change. That is not to say that the change won't ultimately be in the best interest of both the user and the company, just that it is often difficult to facilitate that change.

Now go through each of the user profiles, both internal and external, and rank the cost, benefit, and risk of each application relative to other applications within that user profile. How you do this is up to you, but it's often easy to use a scale of 1-5 for each criterion. You can subtract the cost from benefit to calculate a quick relative value score. Any applications with positive scores are good candidates, and it might be appropriate to defer an app with a negative score (although if that same app provides a positive score in a different profile, it still may offer value to that user profile, since the costs could be covered in the context of the other user profile).

Depending on many different things, including your personality and the culture of your organization, how you factor the risk into the relative value score is up to you. However you choose to do it, though, it's important to rank each app within a user profile to provide a clear prioritization.

Summary

The business value of the iPad is not in the device itself, but rather in the applications built on top of the mobile platform that the iPad provides. As you're developing your enterprise mobile strategy, make sure you have properly identified, organized, and prioritized the applications in your road map to maximize the return on investment potential of the technology within your organization.

Architecture

In This Part

Deciding Whether to Build or Buy

As your mobility strategy is fleshed out, you'll develop a road map of potential applications prioritized according to the business benefit, total cost of ownership, and potential risk. At that point it's critically important to make the appropriate decision about whether to build or buy your enterprise solutions.

The decision to build or buy is one that will stick with your organization long after the initial deployment. The long-term total cost of ownership of your mobile solution will also be greatly affected by the build-or-buy decision.

That being said, it is also important to recognize that most enterprises won't build all their apps, and they probably won't buy all of them either. Most enterprises will likely take a combination of custom-built systems and off-the-shelf applications that can either function in a stand-alone role or be integrated with enterprise systems.

Your organization should develop criteria for determining whether a specific application should be purchased off the shelf or developed as a custom solution. First of all, the big question is whether the application exists as an off-the-shelf option. If so, does it meet most of the requirements? Can this app be customized to meet the needs of the business, or can business requirements be adjusted to take advantage of what is offered by the application? These questions and many more must be examined as you work your way through the decision whether to build or buy.

Finding Potential Off-the-Shelf Options

For any application idea that you're thinking of providing to your users, it's always advisable to see what's available off the shelf. Even if you're confident that a commercially available application won't meet your specific requirements, looking for similar applications in the App Store or from existing software vendors can help you define and develop the requirements for any custom-built solutions.

The App Store

The App Store has applications of all shapes and sizes. By the store's nature, most of these aren't designed for enterprise use, but rather for individual users. As a result, most applications in the store are stand-alone apps or are integrated with cloud-based services. A growing number of apps, though, are designed to integrate out of the box with existing enterprise server-based products, like SharePlus, which integrates with SharePoint, or MicroStrategy Mobile, which integrates with existing MicroStrategy implementations for mobile access to business intelligence. Some apps also feature pre-build integration with a server product that can be implemented in the enterprise environment and facilitate integration on the back end without modification to the mobile application (for instance, Cortado Corporate Server for document management or Roambi ES3 for interactive dashboarding).

As of this writing, there wasn't a way for enterprises to purchase applications in bulk through the App Store. One program, the App Store Volume Purchase Program, allows bulk purchasing for educational institutions, but not for corporations. This is not an issue for the many free iPad apps that are companions to paid back-end enterprise applications or server products, but it's a problem for paid apps. There are a few ways to work around this, though. There are "gift" applications the company can obtain for authorized users. Some app developers offer companies the ability to create a custom build of the application that can then be distributed through the company's in-house app catalog. Alternatively, many companies let users purchase the apps themselves, and in some cases offer reimbursement for the cost of the apps. Apple has been criticized for the lack of a bulk purchase program for enterprises, but one can hope that this will soon change.

Reading through the following list of apps available in the App Store can help facilitate brainstorming about what's possible within your enterprise. Whether the exact app is appropriate or not for your organization, it can help provide an example of how the iPad can be used by your workforce.

Document Management

Since most iPad workers will need to work with various types of electronic documents, many of the following applications are likely to be "must-haves" for your users. Some of these applications are designed as stand-alone document viewers and editors, while others are designed to provide document management and synchronization between an enterprise server and mobile devices.

Pages

Pages (Figure 5-1) is a core application within Apple's iWork suite. It establishes word processing as a mainstay in the mobile market. Dozens of templates make it possible to take business productivity on the road. Yet Pages' streamlined features keep the learning curve short with simple and intuitive interfaces.

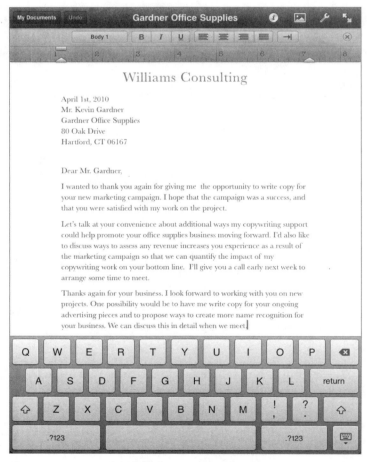

Figure 5-1: Pages is a fully featured word processing app similar to Microsoft Word.

Keynote

Comparable to Microsoft PowerPoint, Apple's Keynote (Figure 5-2) is a powerful application for creating, viewing, and giving presentations. Presentations can be viewed on an iPad for a small group or connected to a projector for a large group. Keynote can both open and save PowerPoint files, so a sales presentation can be created in Keynote and e-mailed to a client who may view it in PowerPoint.

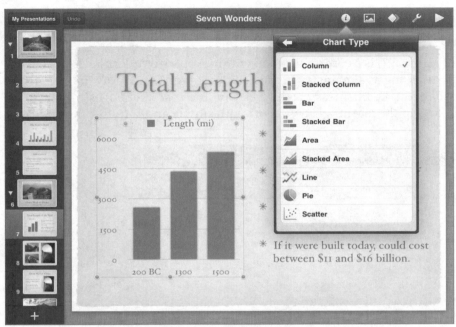

Figure 5-2: Keynote is a must-have presentation app for the iPad.

QuickOffice Connect

QuickOffice Connect Mobile Suite (Figure 5-3) can open and edit Microsoft Office files (Word and Excel) on mobile devices. This suite is especially useful for business professionals who need to manage their Microsoft Office files on the road. The app gives users the ability to create and edit Word, Excel, and PowerPoint documents. It can also be used to give presentations.

GoodReader

GoodReader (Figure 5-4) is a popular mobile document reader that allows you to manage all your documents, including PDF, Office, and iWork formats. You can also make annotations to your documents — highlights, mark-ups, and drawings — and transfer files back and forth to servers.

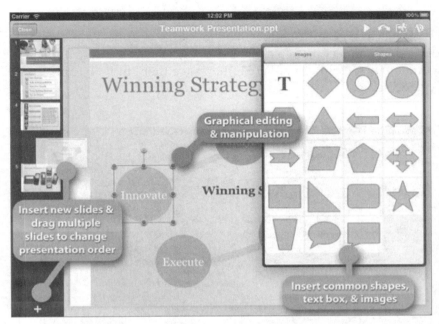

Figure 5-3: QuickOffice Connect can manage, create, and edit business documents on your iPad.

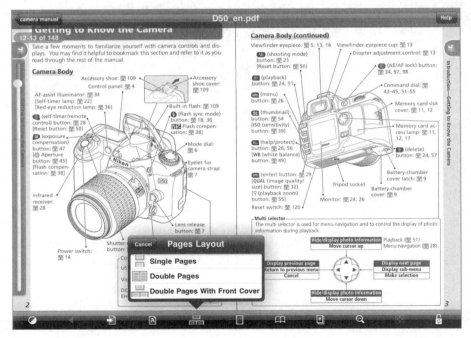

Figure 5-4: GoodReader provides easy viewing access to all your documents with the ability to annotate.

Cortado Workplace

Cortado Workplace (Figure 5-5) allows you to access your desktop computer from your iPad by connecting as a cloud drive. This app can display, edit, and print documents on a printer via Wi-Fi, then save them in PDF format on a central Cortado server.

Figure 5-5: The Cortado Corporate Server lets organizations publish documents that users can access, edit, and print from their iPads.

SharePlus Office

For organizations that have made significant investments in Microsoft SharePoint, the SharePlus Office Mobile Client (Figure 5-6) provides a rich native user experience that is not otherwise available through the browser. The app manages SharePoint data such as documents, calendars, task lists, and discussion boards. It allows users to exchange documents with other third-party applications.

Figure 5-6: The SharePlus Office Mobile Client allows users to synchronize documents and other content to their iPads while on the go.

Workflow Productivity

When you're on the go, you still need to get the job done. Whether you're managing documents and communications while serving on a corporate board of directors, looking up airport terminal information as an airline pilot, viewing three-dimensional CAD drawings as an engineer, or performing home inspections as an appraiser, the iPad can help you get down to business. Here are just a few of the many apps available in the App Store to help information workers stay productive while mobile.

Jeppesen Mobile TC

Airline pilots can use Jeppesen Mobile Terminal Charts (Figure 5-7) to stay up to date on the latest airport terminal information from around the world. This navigation app provides IFR/VFR charts, terminal diagrams, and manuals for airports worldwide. Jeppesen also provides demo charts, chart favorites, and push notifications.

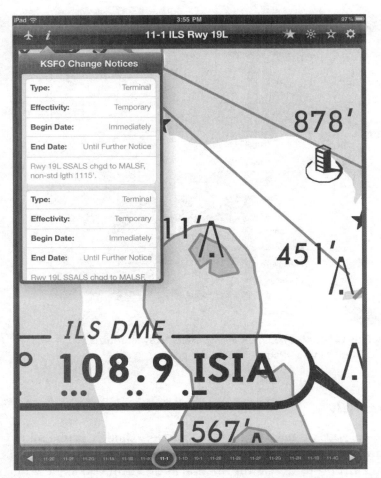

Figure 5-7: Jeppesen Mobile TC brings essential information to pilots' iPads.

BoardVantage

BoardVantage Collaborate (Figure 5-8) keeps your company's leadership team informed by providing secure access to documents and resources for board meetings. BoardVantage is a leader in the board portal market and is used by several Fortune 100 boards. Collaborate is a third-generation product which takes social media and mobility into the corporate boardroom.

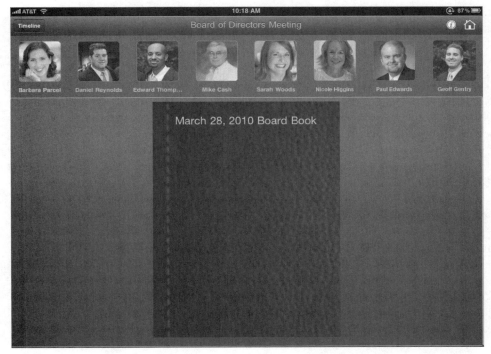

Figure 5-8: BoardVantage gives your corporate board secure access to documents and resources.

Numbers

Numbers (Figure 5-9) is the spreadsheet application in Apple's iWork suite. The onscreen keyboard is designed for working with numbers, formulas, dates, and text. Sixteen templates provide a great starting place to customize your spreadsheet with tables, charts, and even pictures. Users can navigate the spreadsheet by using tabs to move from one sheet to another. The full-screen view can display the finished spreadsheet right on your iPad.

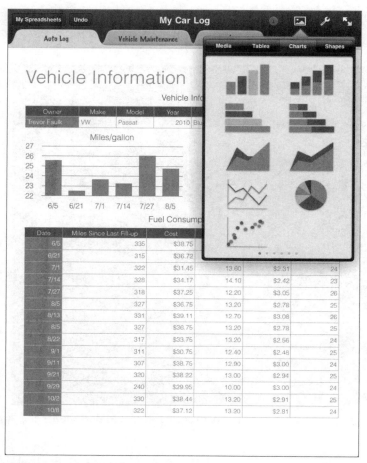

Figure 5-9: Numbers is Apple's spreadsheet app, which can open Excel files and export to Excel or PDF format.

DaVinci

DaVinci (Figure 5-10) is the first field app for appraisers on the iPad. Onsite inspection forms are complete with just a few taps of a finger on customizable data-gathering screens. Appraisers can accurately and quickly sketch floor plans, draw walls, and define areas. They can add photos, sketches, and even voice notes. When the work is done, DaVinci can send the completed file to the office staff long before the appraiser gets back to the office.

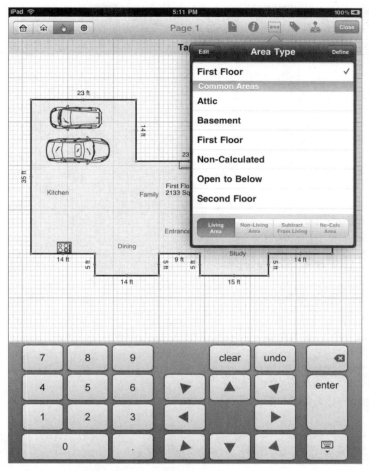

Figure 5-10: DaVinci allows field appraisers to diagram floor plans and perform on-site inspections with their iPads.

FileMaker Go

FileMaker Go for iPad (Figure 5-11) is a powerful application that can check and sync warehouse inventory, manage event registrations, update the status of a manufacturing project, or do just about anything else you can do with a database application. Users can build databases with FileMaker Pro and access the data remotely with FileMaker Go. They can find, navigate, and sort records, as well as add, delete, or edit data for later synchronization.

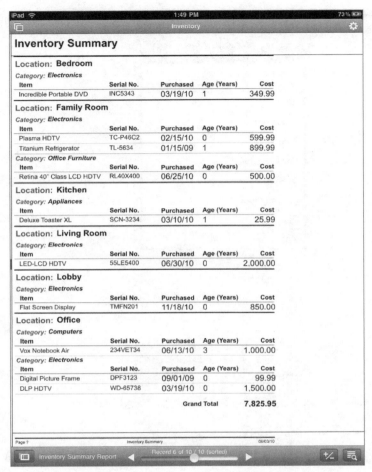

Figure 5-11: FileMaker Go puts your databases on your iPad and lets you remotely access, search, and update information.

AutoCAD WS

You can view, edit, and share your 2D or 3D computer-aided designs (CAD) from anywhere with AutoCAD WS (Figure 5-12). With the touch-and-gesture interface of an iPad, AutoCAD can annotate and revise computer-assisted drawings in the field. It reduces the need to carry around large paper drawings on the road. The application can open, modify, and export CAD documents in the DWG file format.

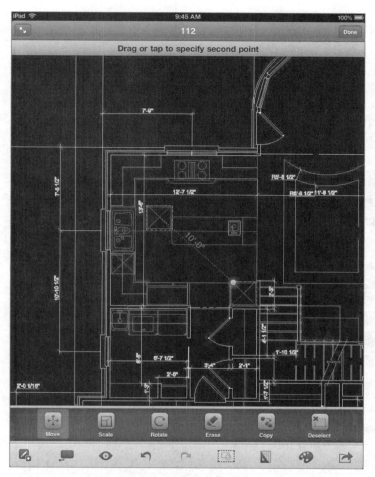

Figure 5-12: AutoCAD WS gives users the ability to access 3D designs on their iPads from anywhere.

Business Intelligence

Today's knowledge workers need constant access to information, and the following applications include some of the most popular iPad-based business intelligence solutions. These solutions allow users to view and interact with dashboards, key performance indicators, and reports for a rich user experience.

Roambi

Roambi Visualizer (Figure 5-13) works with existing business intelligence systems to transform reports and spreadsheets into secure mobile dashboards. The application works on the iPad with taps, turns, and swipes to give users interactive visual reports and graphs of their most important business metrics. You can access, analyze, manage, store, and share your data. Roambi ES3 is an enterprise server product that provides organizations with out-of-the-box integration with the iPad app.

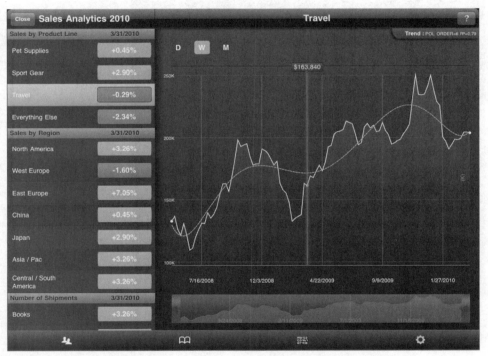

Figure 5-13: Roambi Visualizer allows users to be interactive with charts, graphs, and reports generated from their business data.

SAP BusinessObjects Explorer

SAP BusinessObjects Explorer (Figure 5-14) is a mobile data search and visualization application. The application features simple keyword search and navigation to access all your SAP information regardless of where you are with your iPad.

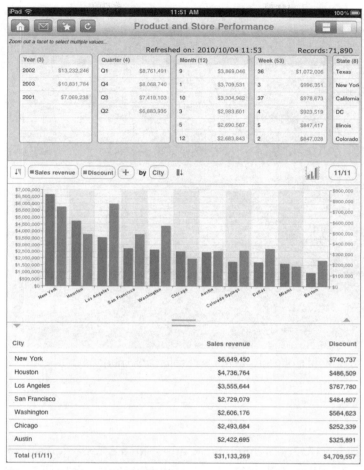

Figure 5-14: SAP BusinessObjects Explorer provides users with mobile access to information for on-the-spot decisions.

MicroStrategy Mobile

MicroStrategy Mobile (Figure 5-15) is a mobile extension for existing business intelligence systems. With MicroStrategy Mobile, users can access business data in multi-touch tables, graphs, charts, and maps. With a connection to a MicroStrategy Mobile server, they can view, edit, and share interactive reports, documents, and dashboards.

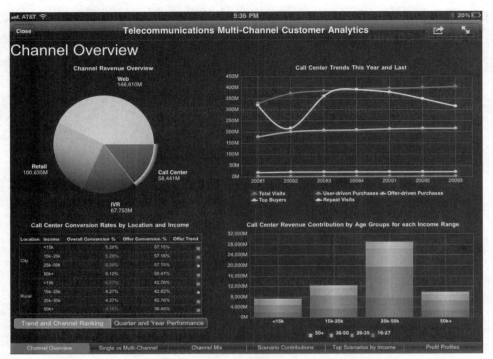

Figure 5-15: MicroStrategy Mobile offers real-time access to data, charts, graphs, and reports.

QlikView

QlikView (Figure 5-16) is a business intelligence app with a companion server product, which offers real-time mobile access to your company's performance and business metrics. The QlikView server provides interactive analysis and sharing and facilitates back-end system integration.

PushBI Mobile

PushBI Mobile Business Intelligence (Figure 5-17) is another application that uses existing business intelligence technology and transforms your vital business data into a mobile, visual format. You can access key performance indicators for your business and find the information you need for business decisions in remote locations. PushBI also provides integration with Microsoft SharePoint.

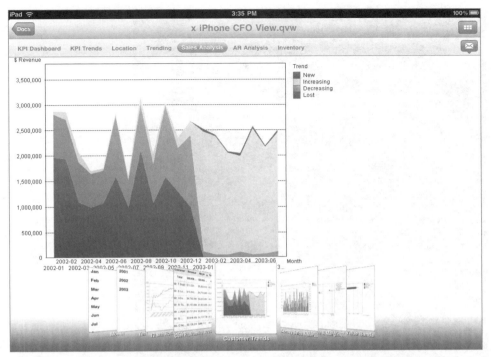

Figure 5-16: QlikView server feeds real-time business intelligence data to the QlikView iPad application for access to current performance and metrics.

Analytics HD

Analytics HD (Figure 5-18) creates and shares web traffic reports with Google Analytics and Adwords data, including traffic volume, length of visit, depth of visit, visitor frequency, and geographical location of visitors. A dashboard provides an overview, and multiple metrics are available for most reports. And of course it's all mobile on the iPad.

Knowledge Management

Whether you're trying to capture ideas or search for thoughts from previous brainstorming sessions, the iPad provides a powerful platform for knowledge management solutions. The following apps include some of the most popular applications for capturing, manipulating, storing, and searching for information.

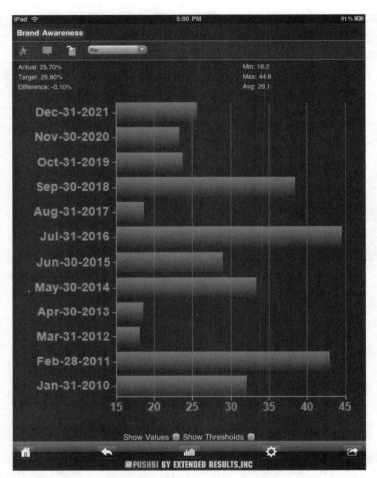

Figure 5-17: PushBI Mobile Business Intelligence creates iPad access to key performance indicators for your business.

Evernote

Evernote (Figure 5-19) captures text, screenshots, and voice recordings and tags the files with geo-location information. It helps you store anything and everything that you need to remember. Evernote captures content and then synchronizes it from your iPad to the cloud as well as your desktop.

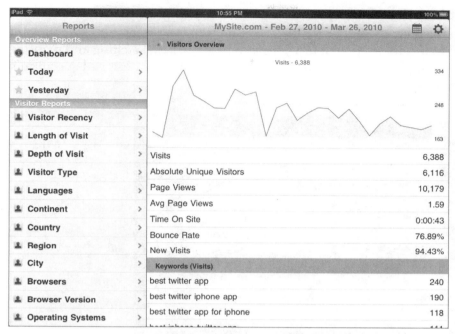

Figure 5-18: You can track website visitors and Google AdWords campaigns with Analytics HD.

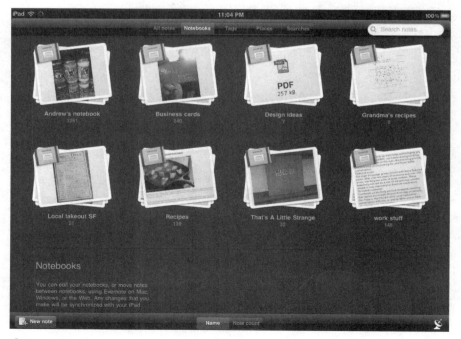

Figure 5-19: Evernote captures notes, diagrams, pictures, and voice recordings, and adds geo-location tags.

SketchBook Pro

Autodesk SketchBook Pro for iPad (Figure 5-20) is a professional-grade paint and drawing application. It provides a complete set of sketching and painting tools through a streamlined and intuitive user interface designed specifically for the iPad.

Figure 5-20: SketchBook Pro can create beautiful sketches and renderings with high-quality artist tools and layers.

OmniGraffle

OmniGraffle (Figure 5-21) creates diagrams, charts, flowcharts, and wireframes on an iPad. The touch screen becomes the canvas for a quick diagram, process chart, page layout, or website wireframe. Multi-touch gestures draw shapes, drag in objects, and style the diagram, bringing ideas to life.

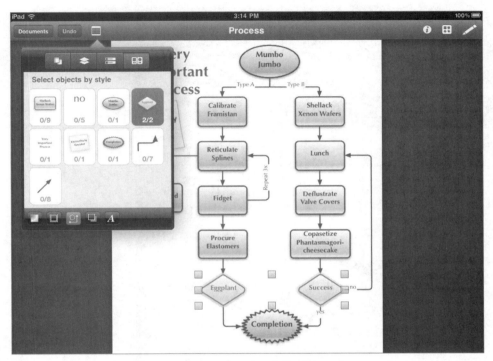

Figure 5-21: OmniGraffle creates attractive visual diagrams, charts, and wireframes on an iPad.

Penultimate

Penultimate (Figure 5-22) is a handwriting application that allows the user to take notes and draft sketches to review and share with others. You can use a pen to take notes, keep sketches, or share an idea. It's like writing on paper, but with digital power and flexibility. Thoughts are stored in notebooks which are easy to browse and edit. Penultimate includes photorealistic paper and an eraser tool that always matches your handwriting size.

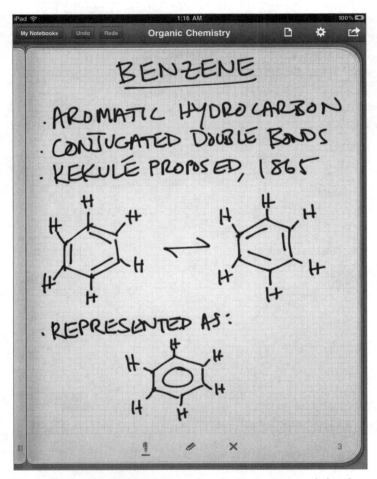

Figure 5-22: Penultimate creates handwritten notes and sketches on your iPad to share with others.

OmniGraphSketcher

OmniGraphSketcher (Figure 5-23) is another application which creates and presents handwritten graphs and charts on iPad. Multi-touch gestures help the user add new lines or change existing ones. Imported data can be used to create precise graphs or charts with text.

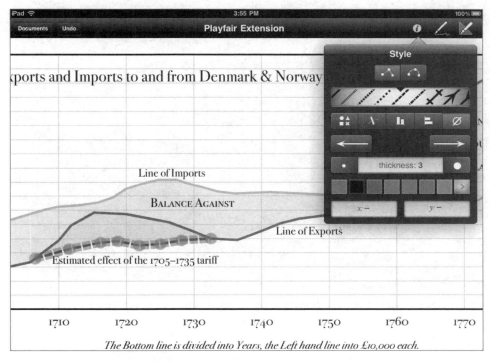

Figure 5-23: OmniGraphSketcher creates and presents detailed graphs and charts.

Dragon Dictation

Voice-to-text transcription is a reality with Dragon Dictation (Figure 5-24), a voice recognition application. You can speak your message and see the text five times faster than typing it on a keyboard. Then you can add your transcribed notes to text message, e-mail, and other applications.

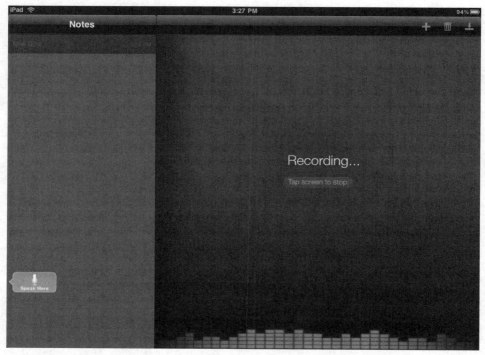

Figure 5-24: Dragon Dictation transcribes your speech to text, which can be attached to e-mail or other apps.

Collaboration

Whether sharing documents and tasks or holding an online meeting, the iPad is a powerful mobile platform for collaboration from anywhere. The following are some of most popular apps in the App Store for online collaboration from an iPad.

Sorted

Sorted (Figure 5-25) is a task management application which assigns each task a custom priority level, a due date, and a reminder. Completed tasks can be repeated or deleted with a swipe. You can sort tasks by priority, due date, or completion date. The alarm makes sure you don't forget appointments.

Figure 5-25: The Sorted application arranges tasks by priority, due date, or completion date.

WebEx

WebEx (Figure 5-26) is a mobile audio and video conferencing application that includes the user in online meetings from remote locations via the iPad. Multiple webcams can show all the participants in the meeting at the same time. Voice-activated video switching highlights the person who is talking at any given moment. The user can view documents shared from any computer with live annotation.

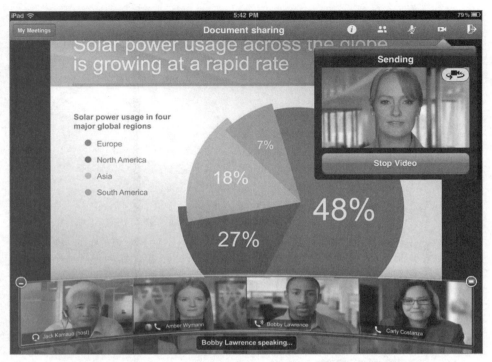

Figure 5-26: WebEx provides audio and video conferencing for online meetings from your iPad.

Things

Things (Figure 5-27) is another task management application which seeks a balance between ease of use and powerful features. It manages to-do lists, due dates, and also notes. A "today" list and a scheduling feature help the user keep daily tasks in proper order.

Dropbox

Dropbox (Figure 5-28) is an iPad application for viewing, saving, and sharing files from your iPad. It can handle photos, videos, documents, and presentations. Shared files can be sent via e-mail or linked with another application. Dropbox also can sync files among all your computers.

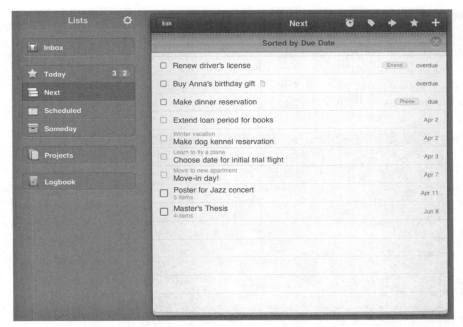

Figure 5-27: Things for iPad is a task management app that puts your "to-do" list at your fingertips.

Figure 5-28: You can view, save, share, and sync files with Dropbox.

1Password

1Password (Figure 5-29) stores usernames, passwords, and website addresses for easy access to your private online accounts. The mobility of the iPad allows you to take all your sensitive information on the road safely, guarded by a single password. 1Password automatically logs you into secure websites without retyping usernames or remembering a multitude of passwords.

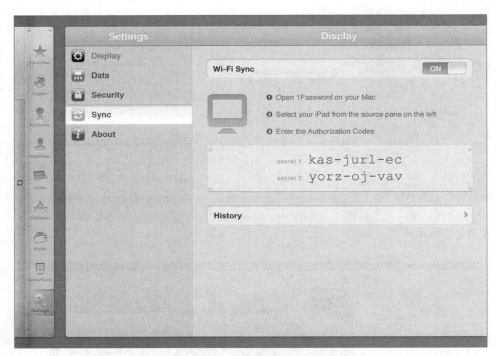

Figure 5-29: 1Password stores, remembers, and syncs all your secure websites, usernames, and passwords.

Fuze Meeting HD

Fuze Meeting HD (Figure 5-30) is an online conference application which starts a meeting, invites attendees, and displays meeting information with documents, images, movies, and presentations. You can designate any attendees as presenters so they can show the group their desktops, and you can mute or unmute each participant, all from your iPad.

Figure 5-30: Start your online meeting, add or remove attendees, and hear from everyone with Fuze Meeting HD.

Medical

The medical profession has always been considered an early adopter of mobile technology, and it has embraced the iPad. There are so many medical apps, in fact, that Apple has provided an entire category in the App Store dedicated to them. Here are just a few of the thousands of applications used by physicians, nurses, medical students, pharmaceutical sales reps, and many other professionals in the health-care industry.

Heart Pro

Heart Pro (Figure 5-31) is a powerful app that provides an anatomically accurate 3D model of the human heart. Users can rotate, spin, cut, and zoom in three dimensions, providing a rich graphical experience. Physicians and medical students can use this app for education and reference or to illustrate difficult-to-explain concepts to patients.

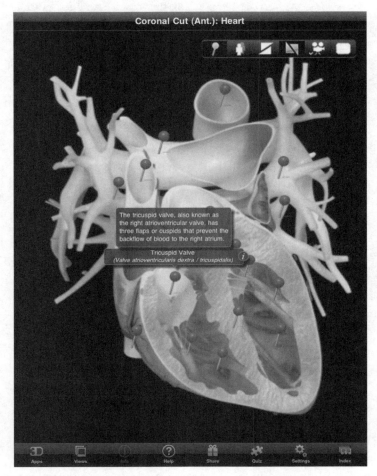

Figure 5-31: Heart Pro gives health-care professionals and medical students an interactive 3-D model of the human heart.

Epic Canto

As one of the leading vendors of electronic medical record solutions, Epic Systems now provides physicians and other caregivers with access from the iPad to Epic Canto (Figure 5-32). The application gives users secure access to clinic schedules, hospital patient lists, health summaries, test results, and notes. Physicians can also use the app for dictation that can be attached directly to a patient record.

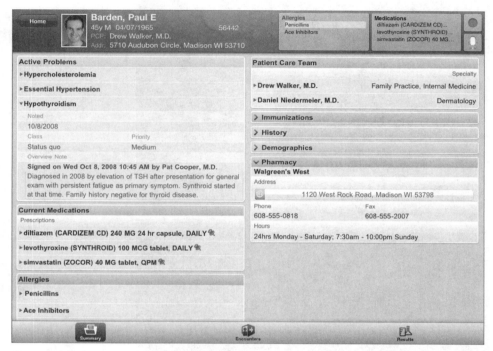

Figure 5-32: Epic Canto lets physicians do mobile dictation as well as access health records and patient information.

AirStrip Patient Monitoring

Airstrip (Figure 5-33) is a remote patient monitoring application designed for clinicians. You can check a patient's current condition on your iPad wherever you are, eliminating delay in assessment and medical treatment. AirStrip records vital signs, cardiac waveforms, lab results, medications, intakes and outputs, and allergies.

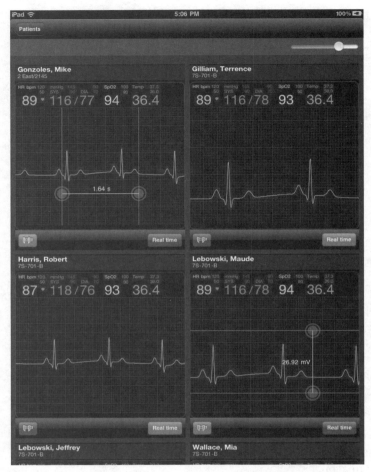

Figure 5-33: Doctors and nurses can monitor their patients' current conditions from remote locations with AirStrip.

Proloquo2Go

Proloquo2Go (Figure 5-34) is an augmentative and alternative speech solution for people who have difficulty speaking. It offers natural-sounding text-to-speech audio, high-resolution symbols, and automatic conjugations. It has an expandable default vocabulary of 7,000 words. Proloquo2Go is useful for people with autism, cerebral palsy, Down's Syndrome, apraxia, ALS, stroke, or traumatic brain injury.

Figure 5-34: Proloquo2Go is a natural-sounding text-to-speech application for people who have difficulty speaking.

iSpine Pain Management

iSpine Pain Management on iPad (Figure 5-35) is an education tool that provides cervical and lumbar spine pain management information to doctors and patients. It includes movies, teaching notes, and medical imaging files and presents diagnoses and techniques for pain management.

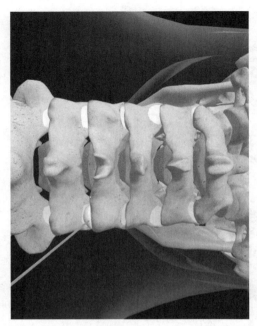

Figure 5-35: Doctors can use iSpine Pain Management for patient education on cervical and lumbar spine pain.

The Merck Manual

The *Merck Manual – Professional Edition* (Figure 5-36) is a mobile resource for health-care professionals to access medical information on the go. The content is downloaded to the iPad, so an Internet connection is not needed to use the Merck Manual, which includes medical images, charts, and figures for symptoms, diagnosis, and treatment of patients. The manual addresses thousands of diseases and treatments displayed by a search-and-browse engine for fast navigation.

Legal

The iPad has revolutionized how lawyers can be productive while not at their desks. The ability to search documents, case histories, and legal research databases from anywhere is changing the way lawyers do their jobs.

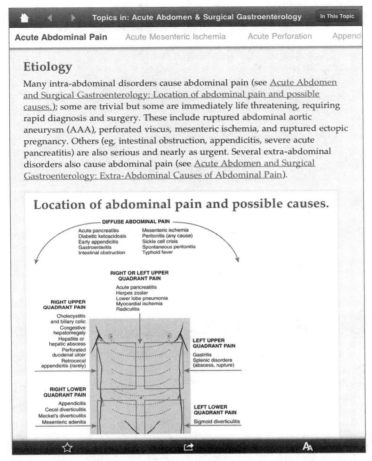

Figure 5-36: The Merck Manual is a fully searchable mobile medical manual for health-care professionals.

WestlawNext

WestlawNext (Figure 5-37) gives users the ability to research legal issues and search documents from their iPads. Documents can be sorted, organized, and annotated from within the application, and content can be selected and e-mailed along with appropriate references. Legal professionals can use the app to perform research from wherever they are.

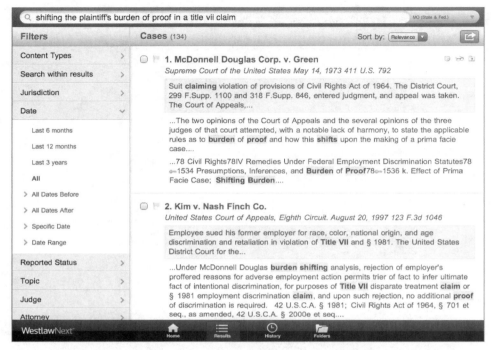

Figure 5-37: WestlawNext provides lawyers and other professionals with a legal research system accessible on the iPad.

DocuSign

Legal contracts and other documents can be managed with DocuSign (Figure 5-38), which gives users the ability to send, track, and sign documents on the go from the iPad. This application takes digital document management to the next level of mobile productivity.

IT Management

Information technology professionals need apps, too, and many are available off the shelf in the App Store. From security monitoring and remote server access to website management and FTP clients, there are many powerful apps for the iPad; here are some of the most popular.

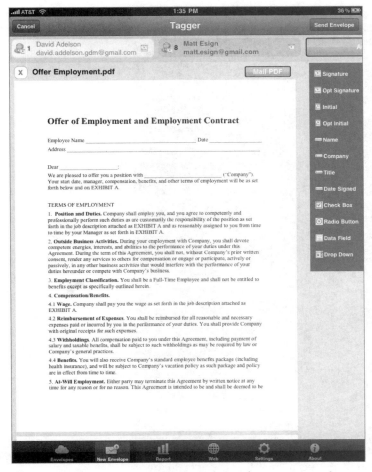

Figure 5-38: You can send, track, and sign documents anytime and anywhere with DocuSign for iPad.

MobileIron Sentry

MobileIron Sentry is a powerful mobile device management solution for administrators (Figure 5-39). The app provides graphical charts and diagrams to visually represent network security threats. It's covered in greater detail in Chapter 20.

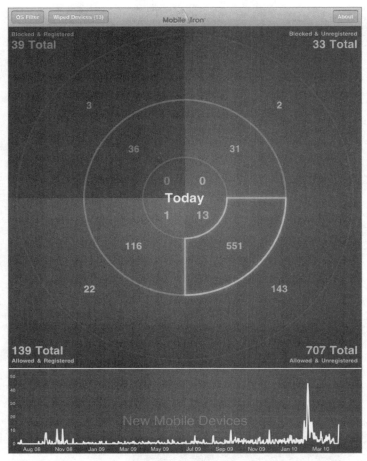

Figure 5-39: MobileIron Sentry lets administrators see real-time security threats on the network.

Wyse PocketCloud

Sometimes you just need to run a Windows program, and with Wyse PocketCloud (Figure 5-40) there's no need to put down your iPad. This application allows users to remotely access their desktop computers from their iPads. Using the Remote Desktop Protocol (RDP), users can connect to a Windows computer and use it as if they were physically there.

Figure 5-40: Wyse PocketCloud provides a remote desktop and RDP client to let users control Windows-based computers and applications from their iPads.

iSSH

If you're a server administrator, there's a good chance that you do your fair share of Secure Shell (SSH), Telnet, and Virtual Network Computing (VNC). With iSSH (Figure 5-41), you can do all of that and more to stay productive from wherever you are with your iPad.

Figure 5-41: iSSH provides SSH, Telnet, and Terminal connections wirelessly with the iPad.

Gusto

Gusto (Figure 5-42) gives web developers with iPads the ability to manage web design and development workflows as well as make changes to web content from anywhere. Website content can be updated and previewed locally. Multiple projects can be managed simultaneously, and content can be published via the built-in FTP/SFTP client.

Figure 5-42: Web developers can maintain their websites from their iPads using Gusto.

FTP On The Go PRO

Whether you're managing a server, updating a website, or moving files back and forth, sometimes you need to use FTP when mobile. FTP On The Go PRO (Figure 5-43) allows users to download, view, modify, and upload files from an iPad via FTP or SFTP.

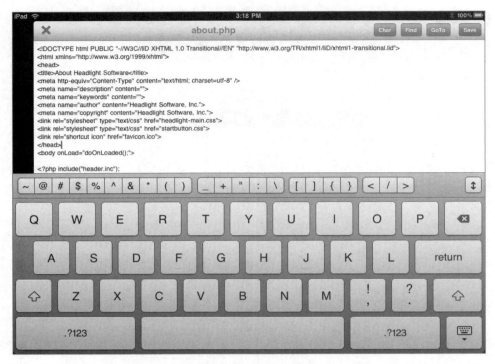

Figure 5-43: FTP On The Go PRO gives users access to their files from anywhere using FTP.

Alternatives to Buying through the App Store

Off-the-shelf applications in the App Store can meet many of your needs, but if you need to make certain specific changes, like custom integrations to back-end systems, adding additional data encryption, or supporting a single sign-on model, you do have alternatives. You might be able to approach the app developer to license an application for in-house enterprise app distribution, bypassing the Apple App Store.

While not every developer will be willing to participate in these types of arrangements, many developers of applications in the App Store are happy to create custom versions for specific organizations to deploy through in-house enterprise deployment models. They might even be willing to license their applications to you through source code or static libraries, so that you can further customize the applications yourself, or potentially even include their functionality within your own custom in-house applications.

For instance, SouthLabs, the developer of the SharePlus client for Microsoft SharePoint, offers enterprise customers several licensing options for custom branding and other application customization, premium customer support, and in-house enterprise app deployment.

Existing Software Vendors

If you're looking to extend the data and/or functionality from existing enterprise systems to the iPad, it's always advisable to talk to the existing software vendors to learn their strategy and view of the iPad.

Many enterprise software vendors are beginning to launch applications in the App Store. Other vendors are taking the approach of developing template applications that specific enterprises can license and then build and distribute as in-house enterprise applications, thus bypassing the App Store.

If you're thinking of developing an iPad version of an existing packaged enterprise software product, you should certainly reach out to the vendor to determine the vendor's road map for a mobile application. If vendors are developing mobile versions of their software, you can determine if what is being developed will meet your needs, and whether it will save you money. On the other hand, a number of enterprise software organizations are using mobile applications to push customers into upgrading to the latest version of their back-end products. In that case, if you're not otherwise planning such an upgrade, it may be more cost effective to build your own mobile extension. In any case, it's important to have the channels of communication open with your existing software vendors when it comes to application mobilization.

Understanding the Implications of Building

If the application you need is not available in the App Store or from your existing software vendors, then you may need to build your own custom application. While this is necessary for many different types of situations and use cases, there are significant implications to writing your own applications, and it's important to understand these before going too far down the path of any development effort.

Of course, solution integration and system maintenance are issues with any kind of enterprise application development. With mobile development, though, these challenges can be amplified for a number of reasons. Since most mobile development will require data access from outside the corporate firewall, there is a whole set of unique challenges to facilitating secure, reliable, and high-performance mobile application integration.

Solution Integration

Integrating a mobile application with a back-end system is always a double-edged sword. In many ways, back-end integration is necessary to give mobile applications the information they need to be functional and powerful in an enterprise context. But integrating a mobile application with back-end systems can be costly, complex, and time-consuming. The cost can be many times more than that of developing the mobile application itself. Mobile enterprise applications often cost significantly more than what might be estimated at first glance. The mobile applications themselves are often quite simple, but giving those applications access to back-end data, systems, and functionality is often a very difficult, long, and expensive process. This is not said to discourage development efforts, but simply to raise awareness of how complex these mobile integrations can be. A business should make a conscious decision when choosing to move forward with a custom development effort.

System Maintenance

Another important consideration in the decision to build versus buy is the long-term cost, time, and effort associated with system maintenance. Any time the solution changes, either on the back end or the client side, both sides of the integration must be kept in sync.

Unlike traditional enterprise software deployments, where the organization can control the client devices by requiring a specific version of the browser or operating system (like Internet Explorer 6 or Windows XP), today's mobile landscape gives users the ability to update the operating systems on their own devices. For companies that support the iPad, users will be able to update the operating systems of their own devices through iTunes at home, and there's currently not a way to prevent users from doing that.

Enterprise developers, like any others, must update their applications published in the App Store whenever Apple releases a new iOS version that changes or breaks the behavior of these applications. Apple gives developers access to pre-release versions of the operating system so that applications can be tested for compatibility and any issues resolved before the OS is released. Since this provides only a few weeks or, at most, a few months of advance notice, enterprises doing mobile development need to follow the same timeline as App Store developers. This often requires higher-speed development than enterprise developers are traditionally used to.

Before building an iPad application, it's critical that the organization understands the ongoing system maintenance that will be required, as well as the often accelerated timeframe.

Summary

As users demand more and more applications to run on their iPads, many apps will likely come from the App Store, while others may be custom-developed in-house applications. In this chapter, you looked at some of the many popular apps available for the iPad, which can help raise awareness about what's currently out there as well as what's possible for the iPad. It's important to stay on top of what products are available off the shelf in order to know what applications must be built.

In the next chapter, we'll examine some of the different types of application architectures that are available for both off-the-shelf apps and in-house custom development.

Evaluating Potential Architectures

Now that you know the applications that you need to build, you need to decide on the appropriate architectures for those applications. Sometimes the architecture is clear-cut because only one kind of architecture is capable of meeting the application's requirements. Most of the time, though, selecting the best architecture is not an obvious decision. Multiple architectures can meet the technical requirements, but have different ramifications when it comes to usability and the total cost of ownership (TCO).

Software architecture is often one of the most hotly debated topics in application development groups within the enterprise; it's important to recognize that mobile development, for the iPad specifically, as well as for mobile software development in general, introduces two variables that might be new to most enterprise architects: limited connectivity and emphasis on usability. As a result, you should look at these architectural discussions through the eyes of a mobile user, not just the typical user of traditional enterprise software.

In this chapter, we'll take a look at the two primary dimensions of mobile architecture: first, the approach of platform-specific coding vs. cross-platform application development, and second, the native vs. web vs. hybrid application architectures.

Architectural Approaches

When it comes to selecting the best architecture for your specific application(s), the criteria come down to environment, context, and usage. For instance, if you're developing a single application to be used only by a single type of user on a corporate-owned iPad that will integrate with just one back-end data source, as illustrated in Figure 6-1, the overall solution architecture may be very simple.

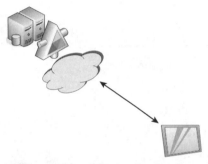

Figure 6-1: Developing iPad-only applications that integrate with a single back-end data source can allow for simplified architectures.

On the other hand, if your mobile environment looks more like Figure 6-2, with multiple applications running on multiple devices that are integrated to multiple back-end systems and data sources, then it's likely that every architectural decision you make will have a ripple effect involving the difficulty, cost, and timeframe of development, as well as maintenance and support of your applications. Every new application, back-end data source, device, or platform will have an impact on the overall solution, and the goal is to minimize the negative impact.

By having a clear understanding of the context, not just today, but of how your users will expect to use their applications in the future, you will be in a better position to make the architectural decisions that will impact the long-term flexibility and viability of your architectural solutions.

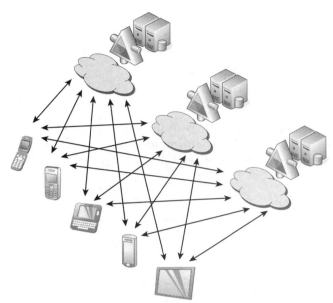

Figure 6-2: If there is a complex back-end and application environment, a more strategic architectural approach is recommended.

Device-Specific Applications

It's necessary to make certain applications device-specific. If the feature set is applicable only to the iPad, for instance, and not other iOS-based devices like the iPhone or iPod touch, then this may be an appropriate approach (Figure 6-3).

Figure 6-3: Developing an iPad-only application may use device-specific features and capabilities.

Platform-Specific Applications

Even though there are certain circumstances where device-specific applications are appropriate, it's usually advisable to develop your applications in such a way that they will support any devices powered by a specific platform (Figure 6-4).

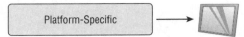

Figure 6-4: Even if the application will be used initially only on the iPad, it may be a good idea to develop it as a "universal" app so that it can run on other iOS devices in the future.

For example, you may be designing and developing an application specifically for the iPad, but if designed properly according to Apple's guidelines for creating "universal" applications, the application will also run just fine on an iPhone or iPod touch (Figure 6-5).

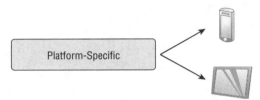

Figure 6-5: Optimizing the iPad application as a "universal" app will allow it to be highly usable on the iPhone and iPod touch as well.

A platform-specific approach is often necessary, but it's also important to remember the ramifications if the applications developed for a specific platform ever need to be supported on multiple platforms in the future (Figure 6-6).

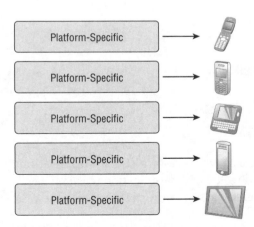

Figure 6-6: If additional devices and platforms need to be supported, a platform-specific approach will require multiple development efforts potentially using completely different programming languages and technologies.

Many organizations have ended up in the position of supporting multiple platform-specific versions of the same application because when the project began there was only a need to support a specific device or platform. But as time went along, the need to support additional devices and platforms was added to the requirements. Even if there is not a need to support multiple platforms today, it's important to determine if there will be such a need in the future, and if a platform-specific architectural approach is still the best choice.

Cross-Platform Applications

For those applications that need to support multiple platforms from day 1, or where it is clear that there will be a need to support additional platforms in the future, a cross-platform architectural approach, as illustrated in Figure 6-7, should be examined and evaluated to determine if this is appropriate for your application(s).

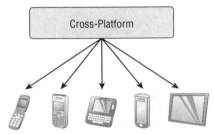

Figure 6-7: If other devices and platforms need to be supported, a cross-platform architectural approach should be considered.

It's important to note that a cross-platform development approach does not necessarily mean "write once, deploy to many." While significant amounts of code and logic can often be shared across multiple platforms, it is sometimes necessary to customize and optimize the user experience for each specific device, form factor, and/or platform. This is discussed in greater detail in later chapters.

Application Architectures

In the context of those architectural approaches, there are several basic kinds of mobile application architectures: thin-client, web app, hybrid app, and native app. Each of these architectures is appropriate for different situations, but it's important to fully understand the strengths and weaknesses of each approach in the context of your solution before making a decision.

Thin Client

Thin-client architecture comes into play when applications are installed and executed on a remote server. This is the modern equivalent to the "dumb terminal," as all processing is performed on the server. The thin-client iPad app, like Citrix Receiver, shown in Figure 6-8, is responsible for transmitting keystrokes and touch screen interactions, as well as receiving and displaying the visual user interface that is transmitted from the server. This allows a single thin-client application installed on the iPad to provide access to potentially hundreds of pre-existing Windows applications running on a server.

Figure 6-8: Citrix Receiver allows iPad users to access any Windows application delivered through the Citrix XenApp virtualization environment.

Advantages

For organizations that have already made significant investments in thin-client architecture and infrastructure, the thin-client approach for iPad applications can be very appealing. Significant numbers of existing Windows-based applications can be exposed to iPad users for a relatively small cost.

Also, if there are Windows applications that have been specifically optimized for the iPad (or even the tablet form factor more generally), for both the display resolution and the touch screen instead of a mouse and keyboard, then usability can often be quite acceptable in environments with fast and highly available local wireless connectivity.

Disadvantages

The downside to thin-client applications, though, is that they are completely dependent on the availability of a wireless connection. Additionally, due to the technical requirements of this architecture, the application performance will be greatly affected by both connection latency and bandwidth.

The other major issue is directly related to the primary value proposition of this architecture. Thin-client architecture lets you mobilize the applications that you already have, but these applications were probably not designed with the iPad in mind, so usability is often quite poor. Most existing applications are designed for use with a mouse and keyboard, not a touch screen. As a result, a thin-client architecture can often very easily and inexpensively give your users access to existing functionality, but if the usability is poor, then they simply won't use it.

Before making a decision to go with a thin-client architecture, it is highly recommended that you do a pilot with your users to get their feedback and determine if this architecture will be accepted by them.

Web App

Web app architectures have been extremely popular in most enterprise application development groups for quite a few years. The reasons are extremely compelling. Web apps need to be updated in only one place on the web server, and there's no need to manage distribution, installation, and updates to client-side applications. The applications are also usually quite portable, supporting virtually all browsers and operating systems if designed properly.

As a result, most existing enterprise web applications and those from third-party Software-as-a-Service (SaaS) providers, like salesforce.com, pictured in Figure 6-9, will work just fine on an iPad.

Advantages

Web applications have many advantages, but the biggest is the fact that so many existing enterprise web apps will already work on the iPad — and if they won't, relatively minor refactoring will usually fix any CSS or JavaScript issues. Your existing infrastructure, development capabilities, and build processes will likely work "as is" when developing web apps for the iPad.

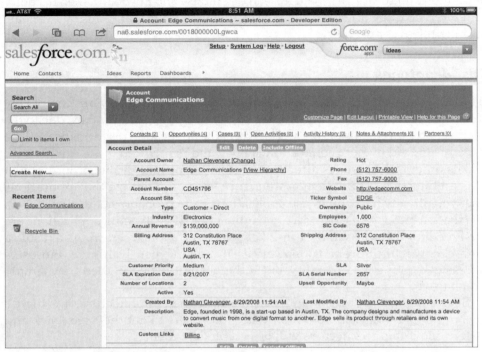

Figure 6-9: A Web app, like salesforce.com, shown here, is built using HTML, CSS, and JavaScript and is used through a web browser, like Safari, on the iPad.

You don't need to deploy or update anything on the client devices in order to maintain the web app, but it is possible to deploy a "web clip" for iOS that gives users an icon on their home screens to make the web app feel a little bit more like a native app.

Additionally, there are many HTML5 capabilities and graphics-accelerated CSS transitions for Apple iOS–specific hardware, which greatly enhance the capabilities, performance, and look-and-feel of these applications on the iPad. Through HTML5 these web applications can take advantage of geolocation, offline functionality with HTML5 cache manifests, and much more.

Disadvantages

Web apps have several disadvantages, namely connection dependence, lack of access to native features and capabilities, and often lower levels of performance and usability than native applications with similar feature sets. HTML5 has a number of features that can provide for disconnected use of the application, and while that usually works quite well for accessing static data, it's very difficult to maintain transactional integrity of data operations that must be performed in a disconnected state.

As with thin-client architecture, one of the biggest disadvantages is directly linked to one of the most significant advantages, namely that existing web apps can often run without modifications. These web apps were usually designed for always-connected use on a computer with a relatively large screen, mouse, and keyboard. Therefore, the user experience, performance, and usability may not be as good on an iPad as it is on existing desktop or laptop computer form factors, and may require additional tweaks and optimizations to improve the experience.

Hybrid App

A hybrid application is the combination of a native app with a web app. This allows for a full spectrum of hybrid applications, in which hybrid apps can be mostly native, mostly web, or something in the middle.

On one end of the spectrum, a hybrid application could be 99 percent web and just 1 percent native, with the native app doing nothing more than containing a web browser that points to the remote web server. On the other hand, a hybrid app can consist of mostly native application code, but can expose certain user interface components that are generated from HTML, CSS, and JavaScript from within a web browser object. A hybrid app can also be somewhere in between.

In Figure 6-10, the web app on the left is made entirely of HTML, CSS, and JavaScript and consumed through the web browser. The native app on the right is built entirely with iOS-specific native user interface using Apple's CocoaTouch APIs. The hybrid app in the middle is a combination of native and web, with the native application providing the native tab bar (UITabBarController) on the bottom of the display and everything above the tab bar being a web browser (UIWebViewController) that is displaying content delivered from a remote web server.

The native app "container" or "wrapper" for the web application can also provide hybrid applications with access to native device or platform-specific functionality through a JavaScript interface, as illustrated in Figure 6-11. The web app can interact with the native functionality through a pre-defined JavaScript interface that allows the web app to pass information and receive data through a callback. Additionally, the native application can interact with the web app through JavaScript or can interact with the web app's HTML Document Object Model (DOM).

100% Web App

100% Native App

Hybrid App

Figure 6-10: The "hybrid spectrum" ranges from web apps to native apps, with hybrid apps being anything in between.

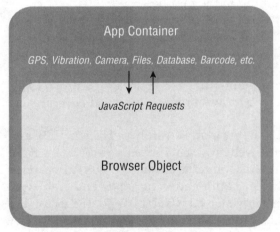

Figure 6-11: Hybrid apps can contain their own embedded web browser and provide the web apps with access to native device and application functionality.

PhoneGap, an open-source hybrid container project, provides a unified JavaScript interface for accessing native features from a wide variety of mobile platforms. This allows web developers to access native features like the accelerometer, camera, compass, contacts, file system, geolocation, audio recording, media playback, and more from HTML/CSS/JavaScript hybrid applications.

Advantages

Hybrid applications have many of the benefits of both web and native applications. As with web applications, hybrid applications can allow existing web functionality, infrastructure, and developers to be used in a mobile context. As with native applications, hybrid applications can access native device and platform-specific APIs and can be distributed through the App Store in in-house application catalogs.

Disadvantages

Since a hybrid application is essentially a native application that serves as a "container" or "wrapper" for a web application, it requires that an application be deployed and installed to the mobile device.

Even though hybrid applications can provide access to native functionality, most of the user interface is usually supplied through web browser objects rendering HTML, CSS, and JavaScript. While this is perfectly acceptable for many applications, it won't provide the same performance and rich user experience as a fully native app.

Native App

Native applications are compiled to and executed on a local mobile device. In recent years, the popularity of client-side software had begun to wane, but in combination with the incredible momentum provided by the explosive growth in the App Store, native apps are making a dramatic comeback. For many types of business applications, native apps are necessary to deliver the necessary performance and user experience. For instance, Roambi (pictured in Figure 6-12) is a mobile business intelligence application that provides rich graphical interaction with data visualizations.

While native apps require that the application be compiled to target a specific platform, it's important to recognize that not all native applications are platform-specific, and that there are a number of cross-platform development approaches and architectures that allow significant sharing and reuse of application code across other platforms. This will be discussed in much greater detail in later chapters.

Advantages

Apple has repeatedly demonstrated that success with mobile apps is all about the user experience, and nothing beats the user experience of a native app. Native applications provide the high bar of performance and user experience that most iPad users have grown to expect.

Additionally, for applications that require access to and synchronization of offline data to ensure transactional integrity, native applications are often the only way to go.

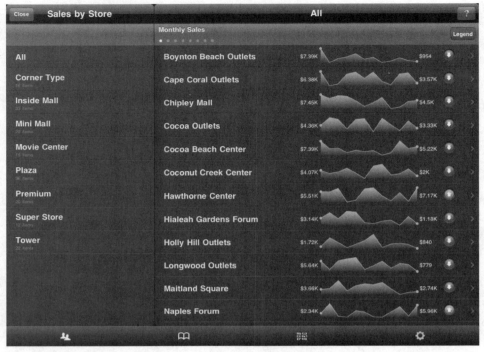

Figure 6-12: Native applications can provide a very rich user experience and can remain fully functional when a wireless connection is not available.

Disadvantages

Native applications must be deployed to the device. Since any changes or updates to the source code require the application to be recompiled, the resulting binary must be redeployed to the device. While iOS supports over-the-air application deployment, it is still generally more complicated to update native applications than web applications.

Also, in order to get the best user experience possible for the iPad, it usually means doing device- and platform-specific optimizations to take advantage of the unique capabilities of the device. This enhanced usability usually comes at an increased cost for application development and maintenance.

Selecting the Best Architecture for an App

When it comes to selecting the best architecture for an application, it's not always a decision based on straightforward objective criteria. A number of subjective criteria and opinions usually come into play. For this reason, many organizations have found it valuable to develop a standardized decision tree, like the one illustrated in Figure 6-13. This tree is defined by those in architecture leadership positions within the organization, and it can help to provide more objective criteria for evaluating a specific application and determining the best architecture.

In the same way that most organizations will have a mix of off-the-shelf and custom applications, they will also have a mix of application architectures. There is no overall "perfect" mobile application architecture, but there is usually an optimal architecture for any given application when taking into consideration its functionality and user profile.

Taking the time to develop an architectural decision tree can help to establish certain standards and consistency when it comes to mobile application development across an enterprise.

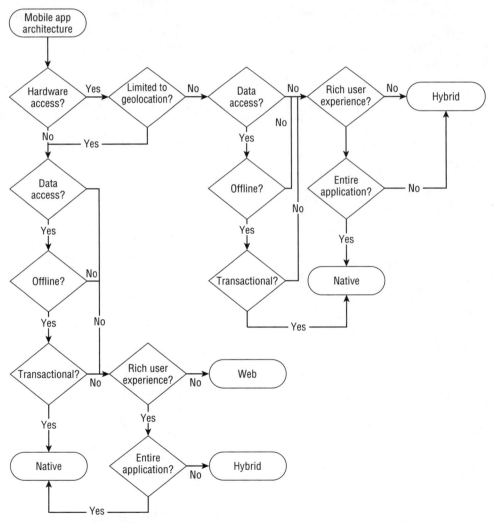

Figure 6-13: An example decision tree for selecting the optimal mobile application architecture.

Summary

There are two primary dimensions to mobile enterprise architecture: platform-specific vs. cross-platform, and web vs. native vs. hybrid. Across both of these dimensions there is full flexibility (i.e., you can have platform-specific web apps or cross-platform native apps). There is no single architecture that's better than the others, as each architecture presents its own unique set of strengths and weaknesses. It's important to weigh the advantages and disadvantages of each architecture in order to determine the best approach for any given application.

In this chapter, you studied the different types of application architectures involving native, web, and hybrid, as well as how to evaluate the best option for any given application. In the next chapter, you'll explore more of the architectural details concerning platform-specific and cross-platform development approaches.

Creating Enterprise-Friendly Solutions

- Maximizing your existing technology investments
- Porting your existing mobile applications to the iPad
- "Future-proofing" your new mobile development efforts
- Selecting the best programming language for your apps
- Allowing for code portability and reuse with proper design
- Ensuring the security of your mobile applications and data

Now that you've developed an enterprise mobility strategy, identified potential applications, determined which ones you need to build vs. buy, and selected the appropriate architecture, it's time to make sure that your app will be designed to be enterprise-friendly. What does that mean? Your new application development efforts should take as much advantage as possible of existing IT investments, infrastructure, and reusable software components. While the iPad is the most popular device right now, you should be certain that the investments you make on the platform are potentially portable to other platforms if the need should ever arise. Finally, you should make sure that you are properly securing your application sandbox with authentication and encryption, so that a breach of device security does not necessarily mean a breach of application security.

Leveraging Existing IT Investments

When it comes to innovative and disruptive technologies, one factor that often prevents enterprise adoption is the perception that existing investments must be discarded and replaced with new investments. While this is often the case, it doesn't always have to be. Strategic technology evaluation and architectural planning can maximize the investments that can be reused and minimize the investments that need to be thrown away.

These investments include web services and integrations to back-end enterprise systems and software. Getting access to back-end data and functionality is usually the most difficult and expensive aspect of mobile enterprise application development, but reusing existing web services can often soften this expense. Existing web applications can often be reskinned to be optimized for the iPad and take advantage of its unique user interface paradigm. Existing mobile applications can often be ported to the iPad while reusing significant amounts of existing code.

Web Services

As mentioned previously, the vast majority of the total cost of ownership of a mobile application is not in the development of the mobile application itself, but in the integration with back-end systems, data, and services. As Service-Oriented Architecture (SOA) has grown in popularity over the last decade, the wide availability of loosely coupled web services infrastructure has reduced the effort associated with developing and maintaining system integrations.

Even where the existing services are not necessarily optimized for mobility due to their architecture, protocol, or verbosity, it's often a straightforward process to build a mobile-friendly web services layer on top of existing infrastructure and services. Of course, it's not always appropriate to reuse existing systems if they are not scalable or flexible, but it's important to carefully examine your environment to determine what can possibly be reused within your existing infrastructure and investments.

Existing Functionality

Since most general enterprise application development today is done with browser-based web application architectures, the most common type of functionality reuse with the iPad involves web applications. As long as there are no browser-specific issues, most enterprise web applications are easily portable to the iPad. Unfortunately, many enterprises have had trouble upgrading from Microsoft Internet Explorer 6.0 (IE6) because their web apps are only compatible with IE6. As a result, CSS and JavaScript refactoring is sometimes required for the application to function properly on the iPad.

Although most web applications were not designed with the iPad in mind, there are often a number of relatively simple CSS and JavaScript tweaks that can be made to dramatically improve user experience on the iPad. When the user interface is beyond repair, mobile HTML 5.0 frameworks like Sencha Touch can be used to rewrite the presentation layer of existing web applications into rich iPad-optimized mobile web applications that can also be compatible with iPhone, iPod touch, Android, BlackBerry, and other devices. Sencha Touch, as illustrated in Figure 7-1, uses many HTML5 and CSS3 features to deliver rich mobile web apps that can look and feel like native applications.

Figure 7-1: Sencha Touch is a powerful mobile HTML5 framework for optimizing web applications for the iPad.

While the iPad is certainly helping to take the concept of mobile enterprise apps mainstream, custom line-of-business mobile applications have been used by many industries for more than a decade. Between Windows CE and Windows Mobile, Microsoft has held a virtual monopoly on the platform for these types of devices and applications.

Thankfully, though, for the many organizations that have made significant investments in developing C# .NET Compact Framework applications for Windows Mobile or Windows CE, it is often possible to reuse much of this code when porting to iOS. As shown in Figure 7-2, MonoTouch offers the ability to compile C# .NET code for iOS, so while the user interface and presentation layer will need to be redeveloped, the underlying logic and data access code can be reused.

If these applications were developed in such a way that the business logic and data structures are not encumbered by device- and platform-specific dependencies, then those classes should be quite portable to iOS via MonoTouch with minimal, if any, refactoring required.

Of course, this does not mean that every C# .NET Compact Framework application can or should be ported to iOS. Sometimes if the application was not designed properly, it will be more work to port and refactor the app than simply to throw it away and start from scratch. This is all the more reason, though, to ensure that applications and architectures are properly designed to maximize code portability.

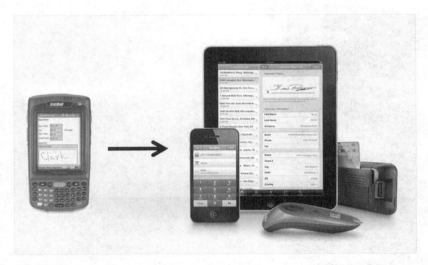

Figure 7-2: MonoTouch makes it possible to reuse existing C# Windows Mobile application code and functionality on iPads, iPhones, and iPod touches.

Future-Proofing Application Investments

It took only a few months after the launch of the iPad for corporations to begin deploying the devices en masse. Given the industry trend toward consumerization of IT, the only thing about the mobile market that can be known for sure is that it will change. While the iPad is extremely popular today, will it still be as popular in six months? What about a year, or two to three years? What about the competition from RIM, HP, Google, Microsoft, and others?

The mobile landscape is changing so rapidly that it's impossible to predict how things will look in just a few years. For organizations looking to make investments in developing and deploying applications for the iPad, this can be a very disconcerting thought.

How can you "future-proof" your application investments so that you won't have to start from scratch if you ever need to support something besides the iPad? While there is no silver bullet for perfect and complete "future-proofing" of your applications, there are a number of strategies that can maximize the long-term return on your application development investments.

Development Languages

One very important decision that will affect the "future-proofing" of your applications is your choice of a development language. While Objective-C is the preferred development language for native applications, according to Apple, the language is supported only on Apple's iOS and Mac OS X operating systems. Unfortunately, this does not provide organizations with much code portability, should the need arise to support non-Apple devices or platforms.

As mentioned earlier in this chapter, a very interesting development within the industry has been the emergence and maturation of the Mono framework. Mono is an open-source implementation of the Microsoft .NET framework that allows C# .NET code to be compiled and run on Linux, Mac OS X, and Unix-based operating systems. This is commonly used to allow .NET Active Server Pages (ASP.NET) web applications to run on Linux instead of Windows web servers, but it also brings C# .NET code portability to mobile application development.

MonoTouch, a commercial framework developed and supported by Novell, provides .NET developers access to Apple's entire collection of iOS CocoaTouch APIs from C# code. This allows .NET developers to bring their existing development skills to the iOS platform, as well as reuse existing C# .NET code and libraries.

For server-side applications, most development groups will want to utilize the technology stacks they're most familiar with. Within the enterprise, this generally means either Java/J2EE or C# /.NET. As of mid-2011, there is not a good way to develop native iOS applications in Java. While this is likely to change in the future, it complicates things for Java shops at present. Microsoft .NET shops have a much clearer decision, though, as C# .NET is very portable, not just between mobile platforms but also between client-side native applications and server-side web applications. Although Ruby is not as popular in the enterprise as Java or .NET, Ruby shops will be glad to know that there is mobile portability of Ruby code with a framework called RhoMobile.

Another approach is to use a Mobile Enterprise Application Platform (MEAP) like the Sybase Unwired Platform, Antenna Mobility Platform, or Pyxis Mobile Application Studio. MEAPs provide a middleware integration layer and allow development to be performed in fourth-generation programming languages (4GL). Each of these platforms provides high-level drag-and-drop development environments that are popular because they can often be maintained by non-programmers like business analysts. While Antenna and Pyxis offer user interface abstraction layers, Sybase's approach uses code generation to translate its proprietary 4GL into platform-specific source code. For iOS, the Sybase Unwired Platform generates Objective-C code that allows developers to create custom iPhone or iPad user interfaces that access the Sybase data objects and middleware.

Although not exactly a MEAP because it uses C# instead of a higher-level proprietary fourth-generation language, iFactr is a .NET-based mobile cross-platform framework that provides data synchronization middleware and user interface abstraction. iFactr provides native, web, and hybrid applications from a single C# .NET application code base.

Additionally, there are iOS-compatible cross-platform development environments and frameworks that provide code portability for the JavaScript and Ruby languages. Appcelerator Titanium Mobile translates HTML, CSS, and JavaScript into native mobile applications, and RhoMobile provides device-side native execution of compiled Ruby applications, although, unlike Appcelerator, the user interface is presented using HTML, CSS, and JavaScript. RhoMobile also provides an enterprise-friendly data synchronization framework called RhoSync.

Layered Architectures

In a single-tier application, the user interface, business logic, and data access code are tightly coupled. Interweaving code like this is generally regarded as problematic, since a change to any one of those things can greatly affect everything else. It also limits the reuse and portability of the code.

As a result, it is considered to be a best practice in enterprise software development to cleanly separate the code for these different processes into discrete layers. By providing well-defined interfaces between layers as shown in Figure 7-3, this approach allows for any of the layers to be upgraded or replaced independently of the others.

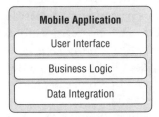

Figure 7-3: Developing software with cleanly separated layers is important for code reuse and portability.

In the context of a mobile application, the user interface layer provides the presentation of content and functionality, allowing the user to interact with the application. The business logic layer should contain the core functionality of the application with respect to workflow, logical execution, and processing. The data integration layer should provide the business logic layer with access to data, from either web services or a localized cache of data.

Portable Code

When it comes to writing software code that is portable between platforms, it's critical that platform- and device-specific code and references be limited to the user interface or presentation layer, as described in Figure 7-4. If the business logic and data integration layers are not encumbered with APIs and dependencies that are only available on a specific platform, then that code is highly portable and can allow for applications targeting different platforms that share significant amounts of code.

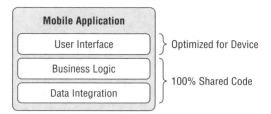

Figure 7-4: While the user interface and presentation logic will need to be different, carefully designed mobile applications can provide significant code reuse and portability.

Sometimes there is a need to access a device- or platform-specific feature from the lower business logic or data integration layers. In those situations, an abstraction layer should be introduced so that the code in the business logic and data integration layers operates against an abstract interface that can have a platform-specific concrete implementation. These business logic and data integration layers can be packaged as portable shared code libraries that are referenced and used by platform-specific applications with customized user interfaces and presentations.

Whether you're trying to target multiple devices in a cross-platform manner or simply to develop iPad applications, it's still highly recommended to properly layer and abstract your applications. With the unprecedented rate of change currently occurring in the mobile industry, if you want to develop enterprise-friendly solutions that will be around for more than a couple of years, you need to plan and prepare for change. That way, the majority of your application development investment is reused if you need to support another platform in the future, as shown in Figure 7-5.

The open-source MonoCross project provides an excellent example of this pattern with a cross-platform Model View Controller (MVC) design pattern. In this C# .NET-based framework, the models and the controllers are developed in a device-agnostic manner, while each view is an abstract class with a device- or platform-specific concrete implementation. This allows applications to not only share their models and controllers between platforms, but also implement platform-specific views for iPad, iPhone, Android, and Windows Phone, giving the application a user experience optimized for each platform.

Whether you're planning on supporting multiple platforms or not, you never know what the future will hold, so you should try to design your applications so that your code is as portable as possible.

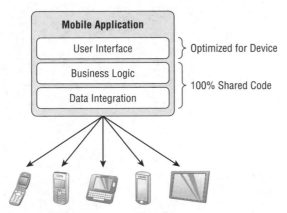

Figure 7-5: By ensuring that no device- or platform-specific code resides in the business logic or data integration layers, those layers can be shared by applications targeting different devices and platforms.

Architectural Flexibility

In addition to planning and providing for portability between client-side native applications on various platforms, it's also important to consider the portability of code between client-side and server-side contexts as illustrated in Figure 7-6. Of course, most server-side code is written in such a way that it's not appropriate for execution on a mobile device, but moving code in the opposite direction is usually much easier. If you optimize your code and are sensitive to performance and memory consumption, as is necessary with mobile development, then your portable code libraries can be easily moved from client-side to server-side contexts.

MonoCross also demonstrates this type of architectural flexibility by supporting both device-side native C# applications and server-side web-based C# applications using ASP.NET. One of the ways this is accomplished is by unifying the navigation paradigm so that both native and web applications use a URI-based navigation. Since web applications have more limitations on state and navigation, using the same relative-URI navigation approach allows business logic and data integration code to be shared between native and web applications.

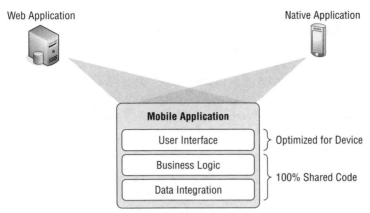

Figure 7-6: Properly designed business logic and data integration layers can also be portable between client-side native applications and server-side web applications.

Ensuring Application Security

For almost all internal-facing business applications, ensuring the security of the data and functionality is of the utmost importance. That said, security is often provided at the expense of usability. For example, multi-factor authentication with a hard token will improve application security, but it will dramatically reduce the usability and harm the user experience. And with mobile applications, usability is critically important. Most mobile applications are not "required-use" apps, but applications that help users do their jobs better. If the usability is reduced below what users are willing to endure, they simply will not use it. I have unfortunately observed too many enterprise mobile solutions that were deployed with overly burdensome security to the user, and the users just didn't use them. It's important to keep all this in mind as you approach security for your application.

Application Sandboxing

While traditionally a lot of the focus of mobile security within the enterprise has been on securing the device, there is a growing focus on securing the application sandbox. That's not to say that the device cannot or should not be secured, but as consumerization continues to bring more individually owned mobile devices into the enterprise, there is an additional emphasis on separating personal information and applications from business data and applications.

Even if the device is being secured and managed, it's still a good idea to think of it as being potentially compromised and therefore to treat the application sandbox as if it is its own fortress, providing application-level authentication, authorization, encryption, and even self-destruct capability.

Rather than focusing on potential security issues with the device or the platform, you can ensure the security of your organization's data by managing security from within the application sandbox.

User Authentication

A lot of enterprise application development in the past has revolved around device-level authentication. A user is authenticated by logging in to a computing device, and once logged in has access to applications without additional authentication.

As personally owned devices grow increasingly common, personal and business uses of mobile devices are mixed together. It's important for mobile applications to ensure and manage their own security. This does not necessarily mean that users will be forced to log in every time they launch applications. Single Sign-On (SSO) solutions can be used so that a user can log in to one enterprise-controlled application sandbox, and then switch execution to another app with the authorized session token being passed between applications. This way the user doesn't need to re-authenticate within a predetermined time-out period.

Encrypting Data in Motion

For most mobile applications, data communication to back-end web services can easily be secured through an encrypted HTTPS connection over Secure Sockets Layer (SSL). In situations where this is not acceptable, either for security reasons or when the web services cannot be exposed externally outside the firewall, an L2TP, PPTP, or IPSec VPN connection can be used. For both usability and performance reasons, this is not always an ideal situation, but it does work.

If neither of those solutions provides adequate protection, you can take a double-envelope approach with an HTTPS/SSL connection embedded inside a VPN connection. Again, this can lead to issues with communication overhead, usability, and often performance, but it can be done if necessary to meet security requirements.

Encrypting Data at Rest

While iOS provides a number of APIs that applications can use for hardware-based encryption of data, the security of your persisted data is ultimately the responsibility of your application. Whether you want to use the Apple-provided

APIs, your own implementation of open-source encryption algorithms, or some combination of the two, it's up to the application developer to implement the level of encryption security necessary, given the sensitivity of the underlying content.

If you're dealing with especially sensitive information, it's also questionable whether it's necessary to persist any information at all to the device. Of course, device-side persistence is necessary for disconnected application execution, but a delicate balance must often be struck between application availability and security.

Data Self-Destruction

Whenever data is stored locally on the device, it is a good idea to implement a self-destruction capability. Whether the data expires after a period of time or after a certain number of failed login attempts, this is a fairly straightforward technique to implement. It is important to recognize, though, that like most security techniques, it is not foolproof, but just one simple mechanism that contributes to overall higher levels of security.

Summary

Even though the iPad is disrupting many aspects of the technology industry and IT itself, it doesn't diminish the need for your ongoing mobile development efforts to "play nice" within the enterprise environment. This means reusing as much existing investment as possible, designing your applications with "future-proofing" in mind, and ensuring that your apps and data are appropriately secured. The iPad is an uncomfortable platform for many in IT, but these approaches will help ensure that the iPad is as enterprise-friendly as possible.

In the next chapter, we'll examine how to best provide mobile access to back-end systems and data through web services.

Exposing Data and Web Services

Almost by definition, enterprise software is data-driven, and mobile apps are no exception. Mobilizing your data, though, can be more difficult than it might appear at first glance.

This chapter will examine the best approaches for optimizing your data models for consumption from iPad applications. Even though the iPad is a powerful mobile computing device, there are still a number of constraints introduced by mobile and wireless technologies that must be appropriately managed to maximize performance, scalability, and usability. You'll learn some of these "mobile-friendly" concepts and some general approaches to implementing them.

You'll then examine web service architectures with SOAP and REST, including the primary differences between these approaches, as well as the strengths and weaknesses of each.

Finally, you'll look at the different types of wireless connectivity provided by the iPad, and the four primary connectivity models that mobile applications can take: always connected, usually connected, occasionally connected, and never connected.

Optimizing Your Data Model for Mobility

When the data models of your enterprise applications need to be mobilized, it requires a different kind of approach than the typical enterprise integration project. When it comes to mobility, even with hardware that has as much computing power as the iPad, it's important to recognize that mobile devices have many more constraints than the servers in the data warehouse that normally execute the applications facilitating integration between enterprise systems. As a result, in order for mobile applications to be successfully integrated into an enterprise environment, the integration should occur in such a way that the web services and data models are optimized for consumption on a mobile device via a wireless connection.

Mobile User-Centric

The data models in your back-end data warehouses are designed to model and store information from the perspective of the overall needs of the system and the enterprise. When this data is mobilized, though, the data model should be designed from the perspective of the user.

This can be accomplished starting from the existing data model and reworking it to include only the data structures and elements that are needed for the mobile application. But it's usually easier and more effective to start with a clean slate and simply define what the user needs.

By looking at your data requirements from the outside-in as opposed to the inside-out, it's often possible to keep things clean and simple, and to then use the mobile-friendly data model to define an interface that can hide many of the data-related complexities behind the services.

Data Flattening

In a world of relational databases and enterprise best practices for database design that stress data normalization, it's important to remember that when it comes to mobility and web services in general, many of these overall guiding principles about database design don't necessarily apply.

While your back-end data model might have many small tables that can be joined together whenever data is queried, when it comes to exposing that data via a web service to a mobile application, all of the heavy lifting should be performed on the server side. Rather than pulling down all the different objects from the server and joining them on the client side, it is usually more effective to manage this in the service.

For example, you might have a data model with Company objects:

```xml
<?xml version="1.0" encoding="utf-8"?>
  <Company>
    <ID>1</ID>
    <Name>Ashtree Software</Name>
    <Website>www.ashtreesoftware.com</Website>
    <PrimaryPhone>(612) 852-7900</PrimaryPhone>
  </Company>
```

And with Contact objects:

```xml
<?xml version="1.0" encoding="utf-8"?>
  <Contact>
    <ID>2</ID>
    <CompanyID>1</CompanyID>
    <FirstName>Scott</FirstName>
    <LastName>Olson</LastName>
    <Title>Chief Architect</Title>
    <Email>scott@ashtreesoftware.com</Email>
    <OfficePhone>(612) 852-7964</OfficePhone>
  </Contact>
```

As well as Address objects:

```xml
<?xml version="1.0" encoding="utf-8"?>
<ArrayOfAddress>
  <Address>
    <ID>3</ID>
    <CompanyID>1</CompanyID>
    <Description>World Headquarters</Description>
    <Street1>520 Marquette Ave.</Street1>
    <Street2>Suite 500</Street2>
    <City>Minneapolis</City>
    <State>MN</State>
    <Zip>55402</Zip>
  </Address>
  <Address>
    <ID>4</ID>
    <CompanyID>1</CompanyID>
    <Description>Regional Sales Office - East</Description>
    <Street1>520 Lexington Ave.</Street1>
    <Street2>Suite 125</Street2>
    <City>New York</City>
    <State>NY</State>
    <Zip>10022</Zip>
  </Address>
</ArrayOfAddress>
```

In order for this to be consumed by a mobile device, though, all three objects must be downloaded to the device and joined together on the client side. As a result, it's often better for mobile consumption if the data is flattened, or denormalized, from the perspective of the mobile user, so that the data joins are occurring on the server. In that case, you might see something like:

```xml
<?xml version="1.0" encoding="utf-8"?>
<Company>
  <ID>1</ID>
  <Name>Ashtree Software</Name>
  <Website>www.ashtreesoftware.com</Website>
  <PrimaryPhone>(612) 852-7900</PrimaryPhone>
  <PrimaryAddress>
    <ID>3</ID>
    <Description>World Headquarters</Description>
    <Street1>520 Marquette Ave.</Street1>
    <Street2>Suite 500</Street2>
    <City>Minneapolis</City>
    <State>MN</State>
    <Zip>55402</Zip>
  </PrimaryAddress>
  <Addresses>
    <Address>
      <ID>3</ID>
      <CompanyID>1</CompanyID>
      <Description>World Headquarters</Description>
      <Street1>520 Marquette Ave.</Street1>
      <Street2>Suite 500</Street2>
      <City>Minneapolis</City>
      <State>MN</State>
      <Zip>55402</Zip>
    </Address>
    <Address>
      <ID>4</ID>
      <CompanyID>1</CompanyID>
      <Description>Regional Sales Office - East</Description>
      <Street1>520 Lexington Ave.</Street1>
      <Street2>Suite 125</Street2>
      <City>New York</City>
      <State>NY</State>
      <Zip>10022</Zip>
    </Address>
  </Addresses>
  <Contacts>
    <Contact>
      <ID>2</ID>
      <FirstName>Scott</FirstName>
      <LastName>Olson</LastName>
      <Title>Chief Architect</Title>
```

```
        <Email>scott@ashtreesoftware.com</Email>
        <OfficePhone>(612) 852-7964</OfficePhone>
      </Contact>
    </Contacts>
  </Company>
```

As a result, the client does not have to make multiple calls to construct a single view of the data (which is important because wireless latency is often a performance choke point). The client does not have to perform complex joins or data manipulations (avoidance of which can dramatically improve performance and battery life). And the client can also centrally manage the logic to facilitate this call (as opposed to having to distribute the logic to each mobile client and keep it up to date).

Concise and Lightweight

Although the data in that sample XML was not incredibly bloated or heavy, it is quite common within enterprise environments for data structures to be extremely complex and heavy. When mobilizing the data, it's important to remember that you need to provide only the data that is necessary for the user and the mobile application. While all of the above data is perfectly valid, if some of it is going to be ignored and not used, then there's no reason to send it unnecessarily over the wire:

```xml
<?xml version="1.0" encoding="utf-8"?>
<Company>
  <ID>1</ID>
  <Name>Ashtree Software</Name>
  <Website>www.ashtreesoftware.com</Website>
  <PrimaryPhone>(612) 852-7900</PrimaryPhone>
  <PrimaryAddress>
    <ID>3</ID>
    <Description>World Headquarters</Description>
    <Street1>520 Marquette Ave.</Street1>
    <Street2>Suite 500</Street2>
    <City>Minneapolis</City>
    <State>MN</State>
    <Zip>55402</Zip>
  </PrimaryAddress>
  <Addresses/>
  <Contacts/>
</Company>
```

This mobile-friendly data design should be done in the context of the design of the mobile application, as it's very difficult to view the data from the perspective of the user without the context of a specific workflow and use case.

Web Services and Mobility

While there are many ways to deliver data to iPad applications, web services are the most common approach. As mentioned in a previous chapter, Dr. Donald F. Ferguson, chief technology officer at Computer Associates, has a vision of how mobility and web services will impact enterprise IT departments. According to Ferguson, "Traditional IT has provided a modest number of applications to customers and employees. IT will evolve to provide data and API calls to an unknown galaxy of applications that employees and end-users download from app stores."

This implies a very mature and mobile-friendly web services infrastructure, and that isn't something that can happen overnight. If you believe in that vision of service-oriented mobility, there are many things you can do to begin preparing your organization for that future. You can begin by establishing a mobile-friendly enterprise services platform.

First, you can make some fundamental architectural decisions. Let's look at the two primary technological approaches to web services: SOAP and REST.

SOAP

SOAP, or Simple Object Access Protocol, remains the most common web services protocol in many enterprise environments. SOAP is typically used like a Remote Procedure Call (RPC) where the service exposes the ability to execute a function on a remote service provider, as shown in Figure 8-1.

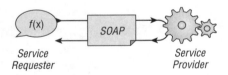

Service Requester   Service Provider

Figure 8-1: SOAP web services typically follow a remote procedure call model of executing a function on a server and returning the results.

In the context of a SOAP service, typically both the "verb" and the "noun" are defined to build a new vocabulary (for example, getCustomers() or performCreditCheck(customerId)) that can be essentially defined without inherent constraints, as the HTTP POST verb is used to communicate all service requests.

Many SOAP implementations follow the convention of publishing Web Service Description Language (WSDL) files that can be used to automate the generation of proxies to facilitate the client's integration with the service.

Here is an example of a SOAP-based service request:

```
POST /Customers HTTP/1.1
Host: www.example.org
Content-Type: application/soap+xml; charset=utf-8
Content-Length: 827


<?xml version="1.0"?>
<soap:Envelope
xmlns:soap="http://www.w3.org/2001/12/soap-envelope"
soap:encodingStyle="http://www.w3.org/2001/12/soap-encoding">

  <soap:Body xmlns:m="http://www.example.org/Customers">
    <m:GetCompany>
      <m:company>1</m:company>
    </m:GetCompany>
  </soap:Body>
</soap:Envelope>
```

And here is the corresponding response:

```
HTTP/1.1 200 OK
Content-Type: application/soap+xml; charset=utf-8
Content-Length: 1897


<?xml version="1.0"?>
<soap:Envelope
xmlns:soap="http://www.w3.org/2001/12/soap-envelope"
soap:encodingStyle="http://www.w3.org/2001/12/soap-encoding">

  <soap:Body xmlns:m="http://www.example.org/Customers">
    <m:GetCompanyResponse>
      <Company>
        <ID>1</ID>
        <Name>Ashtree Software</Name>
        <Website>www.ashtreesoftware.com</Website>
        <PrimaryPhone>(612) 852-7900</PrimaryPhone>
        <PrimaryAddress>
          <ID>3</ID>
          <Description>World Headquarters</Description>
          <Street1>520 Marquette Ave.</Street1>
          <Street2>Suite 500</Street2>
          <City>Minneapolis</City>
          <State>MN</State>
          <Zip>55402</Zip>
        </PrimaryAddress>
        <Addresses/>
        <Contacts/>
```

```
        </Company>
      </m:GetCompanyResponse>
    </soap:Body>

  </soap:Envelope>
```

Advantages of SOAP

The most significant advantage of SOAP is that SOAP-based services are often widely available in many enterprises, so when integration is required with a new mobile application, the services may already exist. If the services are not overly heavy or complex, and if the development is being done using an environment like C# .NET via MonoTouch (that supports the consumption of C#-based WSDL-generated SOAP proxies), then using SOAP services may be the best option.

Disadvantages of SOAP

The largest disadvantage of SOAP in a mobile context is its verbose and heavy XML format. While bandwidth is not a constraint for most server-to-server interactions in a data center, many enterprise services regularly in use are much heavier and more complex than what is optimal for bandwidth-constrained wireless transmission.

Another disadvantage is the difficulty of caching SOAP web service requests. Because every SOAP-based operation is an HTTP POST verb, there is not an inherent mechanism for caching data requests as there is with the HTTP GET verb.

While most enterprise developers are used to being able to easily consume SOAP services from within their development environments, it is not nearly as simple or straightforward to consume SOAP services for iOS development. For example, if you are developing your applications using Objective-C, Apple's Xcode development environment does not provide the ability to directly consume WSDL. There are open-source WSDL parsers that generate iOS-compatible Objective-C.

Also, if you are taking an HTML5-based development approach where AJAX is used to make data requests, it is quite difficult to consume SOAP-based services from within JavaScript.

REST

REST, or REpresentational State Transfer, is a style of web service architecture that utilizes both the capabilities and the constraints of HTTP (HyperText Transfer Protocol).

Rather than defining new "verbs" as is commonly done with SOAP-based web services, RESTful web services use the four basic HTTP verbs: GET, POST, PUT, and DELETE.

The "nouns" can be defined to be whatever they need to be, but the predefined verbs translate to the commonly known CRUD operations (Create, Read, Update, Delete), where Create uses the POST verb, Read uses the GET verb, Update uses the PUT verb, and Delete uses the DELETE verb.

Here is an example of a REST service request:

```
GET /Customers/1 HTTP/1.1
Host: www.example.org
```

And here is the corresponding response:

```
HTTP/1.1 200 OK
Content-Length: 977
Content-Type: application/xml; charset=utf-8

<Company>
  <ID>1</ID>
  <Name>ITR Group, Inc.</Name>
  <PrimaryAddress>
    <City>Mendota Heights</City>
    <Description>World Headquarters</Description>
    <ID>1</ID>
    <State>MN</State>
    <Street1>2520 Lexington Ave. So.</Street1>
    <Street2>Suite 500</Street2>
    <Zip>55120</Zip>
  </PrimaryAddress>
  <PrimaryPhone>(651) 757-4500</PrimaryPhone>
  <Website>www.itrgroupinc.com</Website>
  <Addresses/>
  <Contacts/>
</Company>
```

Because RESTful services are often consumed by JavaScript-based applications, and because JavaScript Object Notation (JSON) is more lightweight than XML, REST services often use JSON, as in the example shown here:

```
HTTP/1.1 200 OK
Content-Length: 297
Content-Type: application/json; charset=utf-8

{ "Addresses":[],
  "Contacts":[],
  "ID":"1",
  "Name":"Ashtree Software",
```

```
"PrimaryAddress":{ "City":"Minneapolis",
                   "Description":"World Headquarters",
                   "ID":"3",
                   "State":"MN",
                   "Street1":"520 Marquette Ave.",
                   "Street2":"Suite 500",
                   "Zip":"55402" },
"PrimaryPhone":"(612) 852-7900",
"Website":"www.ashtreesoftware.com" }
```

Advantages of REST

The biggest advantage of REST from the perspective of mobility is that it is generally more lightweight and easier to consume than SOAP services. And because it leverages the basic foundation of HTTP, the ability to cache requests is dramatically simplified as compared to SOAP.

Since SOAP is difficult to consume from JavaScript, and REST is relatively easy to consume in web applications, RESTful services have become the foundation of most AJAX-based services. And with new capabilities of HTML5, like the cache manifest that instructs the consumer to pre-fetch and cache certain resources, RESTful service endpoints can be pre-cached to dramatically improve the performance of web applications.

Disadvantages of REST

Many enterprise developers feel the biggest disadvantage of REST is the lack of an automated proxy stub generator comparable to the WSDL commonly used for SOAP-based services. Another complaint is often about the constraints imposed by requiring the use of only the four HTTP verbs, but this subject is hotly debated; some say that the constraints of HTTP verbs simplify the creation and consumption of RESTful services.

Choosing between SOAP and REST

Generally speaking, for all of the reasons mentioned above, REST-based services are preferred in iOS application development. That being said, there are situations where it is appropriate to go with a SOAP-based approach.

If you're developing your web services from scratch, you should seriously consider taking a RESTful approach to your mobile data. If you already use existing SOAP-based services, you should evaluate how mobile-friendly they are. If they are relatively lightweight, and issues of request caching and proxy generation for consumption are not problems for your specific application, then there is probably no reason not to use the SOAP services for your mobile apps.

If there are mobile-related SOAP consumption issues, there are often ways to easily get REST services. For instance, if the SOAP-based services were developed in .NET WCF, it can be relatively simple to publish those same services as REST using Microsoft's WCF REST Starter Kit. Otherwise, a RESTful mobile services layer can often sit on top of the existing SOAP-based enterprise services and provide a clean and lightweight, mobile-friendly services interface.

Understanding Connectivity Models

Before developing an enterprise mobile application, it's critically important that you understand the connectivity model appropriate for the app.

Even though "mobile" and "wireless" are used by many as synonyms, there is actually a very important distinction. While "wireless" apps require connectivity to wireless networks, "mobile" applications are not necessarily dependent on connectivity.

Network connectivity is primarily established through one of two types of wireless networks: wireless local area networks (WLAN) and wireless wide area networks (WWAN).

The WLAN that has become standard is called 802.11x, or Wi-Fi for short. The iPad supports all the common Wi-Fi standards with 802.11n, 802.11g, 802.11a, and 802.11b.

The WWAN technology supported as an optional iPad component is commonly referred to as 3G, which is short for 3rd Generation Wireless Network. The 3G in the first generation iPad was GSM-only (Global System for Mobile Communications), but the iPad 2 also comes in a CDMA (Code Division Multiple Access) 3G model.

In that context, let's look at the four primary types of connectivity models for mobile applications: always connected, usually connected, occasionally connected, and never connected.

Always Connected

For certain usage scenarios, environments, and applications, it can be either preferred or necessary to utilize an always connected model. If the application architecture is a thin-client model, then connectivity will always be required. Or if the data necessary to function in a disconnected state is either too large or security-sensitive to be cached on the mobile device, then an always connected model is necessary.

Examples of Always Connected Applications

Examples of applications that should utilize always connected models include: point-of-sale applications that require access to payment gateways to process credit cards; loan applications to process credit checks; and electronic health records systems that require access to specific patient files. Always connected models can work quite well for applications that require access to external databases, like financial or credit networks or medical records systems, or ones in which the usage environment is within a physical space where a very reliable local wireless infrastructure can be set up and supported. The problems are introduced when wireless connectivity cannot be guaranteed for whatever reason, for instance if the user is mobile beyond a physical location that's not specifically set up to provide ubiquitous local wireless connectivity.

Always Connected Architectures

Always connected applications can be developed using thin-client, web, hybrid, or native architectures. In an always connected scenario, the appropriate architecture will often come down to the user experience requirements for the application. For instance, native apps will provide a richer experience than web apps or thin-client apps, but because the always connected model supports all of the architectures, the differences will primarily revolve around the required or desired user experience.

Usually Connected

Usually connected applications will generally have aspects of functionality that require connectivity, but the application must be able to elegantly handle the disconnected state. Sometimes this means giving the user an error message that this particular function cannot be performed while disconnected, or sometimes it means leveraging cached data to allow the connectivity state to be managed in the background without the user having to worry about it. Since usually connected applications assume general connectivity, any synchronization types of activities will usually happen automatically in the background.

Examples of Usually Connected Applications

Most heavy data-driven mobile enterprise line-of-business applications that are not used in a single physical location will take a usually connected model. This includes executive dashboards, sales force automation, order entry, and systems along those lines.

Usually Connected Architectures

In a usually connected scenario, native applications can generally provide the best experience by most elegantly handling the disconnected events. It is quite possible, though, to develop web or hybrid applications that can perform well in usually connected situations.

Occasionally Connected

Generally speaking, occasionally connected applications are the opposite of usually connected applications, since they expect the application to be generally disconnected and thus take full advantage of the connection whenever it is available to pre-fetch, synchronize, or store and forward any information that may reside in a queue. While this type of application can also auto-detect connectivity state, the types of usage scenarios are often ones where there is known network unreliability; as a result it is usually optimal to give the user control of when to attempt to "update," "sync," or whatever else is necessary when there is network availability.

Examples of Occasionally Connected Applications

If a heavy data-driven application is used in environments where wireless connectivity is regularly unavailable or unreliable, then an occasionally connected approach must sometimes be taken for many types of applications, like field-data capture and survey collection, that are most common as usually connected ones. This can often introduce more complexity into a situation for certain types of apps. But other types (for instance, survey collection) that naturally work in a store-and-forward queue, or applications with dynamic content (for instance e-learning or training) that don't change all that often, can work quite well in an occasionally connected model without much added complexity.

Occasionally Connected Architectures

In an occasionally connected scenario, native applications will usually provide the best experience by allowing network detection and synchronization when connected. It is technically possible to develop web or hybrid applications that can work in occasionally connected situations, but these architectures are often only feasible if the data model is relatively simple.

Never Connected (Stand-Alone)

If an application does not have any dynamic data requirements and is entirely static in both functionality and data, then a never connected application is appropriate. Or if an application must be used in an environment where connectivity is never available, then a never connected approach is necessary.

Examples of Never Connected Applications

Stand-alone predefined functions like calculators for various specific business purposes, documentation, training, and other types of applications providing access to relatively static content or functionality can often work well in a never connected application. If the content or functionality within a never connected application ever needs to be updated, the application itself must be updated and reinstalled.

Never Connected Architectures

Native applications are usually the preferred architecture for never connected situations, but hybrid apps can also work well if all the web-based content (HTML, CSS, JavaScript, XML/JSON, etc.) is physically stored within the hybrid container. Because a connection is never established, thin-client and web applications architectures are not possible in this type of usage scenario.

Summary

In this chapter, you wrapped up the architecture section of the book and looked at how the best practices concerning mobile data modeling and web services take a different approach than is common with relational database design. You looked at how to design the mobile data objects from the outside in, using the perspective of the user as guidance, as opposed to looking from the inside out and using the existing data infrastructure as the starting point.

You also looked at SOAP vs. REST-based web services, the strengths and weaknesses of each, and why RESTful services are generally preferred for mobile application development. Finally, you looked at the four kinds of mobile app connectivity models: always connected, usually connected, occasionally connected, and never connected. There are many architectural implications of the connectivity model, and it is important to take the best approach for any given application and user profile/environment.

In the next chapter, you'll kick off the next section of the book on design, specifically the best practices for user interface design and Apple's user experience conventions and design guidelines.

Part

III

Design

In This Part

Designing Enterprise iPad Applications

Now that you've developed an enterprise mobile strategy and application road map, selected the top-priority applications, and identified the preferred software architecture for the app, it's time to begin the design process.

So what do I mean by design? That's a very good question, because there are many different definitions. For the purposes of this book, design refers to the creative and artistic process around the visual and functional definition of an application.

I recognize that for many in enterprise IT, the term design often refers to technical software design; for clarity this book dealt with high-level technical software design in the previous chapter on architecture, and aspects of the low-level technical software design will be covered in the next chapter, on development.

In this chapter, we're going to start by describing the paradigm shift that enterprise IT must undergo in order to develop applications for the iPad. The shift is subtle, but it has profound ramifications. Many of the traditional ways of developing enterprise software are not effective in the creation of iPad applications, and so the design and development of iPad apps requires a new approach. Let's take a look at what that is.

Understanding the iPad Paradigm

The iPad is one of those things that you have to hold in your hands and experience in order to understand it. While it does not replace the personal computer, it creates an extremely personal experience that fundamentally changes how people interact with computers.

I asked iPad usability guru Josh Clark, author of *Tapworthy*, about the paradigm shift that enterprise IT must undergo in order to successfully develop business applications for the iPad. He replied:

> *The iPad introduced a new kind of computing, one that I believe surprised even Apple. It might look like a big phone or a little laptop, but its unique physical form creates a context and mindset for computing that is more than either. The iPad is a platform for contemplation and flow, a personal computer that emphasizes the big idea. What could be more important for the enterprise?*

> *The iPad is a terrific device for reading, thinking, sharing, and yes, working. While it's not well suited to traditional office productivity tasks, the iPad does promote big-picture thinking: sketching, note-taking, project planning. It's a less jittery platform than mobile devices, but more creatively expansive than a laptop — like the open freedom granted by a pad of paper. And because the iPad is easily passed around, it's a social device that makes it easy to share and collaborate as a group (with people in the same room, an increasingly rare novelty!). All of these characteristics require new and — for the enterprise, unusual — attention to user experience. A device of creativity and contemplation requires design that features the same.*

> *As designers and developers, we're still working out exactly what this thing is. It's not a laptop, it's not a phone, it's not a newspaper, it's not a book, it's not a web browser. And yet it inherits and mixes qualities of all of them, the precocious child of many parents. We're in an exciting period of experimentation with this device, discovering the apps (and applications) for what is a genuinely important new platform for work and thinking.*

I believe that Clark is right on with his assessment, so what does this mean for enterprise IT leaders and developers who want to develop applications for the iPad?

First, I think it's critical to recognize that while the iPad is technically a "computer" it is a very different type of computer, and things that worked well in traditional computing paradigms may or may not be appropriate for the iPad.

Second, the iPad is optimized for a different kind of productivity. While it is not the best platform for creating spreadsheets, it is an optimal platform for capturing data on checklists and surveys. Even though writing documents on the iPad is not extremely efficient, it makes collaborating on and annotating content very easy. What all this means is that the types of applications and functionality that have been traditionally provided may or may not be appropriate for the iPad. What is optimal for the iPad may not have ever been done before. It requires this fundamental paradigm shift to discover these subtleties.

Third, the iPad requires an emphasis on design and user experience that the enterprise is not used to. This is not an optional capability; if enterprise IT does not invest in creating a good user experience for their applications, then users will simply choose not to use them. Unlike traditional enterprise software where users have been forced to accept poor user experience, iPad users will expect and demand solid user experiences or else they just won't use the applications that the organization invests in. If your organization is unwilling to invest in learning how to do proper user experience design, then you probably shouldn't even be doing iPad app development.

Finally, it's incredibly important to recognize that the iPad, as both a paradigm and a platform, is still rapidly evolving. The process of "experimentation" that Clark described can be frightening but is absolutely necessary for those in enterprise IT. The traditional tendency of enterprise software developers to focus purely on features and functionality, and not think about user experience and usability until the end of the project, if at all, must be flipped on its head. Thinking must be focused on user experience and usability, and allow the features and functionality to fall in and out of scope as necessary. While this may sound like heresy to traditional enterprise software developers, it's important to remember that the iPad is not designed as a replacement for the PC, so iPad applications do not need to have all necessary functionality. If there is a complicated piece of functionality that is not commonly used, the default for iPad applications should be to leave it out. If users need to have that function, they should be able to perform it from a traditional PC and application. The optimal mix of iPad app functionality can be discovered only through experimentation, which must be embraced by enterprise developers.

The Impact of 'Consumerization'

As discussed in Chapter 2, IT is being influenced by consumers (who are also employees and users of IT systems) to use technology that is widely adopted by consumers. And while this phenomenon is most commonly attributed to hardware and devices entering the corporate environment, this trend has significant spillover into the app world as well.

In that previous chapter, we included some perspective on this subject from the editor-in-chief of *Wired*, Chris Anderson, who said, "The App Store just keeps growing. And growing. And growing. Consumers now expect that there's really an app for anything, and then when that consumer goes into work, he's beginning to expect that there should be apps for that too. The Long Tail of mobile apps has altered the mindsets of corporate employees, and IT is having trouble coming to grips with all this."

So what does this mean for corporate IT, which is trying to develop applications to satisfy that demand for apps? It means that your custom in-house enterprise apps will constantly be compared to the dozens or even hundreds of other apps that your users have. Creating the apps themselves isn't enough to satisfy demand, since the apps must have a user experience that is on a par with all other apps the user has. Just building an app and providing it to users won't quiet them down if it suffers from poor usability like most existing enterprise software; they'll just complain more loudly about the poor user experience.

When I sat down with Best Buy CTO Robert Stephens to interview him for this book, he passionately shared with me how he believes that "the apps people are using on their smartphones are raising the bar for what they expect from corporate IT. This should strike fear into the hearts of every IT person. The technology is becoming more human, and in order to approach it, engineers need to get in touch with their design side. They should take an art history class."

This represents a fairly significant shift for corporate IT, which must recognize that it can't be successful in iPad application development if it ignores this element of design and user experience.

Jim Prevo, the CIO of Green Mountain Coffee Roasters, added an additional perspective to the impact of consumerization on user experience design. He said, "I have found the iPad blends my personal and professional lives more significantly than previous technology platforms (photos, videos, apps, mail, etc.). For that reason and since it doesn't completely replace any device in my backpack, we haven't decided exactly how to treat it as a new enterprise tool."

This comment also goes back to the point that we're all still learning what the iPad's true potential is within the enterprise, and sometimes we have to experiment with what's possible in order to discover what really works best.

The Human Interface Guidelines

Apple has published an iOS Human Interface Guidelines document that's a must read for anyone involved in the design of iPad applications. In the document, Apple states both general principles and strict guidelines that developers must follow or risk rejection from the App Store. The subjective nature of some of these guidelines has frustrated many developers in the past when Apple has rejected their offerings, although there is a lot more transparency today with Apple also offering a formal appeals process for rejections.

Even if you are developing in-house enterprise applications that can be distributed without submission to and approval by Apple, following these guidelines is still very important. Following these guidelines helps to supply an intuitive consistency for users, so that every app they use on the iPad has a similar interaction paradigm.

In subsequent chapters we'll dig into some of the specifics within the Human Interface Guidelines, but right now it's simply important to mention that anyone involved in designing or developing iPad applications should spend time getting to know the iOS Human Interface Guidelines, as well as regularly refer to the document as design issues emerge.

Envisioning the Application

Before doing anything else, it's critically important to define the vision and purpose of the application. What does the app need to do? Who will be using the app? How will these people use the application?

With a lot of enterprise software, this definition never really emerges. Applications become holding areas for ever-expanding amounts of features and functionality, and a single application can be used by many different types of users and user groups for many different purposes. With iPad applications, this approach simply does not work. Apps must be simple, straightforward, and have a cleanly defined purpose. This often means that the process of bringing a single existing application to the iPad results in the creation of multiple, more focused iPad applications.

What Is the App's Purpose?

What is the purpose of the application? Why would a user want to use it? This purpose must be simple and straightforward.

While a traditional enterprise application might simply be called "Field Sales Toolbox," for instance, it may contain a wide variety of features and functionalities that may be more suitable on the iPad as multiple stand-alone applications. Rather than a single "sales" application, there may be separate apps for customer information, sales and financial reporting, mileage and expense reporting, order entry, product information, and other stand-alone apps along those lines.

While enterprise developers may resist the concept of multiple applications, it's important to note that these "suites" of applications can share code and data; the distinction has a few subtle technical ramifications but has many significant ones for user experience.

Who Is the User?

Who will be using the application? It's critically important not only to know who the user is, but also to understand as much as possible about the perspective of the user when viewing the application.

If there are multiple user profiles with significant differences, it may very well be appropriate to split the app into multiple versions. Again, this does not necessarily mean forking the code base but rather just offering user group–specific versions of the application. For instance, a product catalog application may need to be used by both in-house sales reps and third-party distributor reps. While the functionality may be very similar or even identical, there may be a compelling case to offer different versions of the user experience.

How Will the App Be Used?

In addition to defining the core purpose of the application and gaining a deep understanding of the user, it's also important to understand how and where the app will be used. Will it be used sitting down at a table? Or standing up and walking around? Will it be used by a single user, or will it be used to facilitate communication and collaboration among multiple users?

Designing an application that is optimized for capturing data on a checklist while the user is walking around is very different than designing, for example, a data entry app requiring text input that will be used while the user is seated. It's also different to design an app for a user to demonstrate to and collaborate with other people, versus an application for a single user. These are important considerations that must be understood before starting a design. Of course, these considerations may change as the application and user experience evolve, but you should have a baseline understanding before getting started.

Thinking from the User's Perspective

In order to design an iPad application, you have to put yourself in the shoes of your user, and think from the user's perspective. This is often easier said than done, which is why you need to involve your actual users in the design and development process from the very beginning. Also, be aware that the feedback from your users will change and evolve as they become more familiar with the iPad and have a chance to experience the first few iterations of any application. This should not be discouraged, and this feedback must be embraced in order to design and develop a successful iPad application.

User Experience Is Everything

Most enterprise developers and IT leaders with whom I speak about user experience often struggle to recognize the importance of that experience. The common thinking is, "My users are simply screaming for mobile access to data and functionality, and if I can give that to them, whether the experience is good or not, then they'll be happy." Unfortunately, this thinking is flawed.

I believe that a big part of this is the confusion of a "rich user interface" with a "good user experience." A flashy whiz-bang interface can suffer from poor user experience just as easily as a clean and simple user interface can have great user experience. As Stephens explained, "Rich user interface is not the metric. A great user interface is measured only by the metric of usage. If a user experience is poor, they won't use it."

When enterprise IT focuses simply on delivering the functionality without considering user experience, then user adoption will be poor and usage will be low. Mobile apps should be built with a strong user experience, or they should not be built at all.

Defining the Workflow

Beyond understanding the purpose of the application and the user of the application, it's also important to understand the greater organizational context of the user's workflow. Often, existing legacy processes continue indefinitely because nobody understands why they were created in the first place. While business process change should never be taken lightly, the time is rarely better than when creating applications for a transformative and disruptive technology such as the iPad.

Model the User's Process, Not the System's

The biggest mistake I see organizations make as they mobilize their existing systems is the tendency to try to "port" their existing systems to a mobile platform like the iPad. Although it is often possible and certainly ideal to port or even reuse application code from "under the hood," it's important to recognize that the "ported application" should be fundamentally different from the original application.

The original application was not designed with the iPad paradigm in mind, and it likely does many things that are not optimally done on the iPad. So the mobile version should fundamentally be only a subset of the original functionality, as the iPad app should not do everything that the original application does.

Additionally, the capabilities of the iPad will almost certainly enable new features and functionality to enhance the user experience in ways that were not possible before.

The mobile application should be designed for optimal user experience, not for the structure of back-end corporate data and systems. Your applications may integrate with more than one back-end system. And likewise, from a user's perspective, it will not be ideal to think of the mobile apps as simply mobile versions of back-end systems. Users should think of specific apps to help them perform specific tasks or information-driven process-specific workflows, and that will rarely model the framework of the existing back-end systems. This is a difficult habit for many enterprise developers to break, but it is important for success in the development of iPad applications.

Follow the Optimal Flow of Information

Say that information is gathered on paper forms, then entered into a back-end application where the data is used to generate even more paper forms to capture more data that is again entered back into a system. That process might have been the ideal way to design the workflow before mobile technology like the iPad, but is it really necessary to have multiple stages to the data collection process? Maybe it is, but maybe it isn't. You should question the status quo and challenge any assumptions you have. Test your ideas. For example, maybe the data just needed to have an interim validation step, and maybe multiple stages of a workflow can be eliminated to create a more optimal and efficient flow of information.

Leverage the iPad's Capabilities

Stop for a moment and think about what's possible with everything the iPad holds within its elegant minimalistic package:

- Touch screen
- GPS
- Compass
- Gyroscope
- Accelerometer
- Microphone
- Speaker
- Headphone jack
- Dual cameras

Then also think about the many types of accessories that can be used with the iPad:

- Stylus
- Barcode scanner
- Magnetic stripe reader
- Wireless printer
- VGA/HDMI adapter

How could these technologies be used to simplify the user experience and optimize the workflow? Could GPS be used to detect where the user is physically located, and perhaps default your sales app to automatically display the nearest customer location when the app is launched? Could the touch screen and a stylus be used to capture signatures? Could a barcode scanner or magnetic stripe reader simplify data input and streamline processes? Could interactive and dynamic content generation plus printing replace a stack of legacy-printed marketing materials?

With the iPad, so many new things are possible that we're only beginning to discover what they are. Dream, brainstorm, experiment, and get feedback from users, and the result may surprise you.

Keeping It Simple

Focus.

Keep it simple.

Remember the Pareto principle, which is also known as the 80-20 rule. In this case it means that 20 percent of the features of an application will be used 80 percent of the time. For iPad applications, since they are usually designed to augment existing enterprise applications and enhance them as opposed to replacing them entirely, you should focus on delivering that 20 percent of the functionality. Yes, that will exclude the app from being used in every situation, but that's much better than complicating the app for everyone else who is just using the core application functionality most of the time.

Example: Gallery of iPad UI Designs

For inspiration it can often help to look at examples of well-designed user interfaces. You can use Figures 9-1 through 9-8 to help jump-start your own creativity.

Figure 9-1: Sales automation with signature capture

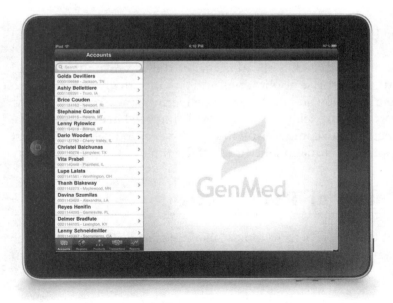

Figure 9-2: Customer relationship management

Figure 9-3: Equipment reporting and telemetry

Figure 9-4: View interactive product catalogs

Figure 9-5: Manage documents and images

Figure 9-6: Interact with real-time charting

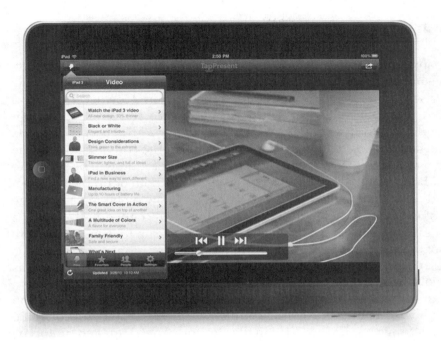

Figure 9-7: Facilitate e-learning with video content

Figure 9-8: Interact with 3-dimensional models

Summary

In this chapter, we defined "design" as the creative and artistic process involving the visual and functional definition of an application. This may be new to enterprise IT, but it's just as important as the high- and low-level technical architecture. The iPad is all about a great user experience, and developing applications for this platform demands a focus on designing a great user experience.

You learned how to define the application, from the core purpose of the application and who the user will be to how the application will be used. We discussed how to think from the user's perspective to both optimize the experience and improve the business process and workflow by taking advantage of many of the unique capabilities of the iPad while recognizing the device's constraints. Challenging yourself and the rest of the team to focus on the core purpose of the application is critical, while ignoring and eliminating all that is not necessary. Finally, you looked at a gallery of some example iPad UI designs to spark your imagination in beginning the design process of your own app.

Are you ready to embrace the iPad paradigm? Are you willing to focus on designing an excellent user experience? If so, the next chapter will cover the process of getting your fingers dirty in the creation of mockups and prototype designs, including rapid-fire paper prototyping.

CHAPTER 10

User Experience Prototyping

Now that you've started to design your iPad application, it's time to get down to actually creating something. It's time to start defining and designing a user experience. As discussed in the previous chapter, it requires a lot of creativity, especially the willingness to let go of preconceived notions about how things should work.

I recently spoke with a user experience expert, Suzanne Ginsberg, who wrote *Designing the iPhone User Experience*. I asked her about the importance of user experience prototyping when developing enterprise apps for the iPad. According to her:

> *Most IT professionals are accustomed to designing enterprise software with little or no user input. Limited resources are the primary reason cited for this approach; however, involving users in the design process can greatly reduce your app iterations and save valuable engineering time. One agile approach to consider is paper prototyping combined with user testing. Prospective users are presented with your iPad app prototype and asked to complete relevant scenarios. Iterating on paper is*

the cheapest and fastest way to go, but many higher fidelity options are available for the iPad, such as HTML, Keynotopia, and even video. Regardless of the medium chosen, the goal is to gather user feedback before finalizing your app design. Quite often, the longer you wait, the harder it will be to address core issues.

In this chapter, we'll examine these very topics, starting with the process of paper prototyping and moving on to realistic mockups and eventually functional user experience prototypes, where you can take your static mockup images and turn them into interactive experiences. We'll also cover the various tools that you can use to accelerate your prototyping efforts, as well as how to ensure that you get feedback from your users as early and often in the process as possible.

Paper Prototyping

You're probably thinking, "Why are we talking about using paper in a book about the iPad?" That's a very good question.

Having been involved in the design process of dozens of iPad applications, I can attest that there's just something about a sketch on a piece of paper that helps to spark creativity and imagination. When you put a paper prototype in front of users, it's not supposed to be perfect, so they don't focus on the details. You can show users a paper prototype and they can see the big picture. They can imagine the user experience. They can provide feedback about the big picture concepts before getting too deep into the details.

There's nothing wrong with prototyping on the iPad using apps available from the App Store, like App Layout and iMockups, both of which I have and would highly recommend. But starting first with a hand-drawn paper prototype can be a very valuable exercise. If you really want to do your prototyping on the iPad itself, you can use a stylus to sketch right on the touchscreen with an app like Penultimate or OmniGraffle, also both great apps.

The bottom line: Once you put a realistic mockup in front of a user for feedback, you'll tend to get lower-level feedback about the details instead of the bigger picture, which is why the process is often most effective if you can start with a low-fidelity paper prototype and iterate a few times before moving to a higher-fidelity realistic mockup.

I fully recognize that the idea of paper prototyping is a foreign concept to most enterprise IT professionals. But if you are willing to let go of your preconceived notions about not only paper prototyping but the application itself, and give the process a chance, I believe you'll be pleasantly surprised with the results.

I will add one caveat to this, though. The iPad paradigm is something that you really have to experience firsthand to understand, and one important prerequisite of any paper prototyping (or realistic mockups) is that the designer have a firm grasp of iPad user interface best practices and the overall iOS Human Interface Guidelines. Without a solid foundation of understanding about what makes a great iPad app, it will be difficult to be successful in any user experience design exercises.

UIStencils.com

There are many great sources for paper-prototyping materials, but one of my personal favorites is UIStencils.com, which has a full line-up of iPad-specific prototyping tools. In Figure 10-1, you'll see an iPad sketchbook that you can use to rapidly create screen designs with a certain level of conformity. Of course, there's no reason why you can't use just a blank sheet of paper, but it can often help to start with a canvas like this.

Figure 10-1: You can use a physical paper-based iPad sketchbook to create paper prototypes.

Even if you don't consider yourself to be an especially skilled artist, don't worry about it; the objective of paper prototyping is to be intentionally vague on very specific details so that the user you're showing it to can imagine the user experience. If you really feel like you need assistance, you can get a stencil kit, like the one shown in Figure 10-2, to easily trace many of the common user interface components as well as gestures and even icons.

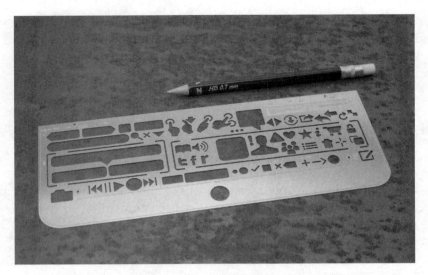

Figure 10-2: You can use an iPad stencil kit to trace user interface controls if you don't consider yourself an artist.

Whether you're drawing your paper prototypes by hand or using a stencil, don't worry about perfection. Give yourself a time limit for each screen that you sketch, so that you don't allow yourself to be sucked into the details of the process. Keep it simple, like the prototype for sketching shown in Figure 10-3, and you'll be able to use a pencil to churn out "screens" in just a few minutes.

As you go from screen to screen, feel free to emphasize the elements that may change between any given screen and a previous one. Remember to focus on the big picture, though, and leave out the details, as in Figure 10-4, where the text is simply represented with scribbles. If you put actual words in many of these areas, the users to whom you show the paper prototypes will focus on the accuracy of the content and completeness of the lists, not the application flow and experience.

As you create your paper prototypes and talk through the experience with your users, remember to take the feedback you receive and iterate on your initial design. Sometimes you can just swap out individual screen designs, and other times you need to throw the entire design out the window and start from scratch. Don't be afraid to start over. The challenge of trying to come up with multiple user experiences and navigation concepts for a single application concept can really help to solidify and refine the vision in your mind as well as in the minds of your users, who will then be better prepared to articulate their feedback.

Figure 10-3: With a sketchpad and a stencil, paper prototypes can be created in minutes.

Figure 10-4: A paper prototype looks enough like a real application for a user to understand, but doesn't look so real that users nitpick specific visual elements.

If you find yourself constantly starting from scratch on the same paper "screen," sometimes a dry erase board like the dry erase iPad template shown in Figure 10-5 can help to simplify the iterative process.

Figure 10-5: Dry erase boards can be used for rapidly changing user interfaces.

As you're going through the process of sketching your paper prototypes, don't be afraid to take inspiration from other apps. You covered some of the best iPad business apps in the App Store in Chapter 5, as well as the gallery of various iPad user interface designs at the end of Chapter 9. Flip through those designs to help spark your own imagination. Many of the designers I work with also like to keep their own personal collections of screenshots of great iPad apps, which they're constantly reexamining for inspiration and focus.

Additionally, it can help to have a printed reference of common icons, layouts, and user interface controls, like the one in Figure 10-6, especially if you're not using a stencil.

One of the other advantages of using a whiteboard, like the one shown in Figure 10-7, is that it makes it very easy to sketch and erase and re-sketch while you are right there with a user, talking through the design. That type of real-time collaboration is the ultimate form of rapid iteration.

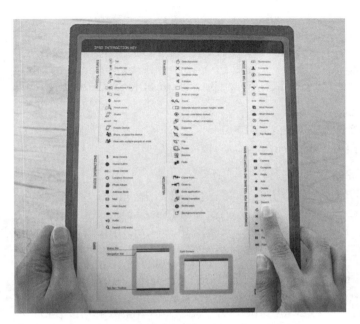

Figure 10-6: It can be helpful to have a printed quick reference of user interface elements for the iPad.

Figure 10-7: With a dry erase board, you can prototype in real time while talking to a user.

Exercise

When you've got your preferred tools and you're ready to create a paper prototype, start by just closing your eyes and imagining the experience of using your applications. It's also helpful if you write out, or at least think through, several things:

- What is the purpose of the application?
- Who is the user of the application?
- How will this application be used?

Once you've defined that, you might want to list the steps of the ideal, "happy path" workflow for a user. Then for each of those steps, think through what might be the ideal iPad app screen. Sketch them out, think about them, refine them. Then once you've got what you think is a good first draft, start showing it to people.

While many people will be excited to provide input, pay special attention to the feedback you get from the actual users who will be using the app after you've developed it. Also, remember the 80/20 rule and that it's impossible to give everyone everything that they want. Keep the app simple.

As you get feedback, keep redesigning the application. Remember, you're dealing with a sketch on a piece of paper, not source code, so now is the time to learn and make mistakes when starting over doesn't take much time or money at all. If you're struggling to get started, one challenge that I personally like to give myself is to come up with as many completely different user experiences for a given workflow as possible. Of course, most of those will turn out to be not very good, but sometimes you have to push yourself to try new things and even make mistakes in order to discover the best possible design.

After you've iterated on your paper prototype and obtained user feedback as many times as you think is necessary, then it's time to move on to a high-fidelity realistic interface mockup.

Mocking Up Realistic Interfaces

By this point in the process, you probably have a pretty good idea about a high-level design for your application. You should, now that the rough design has been articulated by the paper prototype, and you can now go a level or two deeper into the details.

Unlike paper prototypes, the details are very important when creating realistic mockups on the computer itself. When you show these to users, they will notice little things like the color scheme, icons, graphics, and text, including completeness of lists, spelling, and grammar. One of the biggest advantages of the low-fidelity paper prototyping is to allow the design to ignore these details, but now it's important to embrace them. A lot of valuable comments will come out of showing the paper prototype to users.

Iteration is just as important with realistic interfaces, and while the interfaces often take longer to create, since they are digital objects, each subsequent iteration can use the content from the previous iteration to accelerate the timeline.

There are many ways to create realistic user interface designs. Many graphic artists will prefer using Photoshop, but using a presentation tool like Microsoft PowerPoint or Apple Keynote is also a very popular way to do this. As mentioned earlier in this chapter, there are also some great iPad apps that can be used to create mockups right from the iPad itself, including App Layout and iMockups. Let's take a look at some of these tools.

iPad GUI PSD

If you prefer working with Photoshop, you can use a number of templates to accelerate the creation of your mockups. A popular and comprehensive template which is also a free Photoshop template can be downloaded from `http://www.teehanlax.com/blog/2010/12/10/ipad-gui-psd-version-2/`, as shown in Figure 10-8.

Taking this approach, you can go through your paper prototypes screen by screen and convert them to a high-fidelity detailed mockup on the computer. Again, once you've done this it's important to show these to your users early and often to gather feedback about the design.

Keynotopia

If you're not a Photoshop expert, you may prefer a tool called Keynotopia (Figure 10-9), which provides User Interface (UI) templates in both PowerPoint and Keynote formats. This can also be valuable if you want to give the mockups to your users or other folks within your organization to provide their own edits and tweaks to the mockups themselves.

It is important to remember, though, to follow Apple's Human Interface Guidelines and general UI design principles. Anyone working on these designs should be familiar with these concepts as well as with the iPad itself.

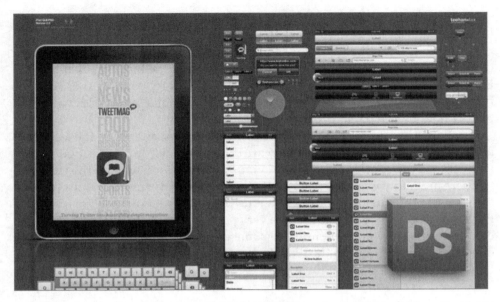

Figure 10-8: Free templates are available for designers who prefer to use the powerful capabilities of Photoshop.

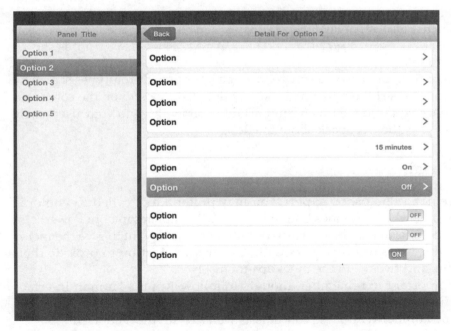

Figure 10-9: Keynotopia provides photo-realistic user interface (UI) components that can be used to easily create mockups.

While Photoshop may be necessary for advanced graphics and complex image manipulations, a lot of apps do not necessarily require that level of complexity, and iPad user interface designs can rapidly and easily be created by dragging and dropping widgets, like those shown in Figure 10-10, from within Keynote or PowerPoint. You can use these graphical components to copy and paste and drag and drop around to create your realistic-looking mockups on the computer.

Figure 10-10: Specific components can be easily "dragged and dropped" in Keynote or PowerPoint.

An Example Prototyping Effort

So now that you know how to do the prototyping and what tools you can use to create the designs, what does this process look like from beginning to end? To help illustrate this, let's walk through the design process of a data collection app for the iPad, as follows:

- The focused purpose of the app is to replace a paper-based form and clipboard with an iPad application.
- The user is a facilities manager.
- The workflow is that of the manager doing a daily walkthrough and inspection of the shop floor, capturing various observations.

The benefit of the application is electronic access to historical inspections, including historical problem areas that should be examined extra carefully, as well as the electronic transfer of information so that the paper-based forms no longer need to be manually re-entered into the database. In the next section, you'll look at paper prototypes; after that you'll go on to see how these translate into realistic electronic mockups on the screen, followed by "functional" prototypes reflecting the user's actual experience.

Paper Prototypes

The first version of the paper prototype started with an almost exact duplicate of the original two-page, paper-based form originally used by the enterprise. But after creating that paper prototype and showing it to users for feedback, more information was gathered about the actual ideal workflow for the users. It was discovered that rather than trying to fit everything on the screen at once, there were about a half-dozen specific inspection topics that were optimal for their own individual inspection screens. It was also discovered that the enterprise had a desire to attach digital pictures to particular inspection items. For instance, if a certain inspection item had a problem, it was much easier to simply mark it as problematic and take a picture with the camera on the iPad 2 than to type, or even to follow the previous process of hand-writing comments.

After a few joint design sessions with the users, the following paper prototypes were ultimately created. In Figure 10-11 you'll see a splash screen (left) to reinforce branding elements, as well as a registration screen (right) to activate the application for the first use. After the initial use, the user was able to log in, even when disconnected, through the use of cached credentials. Note that Figures 10-11 through 10-18 are somewhat stylized versions, for legibility, of what would probably be rougher hand sketches.

In the screen illustrated in Figure 10-12, the application uses a split view, with the master pane describing some of the different elements or variables that need to be captured as part of any inspection. This represents both a logical and functional organization of the application, where the user can select an area for inspection from the master pane to view the details on the pane on the right.

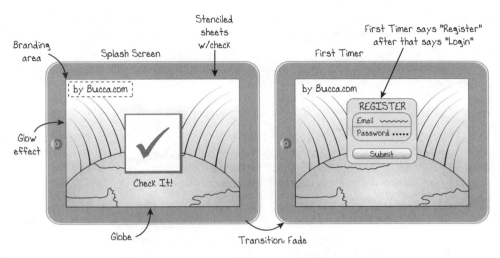

Figure 10-11: An example splash screen (left) and login screen.

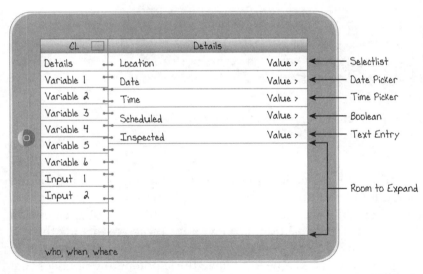

Figure 10-12: Sketch out your interface, but also leave comments and markup describing specific attributes.

Another visual and aesthetic element that was proposed by the designer was the use of a spiral binding so that the virtual iPad application would present a look-and-feel reminiscent of the previous paper-based process. Figure 10-13 illustrates the sketch and comments describing the desired aesthetic background.

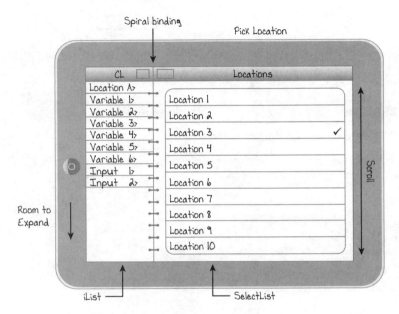

Figure 10-13: Think about aesthetics as well as functionality, like the spiral binding drawn here.

In order for all of the inspection questions to fit on a single double-sided sheet of paper, a lot of the inspection item descriptions were abbreviated. By breaking the inspection up into multiple areas represented by the items in the master pane, we created additional room on the screen to include the full description and detailed explanation for each item, as shown in Figure 10-14.

For each question, there was a need to have three potential responses that represented whether the inspection item was excellent, adequate, or poor. Since the paper-based version of the form had a free-text area to include comments about any items ranked poorly, it was discovered that the use of the camera to capture a picture would eliminate most of the need for that free-text input process. Figure 10-15 is an example of how a specific user interface component can be zoomed in on for greater detail and discussion with users.

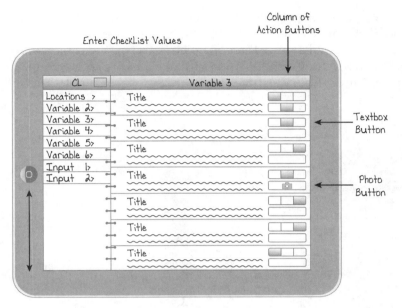

Figure 10-14: Think about user experience through the user's workflow.

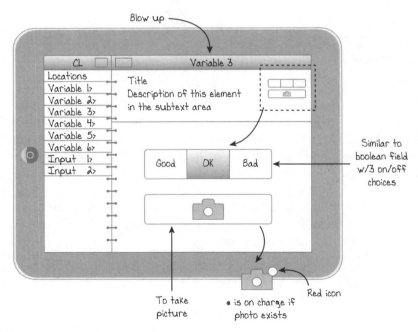

Figure 10-15: If you want to illustrate or describe a specific user interface component, you can draw it in more detail.

From user feedback, it was also determined that a single problem represented in a picture could likely impact more than one item on the inspection. So rather than requiring the user to take more than one picture, when the camera button was pressed the user was given the option to take a new picture or reuse an existing picture. Figure 10-16 illustrates how the user was prompted when selecting the camera icon.

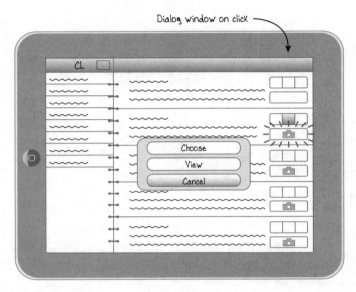

Figure 10-16: You can visually describe responses to user interactions.

Although the vast majority of the application could be used with simple touches to select various items on the inspection form, there was at least one area of the process where text input was required. Remember to account for the size of the keyboard (Figure 10-17) when designing screens that require text input.

When creating a paper prototype, it can also be valuable to visually describe business logic, like the data validation error shown in Figure 10-18 when a user attempts to submit an incomplete inspection.

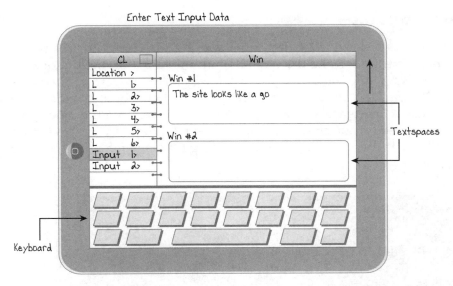

Figure 10-17: If the application requires text input, remember to design the screen with room for the keyboard.

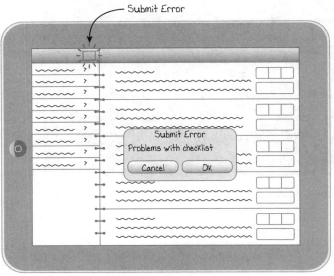

Figure 10-18: Workflow and business logic can also be described visually in a paper prototype.

Realistic Mockups

After successfully developing, iterating, and getting feedback on a paper prototype, it's time to take the next step and create a realistic mockup. Remember that, while the paper prototype was all about getting the high-level details finalized, the realistic mockups should now be able to describe the entire user experience, beginning to end. When creating these designs, remember to create a splash screen (Figure 10-19) followed by a login screen (Figure 10-20), as these are important in setting the stage for a positive user experience.

Figure 10-19: Don't forget the splash screen, as it can be powerful in setting up the user experience.

As you transition from the paper prototypes into the realistic mockups, take advantage of the higher-fidelity graphics as an opportunity to experiment with different aesthetic designs to elevate the user experience. In the screen shown in Figure 10-21, the standard iPad split view was translated into a realistic spiral notebook design. Subtle details like this may seem unimportant, but user feedback has shown that these little details go a long way in improving perceived user experience.

Figure 10-20: The login screen.

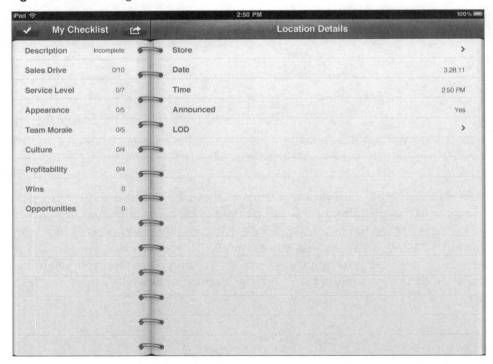

Figure 10-21: Be creative in your application by simulating a natural look-and-feel, like this binding.

As you translate individual screens from the paper prototypes, you will probably discover a lot of missing details in the design and requirements. Use this process to help document items like the lists of contents and menus. When gathering feedback from users, don't forget to ask for comments about the completeness and accuracy of this content, like the text detailed in the screen of Figure 10-22.

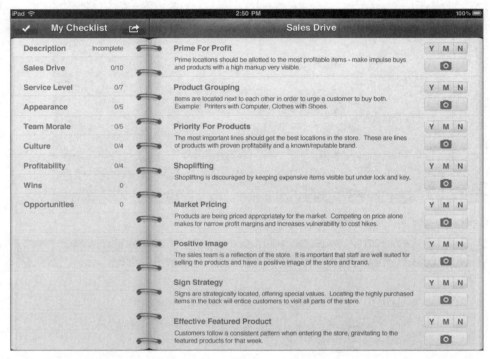

Figure 10-22: With a realistic mockup, users will critique every detail, so try to complete as many details as possible in this high-fidelity phase of design.

As you create the individual screens to describe the user experience and workflow, try to pay attention to subtle details that can improve usability. In the example shown in Figure 10-23, the existing paper-based process of simply checking the box didn't necessarily allow the "score" to visually jump out at the user. But by color-coding the selections green, yellow, and red, users can easily see their own progress through the inspection as well as enjoy aesthetic contrast.

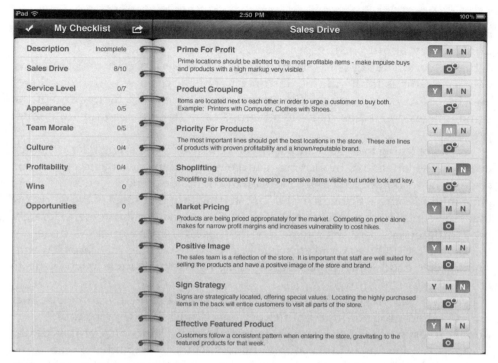

Figure 10-23: Think about how the user experience can be enhanced visually, as through these color-coded green, yellow, and red data capture elements.

While this process may seem much more "creative" and "artsy" than most people in enterprise IT might be comfortable with, the usability and, ultimately, user adoption will be tied to the success of the user experience design. If you don't prototype and get feedback early and often, you won't hear the comments from users until after you've already completed development, at which point the cost of change will be exponentially higher.

Creating Functional Prototypes

For many types of iPad applications, it can be valuable to create a functional prototype. A functional prototype can provide a user with a simulated user experience through actual interaction with the application as opposed to the static nature of mockups.

The key to successfully creating functional prototypes is to recognize and embrace the fact that the prototype will be thrown away. As a result, don't worry about coding practices, or even creating applications that actually work. The key is to "simulate" the user experience; the most effective way to do this is for a graphic designer to sit side by side with a developer and use hard-coded images for almost every screen. In fact, many of the same images created as realistic mockups can often be used for functional prototypes.

Instead of trying to create buttons that actually work, you might take any touch event on the left side of the screen near the master pane and navigate the next stage of the workflow. Any touch event on the right side of the screen in the detail pane might progress through individual steps within that stage of the workflow that represents "happy path" usage. If there is a fork within the usage, you might try to differentiate between interactions for those different workflows, but again the key isn't actually to write any code or even wire up user interface elements. The secret to good, rapid, functional prototyping is to use simple touch events to move through static images.

I've seen this process move amazingly quickly. A skilled graphic designer and a skilled programmer, both experienced with this type of rapid functional prototyping, can sit side by side and turn out a functional prototype of a 20-screen application in just a couple of hours. Then, by immediately capturing user feedback to iterate on the design, I've seen functional prototypes like this go through multiple iterations with user feedback loops within the span of a single day. If your organization plans on developing a lot of iPad applications, it will likely be very worthwhile to invest in developing this unique and rapid prototyping capability within your internal IT staff.

Getting User Feedback

It's been mentioned before, but it's very important to get user feedback as early and as often in the design process as possible. Most enterprise software is never put in front of users until it has already been developed, and only then is it discovered what new iPad-specific features might be valuable and what features might never be used, as well as other concepts related to user experience.

Creating prototypes, whether these are low-fidelity sketches, high-fidelity mockups, or even functional user experience prototypes, is a simple yet effective way to accelerate the capture of user feedback. Prototyping is extremely cost-effective, especially when you consider that an early-stage prototyping process will often cost significantly less than a late-stage code refactoring effort to change a missed or misunderstood functional requirement.

Summary

In this chapter, we discussed how to take your application concept and turn it into a user experience prototype. There are many types of prototypes and many different tools that can be used to accelerate this process, from pads of paper and stencils to iPad apps and Photoshop or PowerPoint templates.

Paper prototyping can be used to refine the high-level application concept while ignoring a lot of the specific details. When providing feedback, users are able to focus on the big picture and think about the purpose of the application in the context of an end-to-end user experience.

Realistic mockups can then take your paper prototype to the next level by filling in a lot of the details that are left to the imagination in the paper prototyping process. Those realistic mockups can also be turned into functional prototypes by wiring those static images into an interactive application that allows the user to experience the application workflow firsthand.

Iteratively prototyping your applications and getting user feedback will dramatically improve the success of your iPad app development efforts. Is that something you are ready and willing to do?

In the next chapter, we'll talk in more detail about maximizing the usability of your application through iPad design best practices.

CHAPTER 11

Maximizing Application Usability

The last couple of chapters covered the high-level concepts around designing an iPad application. That discussion started with defining what is the core purpose of the application and who are the users, as well as how and where will the users actually use the app. The process of designing the user experience, from paper prototyping to realistic looking mockups and ultimately through functional user experience prototypes, was also outlined.

In this chapter, we'll build upon those concepts with an emphasis on the overall usability of the application. As I've mentioned before, a lot of the principles of human interface design and user experience are not commonly practiced in many enterprise environments, so don't be surprised if you aren't familiar with these ideas. With a lot of traditional enterprise software development, usability and user interface design was usually a lower priority that was examined near the end of a project. When it comes to mobile software development, though, especially with the iPad, having high usability and a great user experience are absolutely necessary to a successful application, even when deployed to internal employees.

This chapter starts by detailing some of the principles that are important to iPad application design. After that, you'll learn how some of the best practices for web design usability are not necessarily applicable on the iPad, as well as the importance of truly embracing the iOS user interface paradigm when you create your apps. Finally, we'll discuss the importance of following Apple's iOS Human Interface Guidelines, and we'll summarize the most important concepts of these guidelines.

Human Interface Principles

In the world of iOS development, there are six core principles of good user experience design: aesthetic integrity, consistency, direct manipulation, feedback, metaphors, and user control. While many of these principles are universally applicable, these ideas are especially important in the context of iPad application design. Apple is one of the most design-oriented companies in the world, and Apple has painstakingly invested in designing every aspect of the iPad user experience.

When you develop an iPad application, you aren't creating something that will be consumed in a vacuum. Any given iPad application is only one contributing part of the overall iPad experience. While enterprise software does not normally emphasize these types of ideas, enterprise apps on the iPad demand a focus on these principles.

Aesthetic Integrity

While users will absolutely expect a certain level of aesthetic appeal in their iPad applications, aesthetic integrity is more than just looking good. It is all about how well the appearance integrates with the function. For example, it can be very easy to go too far with a flashy user interface that overwhelms the basic purpose of the app. The application should have aesthetic appeal, but the appearance should fit smoothly within the user experience and not overwhelm the user.

Consistency

Unlike many other platforms that do not have a clear set of human interface guidelines, iOS has a very distinct user interface paradigm. Apple was able to elevate the user experience of the iPad above other platforms by creating a consistent experience throughout all the apps running on the iPad. The iPad is able to provide a high level of usability because of this consistency within the platform; your enterprise applications are no exception. They are not in a vacuum, but part of a total user experience of the iPad, and as such, the usability of your applications is directly tied to your consistency with the iPad user interface paradigms. It's important to note that consistency with your existing enterprise systems is less critical than consistency with the iPad experience. It is a common mistake to attempt consistency with your existing systems, but the paradox is that full consistency with the iPad user interface paradigm ensures intuition, and therefore this will have much less impact on the learning curve than might be expected. If you don't believe this, create some functional user experience prototypes of both and test them with users.

Direct Manipulation

One of the most powerful aspects of the iPad user experience of applications is the ability to manipulate representations of physical objects directly on the screen through rotating, stretching, flicking, dragging, and other multi-touch gestures on the touch screen or through the use of the accelerometer and/or gyroscope. As opposed to using separate controls to manipulate the objects, as might be standard practice on other platforms, iPad users expect a more immersive experience through direct manipulation. Although this may not be common in many enterprise applications, this type of capability could be used as part of applications for sales demonstrations, for instance. Taking advantage of this principle can dramatically elevate the user experience of your apps.

Feedback

Users of iPad applications expect feedback from the application as acknowledgement of an interaction. For instance, tapping a list item will result in a brief highlighting of the item. If the application is performing a function that takes more than a second or two, a spinner or a progress bar should be displayed to show movement and progress. These subtle aesthetic elements can greatly improve the user experience of an application.

Metaphors

Most users are familiar with various computing metaphors, for example the "folder" that can be used to hold various "files" or other data. The iPad introduces new metaphors like the On/Off switches that can be slid back and forth to toggle state or the spinning picker wheels to make selections. Using these metaphors within your iPad applications can increase the user experience, but it's also important not to push the metaphors too far or to overuse them.

User Control

With iPad apps, users must always feel in control. The app should be able to guide them through a workflow and allow them to back out or cancel, if needed. If the app needs to perform a potentially destructive operation, like the deletion of data or not saving a document or completing an operation, the user expects to be prompted in order to confirm the action. Also, users expect to be able to grace-fully stop operations in process or even exit the app at any time without data loss.

Rethinking Web-Based Designs

If you are coming from a web development background, it's important to rec-ognize that there are many significant differences between web usability best practices and what is expected by users of iPad apps. Remember, in this case, an "app" could be native, web, or hybrid, which means that even though it may be developed with the same HTML, CSS, and JavaScript technologies as a website, users expect a mobile app to be different.

For instance, many websites are designed be "portals" that present the users with many different navigation options or functions. In an application, the user expects the app to be focused on a single purpose, and expects it to be useful immediately after launching, not after multiple steps of navigation.

One other big difference is that iPad applications should be designed for touch. Don't try to take your web user interface paradigm to the iPad, but rather embrace the iOS user experience paradigm and all the metaphors and user interface components that come along with it.

There are two final big differences — scrolling and navigation. While web designs often stress "above the fold" to prevent the users from having to scroll, iPad scrolling feels extremely natural and there is no reason to try to prevent it (although designers should avoid extremely extensive scrolling). And with regard to navigation, web design paradigms stress a "Home" button that is always visible, but this is not applicable or appropriate in an iOS paradigm. Users of iOS can always tap the status bar at the top of the screen to quickly scroll back to the top of a long list, and since iOS apps generally don't have home pages, there's no reason to create a custom Home button.

Embracing the iOS User Interface Paradigm

As mentioned earlier in this chapter, creating successful iPad applications requires the design to embrace the iOS user interface paradigm. This ensures that your applications will be highly usable and intuitive, and will provide a great user experience.

Of course, this is easier said than done. It's quite easy to create an iPad app. It's much more difficult to create a great iPad app. It requires a paradigm shift, and the sooner you can recognize and embrace that shift instead of fighting it, the better the design, and ultimately the better the final application will be.

Focus on the User Experience

I've said it before, but I'm going to say it again because it is so critically important. When it comes to iPad applications, the user experience is everything. If the application is not usable, it will not be used. The only metric of mobility that matters is usage and adoption, because that is what ultimately drives the return on investment for any application. If your application isn't used because it doesn't provide a good user experience, you would probably be better off not even developing an iPad application in the first place. Developing an iPad application requires an emphasis on user experience and design that enterprise IT is not accustomed to, but is absolutely necessary for the creation of successful iPad applications.

Apple's Human Interface Guidelines

Apple's iOS Human Interface Guidelines (HIG) are the key to creating successful iPad applications. These guidelines are more than suggestions, and if you want to create apps that provide a great user experience, you need to view them as requirements. In this chapter, I've summarized some of the concepts found in the iOS HIG, but it would be wise to use this summary as a guide, and not as a substitute for reading, digesting, and absorbing the full document from Apple. The HIG should be required reading for everyone on the team, since it contains the keys to success in iOS app development.

Focus on the Primary Task

Focus, focus, focus. Simplicity and focus are critical to the design of a successful iPad application. Don't let the app do too much. Cut all the unnecessary requirements. Remember the 80-20 rule, and focus on the 20 percent of the functionality that is used 80 percent of the time. This can be one of the most difficult tasks in enterprise iPad development, but it is a fundamental requirement of success.

Give Users a Logical Path

Users should be able to clearly and intuitively navigate through an application. If sequential navigation is required, always allow the user to "go back" and don't force the user to only "go forward" in the application. You should also try to give users only one navigation path to any given screen, since multiple navigation paths will confuse them and make the app more difficult to use. If there are screens that need to be reused, see if it's possible to use popover or modal views that can be used in multiple contexts.

Use User-Centric Terminology

Although many enterprise applications tend to use a lot of jargon, you should make sure to use words that your users will understand. Use the iPad app design process to simplify complex wording as much as possible. Also, many enterprise data structures and field names are designed from the enterprise data standpoint, not from the perspective of the user. Think about the data, content, and functionality from the user's perspective, and ensure that any labels and messaging are both clear and concise.

Minimize the Effort Required for User Input

While entering text data using the onscreen keyboard on the iPad is certainly easier than it is on an iPhone or iPod touch, it is still much more difficult than it is on other device form factors with full-sized physical keyboards. Think about how free-text input can be minimized by taking advantage of common selections with select lists or other user interface controls that can provide automatic entry of data. This may require adjustment to the functionality of your application or even workflow. Although it is not always possible to eliminate free text entry, it can often be significantly reduced.

Brand Appropriately

With iPad applications, you should incorporate your branding in an unobtrusive manner without taking away screen real estate to display a logo or other branding elements. Think about how the brand can be subtly integrated into the application through the color scheme and background images. Not only is this type of subtle branding more effective, it also goes a long way to enhance and improve the user experience. Remember, though, that the icon and splash screen can be used to clearly communicate your branding. You should spend some time to find the appropriate balance of incorporating branding into your application.

Make Search Quick and Rewarding

Users of iPad applications expect search functionality to be integrated into the core of applications where search is appropriate. As opposed to, for instance, making search a separate tab, you can incorporate a search bar on the top of a list of data. Then, as users enter text into the search field, you can filter the data in real time to create a better user experience. To optimize performance, make sure that your data is indexed appropriately, and if your search is occurring remotely, it is also valuable to search and filter as the user types into the search box, when possible.

One other important consideration is to think of search in a single-box manner however and whenever possible. While many enterprise applications have search screens with many text boxes to search for different elements, iPad users are accustomed to the single "Google" text field search paradigm. For instance, if your application needs to give the user the ability to search customers, you don't need separate text fields to search for company name, customer number, city, state, or zip. Let all of the searchable fields be searched from a single search box. It may require some creative index optimization of your data, but it is what users expect and will provide a much better user experience.

Be Succinct

Cut down on verbose descriptions. Give controls and objects short labels or even symbol icons to minimize text. Simplify as much as possible, and think like you're writing a newspaper headline where you're trying to cut out as many words as you can. This can be difficult, but the resulting improvements in the user experience will be worth it.

Use User Interface Elements Consistently

This is often one of the biggest challenges for user interface design for enterprise iPad apps. Unlike other platforms, iOS has clearly defined usages for standard user interface (UI) components. Users of the iPad will understand these standard UI elements and what the standard action is. Any deviation from the standard behavior will negatively affect usability and the user experience. Additionally, if there is a standard UI element that performs a given action, you shouldn't radically change the appearance of a particular component, because users will struggle to figure out how to interact with it. Also, iOS comes with many standard buttons and icons, and you should never use those elements to do something that is different from the standard default behavior.

Support All Orientations

There is no upside down in the iPad paradigm. Users should be able to hold the devices any way they want, and the application should respond seamlessly. If possible, when users change the orientation of the devices, the application should simply rotate without impacting the screen layout. If the application's layout is too complicated for that, consider how the transition between portrait and landscape orientation can be as similar as possible. Also, you should use subtle animation to visualize changes in the user interface layout when rotating.

Enhance Interactivity

Even though the iPad has a much larger screen than the iPhone or iPod touch, it's still important to resist the desire to add features that are not directly related to the core purpose and focus of the application. Alternatively, consider how the larger screen real estate available on the iPad can provide new ways to interact with the content and functionality. For example, a business intelligence application might find a way to interact with the data without changing context, by pivoting or looking at the same content from a different perspective.

Reduce Full-Screen Transitions

On the iPhone or iPod touch, full-screen transitions are normal and expected, but on the iPad's larger screen, this isn't optimal. Rather than a full-screen transition, there may be a transition in either the master or detail pane of a split view, or maybe the transition animation of a popover or modal view as it appears. Otherwise, consider using the transition within a popover or modal view as opposed to the entire screen. With the iPad, consider all of the other aspects of the user interface paradigm before deciding to go with a full-screen transition.

Restrain Your Information Hierarchy

Although the iPad has a fairly large screen, you should not clutter any given screen with too much information. Focus on the primary purpose of the application and the core content. And take advantage of the iPad user interface elements for structuring and organizing content and navigation. For instance, with a split view, think of the pane on the left as the master view; upon selection of an item, the detail view on the right can change content accordingly. As appropriate, you can also use navigation bars to drill into content on either the left or the right pane of a split view. You can also use popovers to provide additional actions or interactivity with objects on the screen. Segmented controls on a toolbar at the top of the screen can be used to provide different perspectives of the same content, and a tab bar on the bottom of the screen can provide access to different categories or application modes.

Enable Collaboration and Connectedness

The iPad is a unique form factor that very much lends itself to collaboration. Unlike a laptop form factor that can be quite clunky for multiple users to collaborate on, the iPad can be used to enable multi-user collaboration on applications; you should consider if your apps would lend themselves to that type of usage scenario. Additionally, while many apps must be designed to remain usable when not connected to the network, iPad apps should take maximum advantage of network connectivity whenever available. For instance, geolocation could be used to get the current location and load applicable information for this particular physical area, or general data could be pre-fetched and cached in the background.

Add Physicality and Heightened Realism

It can often enhance the user experience for the iPad app to visually represent the physical objects that it may be replacing, augmenting, or simulating. For instance, the contacts application on the iPad looks and feels like a physical paper-based address book. In the example used in the previous chapter on prototyping, a paper-based checklist was replaced with a digital checklist, so the app was designed to look like a paper-based notebook. Think about the physical alternatives to the objects represented in your iPad application, and consider how the app can be designed to provide a higher level of realism to increase usability and enhance user experience.

Delight People with Stunning Graphics

In your applications, don't underestimate the value of using high-resolution photorealistic graphics. Think about how the visual use of high-quality materials like wood, leather, stone, or even precious metals could enhance the aesthetic integrity of your application.

You should not hard-code screen resolutions into your applications. As Apple has evolved the line of iOS devices, there are now three different resolutions. If a future iPad has a higher resolution display, you should be prepared for that and not have to rewrite a lot of existing code.

Consider Multi-Finger Gestures

While multi-finger gestures are not applicable or appropriate for every application, you should think long and hard about how the creative use of gestures like "pinch and swipe" could increase the user experience of your applications. You can also use complex gestures as a shortcut to streamline a process, but you shouldn't require it as the only way to perform that particular task.

If you choose to use gestures, you should always use the standard action associated with a particular gesture to avoid confusing the user. Like user interface element consistency, gesture behavior consistency is just as important for the overall user experience.

Minimize Modality

Modal views (which you may know as child windows) are extremely common in many enterprise applications designed for traditional PCs, and while modal views are available on iOS, they should be minimized and eliminated wherever possible.

Modal views are appropriate in situations where it is important to get the user's attention, or where a task must be specifically completed or abandoned in such a way as to maintain the integrity the data or the workflow process. If that is not the case, then explore to see if the modality can be removed.

Consider Popovers for Some Modal Tasks

While in many ways popover views are very similar to modal views, they have one very significant difference. While a popover view is automatically dismissed when a user touches outside of the popover, a modal view is not dismissed, and touches outside of the modal view are ignored. There are many appropriate uses for modal views, but consider if a popover is a better option when choosing to use a view.

Downplay File Handling Operations

While interaction with "files" are common in a desktop computing paradigm, the iPad does not have the concept of a "Finder" or "File Explorer" that gives users the ability to manage or manipulate files. Therefore, in iPad applications, while files can certainly be used to store information behind the scenes, to pass information between apps, or to access files from e-mail or the Web for viewing or editing, users should not be presented with a complicated file management concept. Any file management that is exposed to the user should be simplified and graphical wherever possible.

Ask People to Save Only When Necessary

With the iPad, users expect applications to auto-save their work so if they exit the application, they will not lose any data. Depending on the workflow, this sometimes requires the use of in-process saving of data, since it wouldn't be appropriate to save an incomplete transaction. This is an important expectation of iPad users, and enterprise developers should be especially aware of how it might impact the design of the application.

Start Instantly

Waiting is not something that iPad users are generally used to, and as a result your applications should take performance, especially start-up time, quite seriously. If your application has to obtain data from a remote source in order to display the first screen, don't wait to display the screen until you have data. Preferably, use cached data from the previous use if possible, but in any case, show that the application has started and provide visual feedback that the application is loading data over the network. The perception of start-up time performance can also be improved by using a splash screen that looks similar to the first screen of the application. Also, simplify the set-up and activation process as much as possible.

Always Be Prepared to Stop

iPad users expect to be able to hit the Home button at any time to exit the application. As a result, your application should save the user's data as often as necessary to prevent data loss. Additionally, save the application's current state when the app receives a notification of a stop event.

Don't Quit Programmatically

While it is not uncommon for applications on other platforms to quit execution programmatically, that concept is not appropriate for iOS. The user interface of an application should not provide the ability to exit the app. The application will exit if another app is launched from within the app or if the user presses the Home button. If your app encounters an error or if your application features are not working for some reason, do not stop execution, but rather handle the situation gracefully and provide the user with an opportunity to respond (for instance, reestablish wireless connectivity and try again).

Summary

In this chapter we discussed many of the best practices and usability principles of iPad application development. A lot of these concepts will be new to those in corporate IT, but it's important to recognize that following these best practices is necessary for creating successful iPad applications. This chapter contains a summary of many of the ideas found in Apple's iOS Human Interface Guidelines, and that document should be required reading for anyone involved in an iPad application project within the enterprise.

Are you willing to give these ideas about user experience design a try? Are you prepared to embrace Apple's iOS user interface paradigm?

In the next chapter, we'll discuss the process of iteration, both within the design process and within the entire iPad application development project itself.

Improving through Iterations

Now that you have a user interface design, have created a series of prototypes, and have worked to maximize application usability, it's time to look at some of the unique constraints around planning and managing iPad application development projects. At first glance, it might seem that running projects for enterprise iPad applications is really no different than any other enterprise software project. While that view might someday hold true, there are a number of factors that make enterprise development projects for iPad applications different at present.

The first fundamental difference is that the iPad is not only an extremely new device, relatively speaking, but it's also the first computing device with a tablet form factor that has truly gone mainstream. As a result, many enterprise capabilities and best practices for the platform are still emerging, and the ones that have been established across the industry are still quite new and immature within most organizations. This means that the first few iPad projects for any enterprise IT department will involve a fair amount of learning for everyone on the team. Mistakes will be made, so it's important to both fail quickly and learn from those mistakes so the projects can continue moving forward successfully.

The second key difference is that users and business customers will express and explain their requirements differently. As Best Buy's CTO, Robert Stephens, was quoted earlier in the chapter on consumerization, "The user now knows what they want, and now they can and will demand it from IT." But rather than communicating those demands through traditional requirements documents, those users will try to describe an experience. And if that description of an "experience" is somehow converted into a traditional requirements document and handed to a development team to create, the "experience" will almost certainly be lost in translation when the final product is handed back to the end user. This means that "experience" must be incorporated into the entire end-to-end development process and the user must be able to iteratively "experience" the application and provide feedback to inform and improve the design and development.

In this chapter, we'll examine how you can work around and even embrace these differences in iPad application development to maximize the success of these projects within your organization.

Advantages of Being Agile

While I do not want to unnecessarily spark an ideological debate about project management methodologies, I feel it's extremely important to share my consistent and repeated experiences in the mobile software development space.

For many reasons that we will discuss here, iPad application development projects will generally be much more successful with an agile development process than a traditional waterfall approach. Let's take a look at some of these contributing factors.

Waterfall Development

Traditional waterfall development follows a process of sequential phases, where each phase is completed before moving on to the next one, as shown in Figure 12-1. Projects start with a requirements definition, which is then used to create a design, which is then provided to developers to be implemented. After development, the deliverables are provided to Quality Assurance (QA) for testing and verification, and once completed the project is delivered and moved into a maintenance state.

Of course, for many projects, like a monitoring system for a nuclear reactor or a guidance system for a deep space probe, waterfall is not only the preferred approach — it's the only way these types of systems can be delivered. Requirements must be clearly documented up front, and every single requirement must be designed, implemented, and verified before the project can be delivered.

Enterprise iPad applications, though, will rarely, if ever, fall into that category of systems. As iPad apps are all about simplicity and experience and delivering the 20 percent of functionality that users need 80 percent of the time, many of the "requirements" cannot be determined until users have had a chance to actually use the system and provide feedback. This presents a paradox for project managers who are used to defining all the requirements up front.

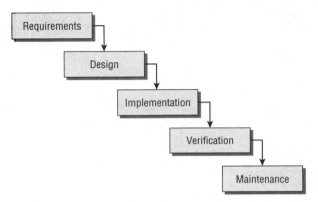

Figure 12-1: The waterfall model follows a series of sequential phases of development.

Agile Development

As an alternative to the more traditional waterfall development approach, agile development is an iterative development approach based on several key principles that make it ideal for iPad application development.

One fundamental principle of agile development is to welcome changing requirements, even late in development, since agile processes can harness change for the customer's competitive advantage. This allows the application to evolve as the user's needs emerge. While traditional waterfall development resists requirements change, agile development embraces change and helps customers discover what their true functional and user experience requirements actually are.

Other agile principles include delivering working software frequently and having business people and developers collaborate daily throughout the project. By delivering working software early in the process and repeatedly throughout development, users are able to clarify in their own minds what they actually need, as well as communicate emerging requirements and explain how the application can be improved. Since this feedback cycle cannot occur until you put working software into the hands of your users, it is much better to do this very early in the development process before a lot of coding has occurred than to wait until the very end of the project when it is delivered. The value of this feedback loop is only amplified on new platforms like the iPad. While the waterfall process fixes scope and flexes time and/or budget, an agile development process fixes time and budget while allowing scope to flex.

In an iterative and agile development process, requirements are drafted and then used to create a design. Implementation and testing should then happen in parallel, and at the end of the fixed time period for iteration, the working software is provided to the customers. This provides a feedback loop into the requirements and design efforts of the subsequent iteration. This process is described in Figure 12-2.

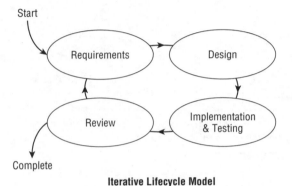

Iterative Lifecycle Model

Figure 12-2: Agile development is based on an iterative approach of creating software and getting feedback by collaborating with users.

As I was writing this book, I talked to Mike Cohn, author of *Succeeding with Agile: Software Development Using Scrum*, about his perspective on iterative development in mobile software. According to Cohn, "With any new and innovative device such as the iPad, users cannot possibly know exactly what they want. They need to work closely with the software developers to figure out what they want and how it should look. Agile software development approaches like Scrum are a perfect fit for the challenges and opportunities created in situations like iPad development today."

Scrum is an agile methodology for software development project management that consists of a series of iterative "sprints" that are typically two to four weeks long. Scrum enables cross-functional and self-organizing teams, but also emphasizes two additional key roles in any project: the Product Owner and the ScrumMaster. The Product Owner is the voice of the customer, representing the business and the users; has authority to make decisions on behalf of the customer; and is ultimately accountable for ensuring the project delivers value to the business. The ScrumMaster is the facilitator of the Scrum process. While not the team leader, the ScrumMaster is responsible for removing barriers to the achievement of the sprint deliverables and for buffering the team from any distracting influences.

Each sprint starts with the creation and/or grooming of the product backlog, which consists of a prioritized list of high-level potential features and functionality. These high-level items are estimated on an order-of-magnitude basis, and are carved into a sprint backlog based on the capacity of resources within the fixed-period sprints. The high-level features on the sprint backlog are broken down into individual tasks and estimated on a lower level by the team in a sprint planning meeting. During each sprint, there is a daily Scrum meeting where team members tell what they've done since yesterday, what they're planning to do today, and if there are any barriers to their progress. A sprint burndown chart is also updated daily to provide complete transparency to actual progress within the sprint to determine if the team is ahead, behind, or on schedule for delivering all the features within the sprint. At the end of each sprint, a working piece of software that is a potentially shippable product increment is to be delivered, and is demoed at a sprint review meeting. There is also a sprint retrospective to identify any lessons learned during the sprint and make constant process improvements. At this point, the project either ends with a shipped project or repeats again with another sprint. This process is illustrated in Figure 12-3.

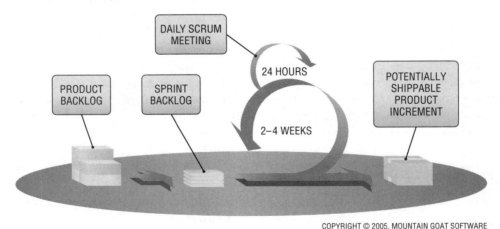

Figure 12-3: Scrum is a popular methodology for agile, iterative-style software development.

While enterprise software is usually more about the functionality, when enterprise applications go mobile it becomes all about the user experience. If certain features or functions are not usable in a mobile context, then there is no point in building them at all.

Gathering Iterative User Feedback

As discussed in Chapter 8, the vast majority of the cost, effort, and time of developing an enterprise iPad application is in the integration with back-end data and systems. The user interface of an application is usually just the tip of the iceberg in total cost, time, and effort, but it's also the most difficult to effectively define and design, especially in a vacuum.

User Experience Prototyping

User experience prototyping, usually conducted in advance or as a prerequisite to a full application development process, is the ultimate in improvement through rapid iterations. This usually works best when a graphics designer is sitting side by side with a programmer, with both having computers to work on their respective prototyping activities: the designer creating images and the programmer hacking them together to simulate actual functionality. A designer and developer who are skilled in this art can often create the initial functional prototype within a couple of hours and then subsequently iterate in 30- to 90-minute loops.

Imagine this happening with one or more users in the same room, so that the designer and developer can quickly build the prototype and immediately hand it to the users to get feedback. Many iterations, often representing very dramatic evolution of the application, can occur within just a couple of days. I've seen many applications come out of this process looking nothing like the concept that was first proposed. Without these rapid iterations of throw-away user experience prototypes, the vastly inferior application concept would have been what was developed and ultimately deployed to users. Bottom line: The return on investment of a properly executed user experience prototyping session should never be underestimated.

Hallway Testing

While hallway testing is not even possible with most types of traditional enterprise software, it can be extremely effective for gathering feedback on iPad applications. Since iPad applications should be naturally intuitive and designed for quick usage sessions, you can hand a random user in the hallway of your company an iPad, describe a workflow or scenario, and ask this user to attempt to use the application. As this happens, observe any areas where the user pauses, makes mistakes, or has to back up. These observations present opportunities to improve the user experience of the application. And as the application evolves, it also helps to "hallway test" with some (but not all) of the same users, as this helps to provide a contrast of the intuitiveness of the application with the overall usability after the learning curve has been achieved.

Focus Groups

More formal than hallway testing, focus groups can also provide a lot of valuable feedback. In addition to handing iPads to individual participants and asking them to do the same sort of workflow and scenario as described in hallway testing, focus groups can provide unique collaborative discussion and feedback. Often, getting a variety of people from different backgrounds and technology skill levels together in the same room to discuss the application can lead to breakthrough ideas that wouldn't have happened with individual-level testing alone. It's always valuable to schedule at least a few focus group sessions throughout the iterative application evolution lifecycle.

Pilot Deployments

In many traditional "pilot deployments" a system is put into testing with a small number of users to determine whether it is appropriate or not to be rolled out to the entire user base. Alternatively, in the context of iterative mobile development, pilots can and should be rolled out for the sole purpose of gathering feedback for the improvement of the application. Rather than using the pilot to make a "go/no go" decision, the pilot should be used to gather feedback for subsequent iterations and deployment of the pilot before a final "go/no go" decision.

Usage Analytics

Configuring your applications to use an analytics tool like Google Analytics in either a pilot or a full deployment can provide extremely valuable information with regard to how users are using the application, how much they are using it, and what features they are or are not actually taking advantage of. This can also provide interesting data contrasts and comparisons when coordinated with a user survey that can highlight differences between perception and reality.

In-App Feedback

One easy way for users to provide feedback about bugs and quirks, suggestions, feature requests, or other comments is to include a "provide feedback" feature within the application. This could be a form from within the app, but one popular way to accomplish this is to simply allow the user to send an e-mail from within the application. When the user selects the "provide feedback" option, a new e-mail message appears with the subject and body pre-populated with any applicable information (device UDID, user id, session token, etc.). There may even be a log file so that any workflow sequences, usage patterns, error messages, and stack traces can be subsequently analyzed.

Many companies have also successfully taken advantage of in-app surveys and feature voting. Say that there are 10 upcoming features on the application road map. Users can be presented with a list and description of all the features, and they can select the top three features they would like. This provides a much more objective kind of feedback, as opposed to random and perhaps outspoken users, who may be speaking from a minority perspective.

Rapid Release Schedule

While somewhat controversial in some enterprise environments, many of the leading iOS application developers maintain very rapid release cycles, often releasing an updated version every two to four weeks. This is especially true as applications are first brought to market, until their features and functionality achieve a baseline and stabilize. This rapid release cycle will work for some enterprise apps, but for other enterprise apps and corporate environments, a release cycle as fast as this is unrealistic, given the constraints and requirements on QA resources for pre-release application regression testing. It's important to note, though, that a release cycle of three to four months is often an undeniable requirement of iOS development, given Apple's own platform release cycle, which may (and often does) introduce issues into existing applications.

Project Planning and Management

From the perspective of the business and project management, there are some best practices to help maximize the success of iPad application development efforts. However you feel about project management methodologies or approaches, following these ideas can make all the difference.

Start Small

It's important to recognize that iPad applications are fundamentally different from traditional enterprise software. An iPad app should have a crisp, clear focus and purpose, and it should not be cluttered with unnecessary or rarely used features and functionality. Not only will a complicated app take much more time and money to develop, but it will face more resistance to adoption as compared to a simple app. That's not to say that you can't develop a complex iPad app, just that it's much easier to deliver a complex app through a series of small releases than through one enormous development and release cycle.

Get Quick Wins

If you start small, you'll likely deliver more quickly and successfully than if you try to start with a huge scope. Once you have achieved that initial success, you can build upon quick wins by delivering repeated iterations of the same application with additional features and functionality (based on prioritized feedback from the actual users) or by introducing additional apps beyond the first one.

Plan for Iterations

If you start small and get quick wins, you need to know how to build upon that. Since many applications are complex and large, it's important to figure out a way to deliver the extensive features and functionality through a series of iterations. As the first iteration or two gets out there, the priority of subsequent iterations and releases is almost certainly going to change, which is why breaking up large and complex apps into smaller apps and projects is so valuable.

Involve Users Early and Often

Again, this has been mentioned many times before but its importance bears repeating. Your users must be involved throughout the entire development process. All too often, development teams are isolated from the users and have trouble getting access to the end customer, but with iPad applications this almost guarantees issues when the users finally receive the application. In order to develop a successful enterprise iPad application, users simply must be engaged throughout the development process.

Summary

In this chapter, you learned the importance of improving the design of your iPad applications through iterations — iterations in early design and prototypes as well as subsequent iterations throughout the entire development process. You compared traditional waterfall development methodology with more agile and iterative processes like Scrum to understand the specific advantages of a more agile approach in developing iPad applications.

You also covered many of the ways that a feedback loop can be created with users, with user experience prototyping, hallway testing, focus groups, pilot deployments, usage analytics, and in-app feedback mechanisms. And you then saw how to take advantage of this feedback through a rapid release cycle.

Even though these approaches are new for most people in enterprise IT, are you willing to give it a try to improve your chances at success in the creation of your iPad applications?

This chapter wraps up the section on design, and in the next section we'll dive into development, with the next chapter discussing how to get started with actually developing iPad applications.

Development

In This Part

Developing iPad Applications

WHAT'S IN THIS CHAPTER?

- Developing web and native apps for the iPad
- Using HTML5 and Sencha Touch to create a web app
- Using Objective-C to create a native app
- Using C# to create a native iPad application
- Using a MEAP to generate a native iPad app
- Understanding the advantages of each approach

In the last several chapters, you learned the process of designing iPad applications to optimize the user experience through prototyping, following best practices, and iterating with feedback from your users.

In this chapter, you'll learn how those designs can be developed into fully functional iPad applications. As discussed in Chapter 6, there are several different application architectures, each with its own set of inherent strengths and weaknesses. In this chapter we're going to focus on introducing the concepts, technologies, frameworks, tools, and development environments for web and native app development.

First, for web applications, you'll take a look at the Sencha Touch framework for creating HTML5 web apps. Then you'll look at creating native apps, starting with Objective-C and Cocoa Touch in Xcode; then using C# and .NET with MonoTouch; and finally using the Sybase Unwired Platform, which is a Mobile Enterprise Application Platform (MEAP).

Building Web Applications

Since the iPad has a relatively large, high-resolution display and is running a modern HTML5-capable WebKit browser, it is capable of successfully running virtually any standards-based web application. That is why popular web-based enterprise software like salesforce.com and NetSuite, for instance, are able to run just fine on the iPad without any changes.

Even though the iPad is capable of running just about any HTML web application, it's important to recognize that the iPad is fundamentally different from a traditional personal computer. As a result, the user experience of web apps can be dramatically improved if they are designed with the iPad in mind.

While there are many ways to theoretically accomplish this, one of the easiest and most popular ways is through a third-party framework to accelerate development. There are quite a few mobile HTML5 frameworks, but Sencha Touch is the first to truly embrace the larger form factor of the iPad, and not just the smaller form factor tablet devices. Let's take a look at this unique and powerful framework.

Sencha Touch HTML5 Framework

The Sencha Touch framework is a relatively simple, but extremely powerful framework for creating mobile web apps. One advantage of using Sencha Touch is that it was designed to support the large form factor display of the iPad, as well as the small form factor smartphone devices. This way your mobile iPad applications can be created using the same framework as web apps you may want to create for smartphone devices.

Development in Sencha Touch is done entirely using HTML, CSS, and JavaScript, so most web developers will feel quite at home with this framework. Sencha Touch includes a collection of user interface controls, or "components," that can be used to quickly create great-looking and touch-friendly user interfaces. The framework also includes a local storage proxy for storing data to the local device; enhanced touch events for tap, pinch, swipe, and rotate; and built-in data integration support for AJAX and JSON. The framework allows developers to rapidly create web apps, like the one shown in Figure 13-1.

Development Environment

Sencha Touch does not have a preferred development environment, per se, as all development in the framework is done in HTML, CSS, and JavaScript. Since those languages are rendered and interpreted at run time, there is not a build process. The HTML, CSS, and JavaScript files can be edited in whatever integrated development environment (IDE) or text editor that you prefer, such as the editor shown in Figure 13-2.

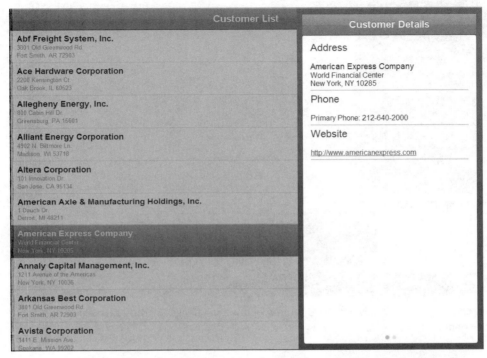

Figure 13-1: Sencha Touch is designed for the development of apps for large form factor mobile devices like the iPad.

Language and Technology Stack

Sencha Touch is an HTML5, CSS3, and JavaScript-based framework, and all application development is performed using those languages and technologies. Unlike some other styles of web app development, though, most of the application development in Sencha Touch is done in JavaScript. In fact, the primary HTML document you create has an empty `<body>` tag, as all the HTML is generated dynamically at run time with JavaScript. Sencha Touch provides a JavaScript-based Model View Controller (MVC) design pattern to help create your applications.

Example

To provide you with a taste of what it's like to develop an application using Sencha Touch, let's take a look at an example.

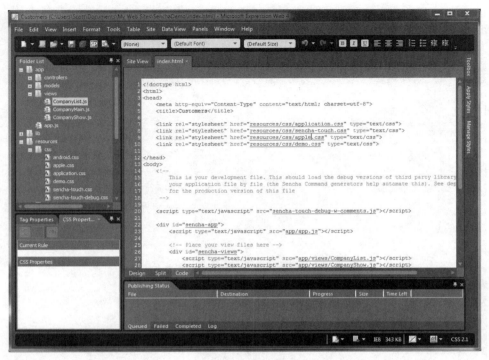

Figure 13-2: Sencha Touch development is done in HTML, CSS, and JavaScript, so any editor can be used.

In the following code snippet, you can see the implementation of a Model called "Company," including the various fields within the Model. It also shows the proxy for making a web services call to retrieve the JSON in order to hydrate the Model:

```
Ext.regModel("Company", {
    fields: [
        {name: "ID",             type: "int"},
        {name: "Name",           type: "string"},
        {name: "PrimaryAddress", type: "object"},
        {name: "PrimaryPhone",   type: "string"},
        {name: "Website",        type: "string"}
    ],
    getGroupString : function(record) {
        return record.get('Name')[0];
    },
    proxy: {
        type: 'rest',
        url : '/customers.json'
    },
```

```
    associations: [
        {type: 'hasMany', model: 'Address', name: 'Addresses'},
        {type: 'hasMany', model: 'Contact', name: 'Contacts'}
    ]
});
```

In the context of the "Customer" Model, here is a View called CompanyList that displays a collection of customer objects:

```
cust.views.CompanyList = Ext.extend(Ext.List, {
    emptyText   : 'No customers matching that query.',
    ui: 'cust',
    itemTpl: new Ext.XTemplate(
            '<div class="company">',
                '{Name}<br>',
                    '<small>',
                        '{PrimaryAddress.Street1}<br>',
                        '{PrimaryAddress.City}, {PrimaryAddress.State}',
                        '{PrimaryAddress.Zip}',
                    '</small>',
            '</div>'
    ),

    initComponent: function() {
        Ext.applyIf(this, {
            store: new Ext.data.Store({
                model: "Company",
                autoLoad: true,
                remoteFilter: true,
                sorters: 'Name',
            })
        });

        cust.views.CompanyList.superclass.initComponent.apply(this,
arguments);

        this.enableBubble('selectionchange');
    }
});

Ext.reg('customerList', cust.views.CompanyList);
```

As you can see, if you are familiar with JavaScript web development, Sencha Touch is a fairly straightforward yet powerful framework for the creation of web apps for the iPad. If you haven't done JavaScript-based development like this, there can be a learning curve. However, if you're planning to do web app development for the iPad, it is certainly worth a look to see if it's right for you and your application.

Advantages

Sencha Touch is an open-source framework under the General Public License (GPL). At the time of this writing, a dual license is available, with a commercial use license also available at no cost, although paid support can be purchased. The framework makes it very easy to rapidly build touch-optimized web applications, as well as support other platforms with WebKit-enabled browsers.

It's also important to remember that web apps, including those developed in Sencha Touch, can access native functionality using a hybrid wrapper application, such as PhoneGap. In the case of a hybrid application, the HTML, CSS, and JavaScript for the app could reside either on a remote web server or within the local application bundle itself.

Disadvantages

As far as web app frameworks go, Sencha Touch is currently best-in-breed. That being said, web apps still do not provide as rich a user experience as native applications, and they require a hybrid wrapper, as opposed to just a web browser, to access native functionality or submit to the App Store. Additionally, while HTML5 supports offline storage and cache manifest pre-fetching, it can still be quite difficult to manage data synchronization and maintain transactional integrity for offline functionality.

Building Native Applications

In this section, you'll cover three different approaches to the creation of native iPad applications. First you'll look at creating native apps using Objective-C and Cocoa Touch. Then you'll look at how native apps can be created in C# and .NET by taking advantage of the C# bindings to the Cocoa Touch application programming interfaces (APIs) in MonoTouch. Finally, you'll look at the process of creating a native app using the Sybase Unwired Platform (SUP) as a Mobile Enterprise Application Platform (MEAP).

Objective-C

Objective-C is Apple's preferred language for developing native iPad applications using the iOS software development kit (SDK). While Objective-C has been a relatively obscure language for most of its existence, the popularity of the iPhone and iPad, combined with the explosive growth of the App Store, has dramatically increased the awareness of Objective-C among developers in recent years.

Xcode Development Environment

The iOS SDK from Apple includes the Xcode development environment (shown in Figure 13-3) along with Interface Builder for designing graphic user interfaces, Instruments for monitoring application performance and memory usage, and the iPhone and iPad simulators for running and debugging applications on a Mac instead of a physical device. Apple provides the iOS SDK for free, but in order to deploy an application to a physical device, you must register for an Apple Developer account (the Standard program is $99/year and the Enterprise program is $299/year).

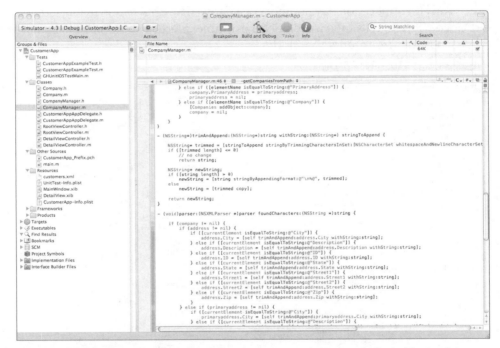

Figure 13-3: Xcode is the integrated development environment included in Apple's iOS SDK.

Language and Technology Stack

Objective-C is a superset of the C language that provides object-oriented extensions. While C++ also implemented object orientation of C, Objective-C is a completely different implementation based on Smalltalk-style messaging.

Cocoa Touch is the collection of iOS APIs that can be used to develop native iPhone, iPod touch, and iPad applications. The framework is based on a Model View Controller design pattern for developing applications.

Cocoa Touch is both a subset and a superset of the Cocoa APIs for Mac OS X development, and they are both primarily written in Objective-C. Cocoa Touch sits on a hierarchical stack of layers within iOS, on top of Graphics and Media (Application Services), then Core Services, and ultimately the Core OS and Mac OS X kernel layer.

Example

To get a feel for application development of a native iPad application in Objective-C and Cocoa Touch, let's take a look at an example. Here is some sample code of a data class that represents the Model:

```
@implementation Company

@synthesize ID;
@synthesize Website;
@synthesize Name;
@synthesize PrimaryPhone;
@synthesize PrimaryAddress;
@synthesize Addresses;
@synthesize Contacts;

- (id)init
{
    if (self = [super init])
    {
            self.ID = [[NSString alloc] init];
            self.Website = nil;
            self.Name = [[NSString alloc] init];
            self.PrimaryPhone = [[NSString alloc] init];
            self.PrimaryAddress = [[NSString alloc] init];
            self.Addresses = nil;
            self.Contacts = nil;
    }
    return self;
}
```

And here is code from within a UITableViewDelegate that is responsible for rendering the above Model in a View:

```
- (NSInteger)numberOfSectionsInTableView:(UITableView *)aTableView {
    // Return the number of sections.
    return 1;
}


- (NSInteger)tableView:(UITableView *)aTableView
```

```
numberOfRowsInSection:(NSInteger)section {
    // Return the number of rows in the section.
      if (companies != nil)
            return companies.count;
      else
            return 0;
}



- (UITableViewCell *)tableView:(UITableView *)tableView
cellForRowAtIndexPath:(NSIndexPath *)indexPath {

    static NSString *CellIdentifier = @"CellIdentifier";

    // Dequeue or create a cell of the appropriate type.
    UITableViewCell *cell = [tableView dequeueReusableCellWithIdentifier
:CellIdentifier];
    if (cell == nil) {
        cell = [[[UITableViewCell alloc]
initWithStyle:UITableViewCellStyleSubtitle reuseIdentifier:CellIdentifier]
autorelease];
        cell.accessoryType = UITableViewCellAccessoryNone;
    }

    // Configure the cell.
      Company* company = [companies objectAtIndex:indexPath.row];
    cell.textLabel.text = company.Name;
      cell.detailTextLabel.text = [company.Website absoluteString];
    return cell;
}
```

Advantages

The primary advantage of developing your application in Objective-C is that it is the approach recommended by Apple, so most documentation and sample source code for iPad development is written in Objective-C.

Disadvantages

While recommended by Apple, Objective-C is proprietary to their technology stack, so application logic is not portable to other non-Apple platforms. Objective-C is not a common skill set within most enterprise IT environments, and while it is growing in popularity, there is currently a shortage of skilled enterprise developers with this skill set.

Additionally, Apple's current Objective-C implementation for iOS does not include garbage collection, a feature present in many modern development languages, which has virtually eliminated an entire category of issues for debugging, that of memory leaks.

C# .NET

Unlike Objective-C, C# .NET is widely used by enterprise IT for application development. In order to use C# and .NET to develop iPad applications, you must take advantage of a framework called MonoTouch. MonoTouch provides developers access to both the Cocoa Touch native iOS APIs and the .NET framework. This allows existing C# code libraries without platform-specific dependencies to be reused for iPad development, and also allows portability of C# code for iPad app development to other platforms. Let's take a closer look at this development approach.

MonoTouch Development Environment

MonoTouch uses MonoDevelop (shown in Figure 13-4) as an IDE. Although most C# .NET developers use Microsoft Visual Studio, MonoTouch development must be done in MonoDevelop on a Mac. Of course, C# .NET business logic and classes can be shared between MonoTouch development on a Mac and Visual Studio development on Windows, but all presentation layer logic, as well as all builds and debugging, must be done on a Mac (because the Apple iOS SDK and compiler chain are also required for all MonoTouch builds). The iPad simulator can be used for debugging, but as mentioned earlier, the Apple Developer Program is required to debug and deploy on physical devices.

Language and Technology Stack

MonoTouch provides access to the Cocoa Touch API from C# via Mono. Mono is an open-source port of Microsoft .NET that provides a C# compiler and run time. While it does provide access to most .NET assemblies, it does not provide access to assemblies that have Windows-specific dependencies, such as Windows Forms or Windows Presentation Foundation. The result is most of the Silverlight assemblies plus some desktop .NET assemblies, with some functionality removed. MonoTouch assemblies are not compatible in terms of the application binary interface (ABI) with existing .NET assemblies, and must be recompiled specifically for MonoTouch. Unlike standard .NET, which is compiled to Intermediate Language (IL) and then uses a just-in-time (JIT) compiler at run time, MonoTouch uses an ahead-of-time (AOT) compiler that compiles the assemblies to machine code at build time as opposed to run time.

MonoTouch uses P/Invoke to provide a managed C# wrapper around the native Cocoa Touch Objective-C APIs, so a MonoTouch project uses the identical iOS APIs via C# that are available in Objective-C.

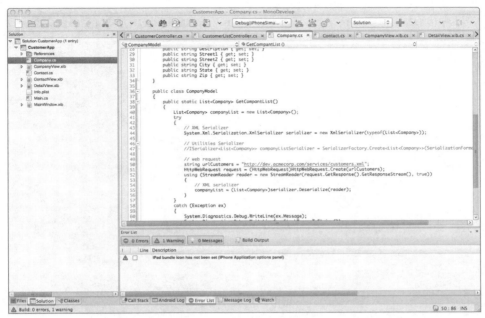

Figure 13-4: MonoDevelop is an IDE similar to Visual Studio that is used for iOS development on a Mac.

Example

To understand what a MonoTouch project would look like, here is some sample code from an example project. A data class represents the Model in this example, as follows:

```
public class Company
{
    public string ID { get; set; }
    public string Name { get; set; }
    public string Website { get; set; }
    public string PrimaryPhone { get; set; }
    public Address PrimaryAddress { get; set; }
    public List<Address> Addresses { get; set; }
    public List<Contact> Contacts { get; set; }
}
```

Now here is code of a UITableViewController that renders the above Model in a TableView:

```
public class CustomerTableViewController : UITableViewController
{
    public CustomerTableViewController ()
    {
        Title = "Customers";

        List<Company> customers = GetCustomers();

        TableView.Delegate = new TableViewDelegate(customers);
        TableView.DataSource = new TableViewDataSource(customers);
        TableView.ReloadData();
    }

    private class TableViewDelegate : UITableViewDelegate
    {
        private List<Company> list;
        public TableViewDelegate(List<Company> list)
        {
            this.list = list;
        }
        public override void RowSelected (UITableView tableView,
NSIndexPath indexPath)
        {
            string uri = list[indexPath.Row];
            Application.Navigate(uri);
        }
    }

    private class TableViewDataSource : UITableViewDataSource
    {
        static NSString kCellIdentifier = new NSString ("CustomerCell");
        private List<Company> list;

        public TableViewDataSource (List<Company> list)
        {
            this.list = list;
        }

        public override int RowsInSection (UITableView tableview, int
section)
        {
            return list.Count;
        }

        public override UITableViewCell GetCell (UITableView tableView,
            NSIndexPath indexPath)
        {
            UITableViewCell cell = tableView.DequeueReusableCell
(kCellIdentifier);
            if (cell == null)
```

```
            {
                cell = new UITableViewCell
                        (UITableViewCellStyle.Subtitle, kCellIdentifier);
                cell.Accessory =
                        UITableViewCellAccessory.DisclosureIndicator;
            }
            cell.TextLabel.Text = list[indexPath.Row].Name;
            cell.DetailTextLabel.Text = list[indexPath.Row].Website;
            return cell;
        }
        public override string TitleForHeader (UITableView tableView,
                                        int section)
        {
            return "Customers";
        }
        public override int NumberOfSections (UITableView tableView)
        {
            return 1;
        }
    }
}
```

Advantages

Assuming you loosely couple your application layers so that the underlying business logic is not encumbered with any platform-specific code, the biggest advantage of using C# .NET is near-universal portability of your code to other platforms.

If you're a .NET development shop, you have an added benefit of being able to remain consistent from a single unified technology stack. In addition, there are many more enterprise developers with C# .NET expertise.

Automatic garbage collection is another advantage that C# and MonoTouch provide over Objective-C.

Disadvantages

If you're a Microsoft .NET shop, you may perceive the biggest disadvantage of using MonoTouch as being that you need to develop on a Mac OS X machine with the iOS SDK in MonoDevelop instead of Visual Studio on Windows. That being said, if you properly layer your code, you can share code between Visual Studio and MonoDevelop, so your developers could develop the business logic and data access code on a Windows machine, and only do the presentation layer development, build, and debugging on a Mac.

If you're not a .NET shop and you're not interested in ever supporting any platforms other than iOS, then just using Objective-C is probably more preferable than C# with MonoTouch.

MEAP

A Mobile Enterprise Application Platform, or MEAP, provides middleware for extending back-end data and functionality out to mobile devices. Sybase, now owned by enterprise software giant SAP, has the industry's leading MEAP with the Sybase Unwired Platform (SUP). To learn how to develop iPad apps using a MEAP, let's take a closer look at this platform.

Sybase Unwired Platform

SUP provides data synchronization middleware as well as a fourth-generation language (4GL) that allows rapid mobile application development. It includes a designer, called the Sybase Unwired Workspace, that is integrated with Eclipse to create Mobile Business Objects (MBOs) that can be visually integrated with back-end data sources (as shown in Figure 13-5).

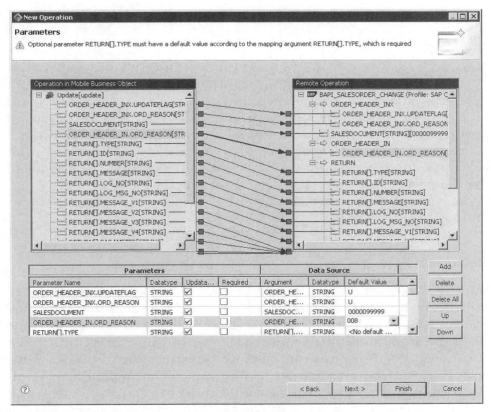

Figure 13-5: Sybase Unwired Platform provides a visual drag-and-drop interface for data integration.

While SUP supports user interface generation for some mobile platforms, the SUP development approach for iOS is to create a native user interface using Objective-C and Cocoa Touch and rely on SUP for the data access layer. Through code generation, the MBOs are converted into Objective-C and can then be used to access data from the native iOS application.

Language and Technology Stack

The SUP technology stack involves a combination of development tools, synchronization frameworks, and data middleware. The 4GL provided by SUP is a proprietary language, but the resulting MBOs can be subsequently converted into the Objective-C code for iOS development through a code generation utility, as shown in Figure 13-6. The generated code can then be added to an Objective-C native iPad application in Xcode, and the SUP synchronization framework can be used to synchronize client-side data on the iOS device with back-end data sources through a server-side middleware layer.

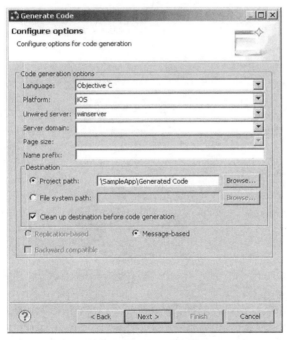

Figure 13-6: Sybase Unwired Platform uses code generation to convert the Mobile Business Object to Objective-C for iOS app development.

Example

Since the user interface of a SUP app uses the same Objective-C and Cocoa Touch as shown earlier in the chapter, we won't focus on the presentation layer of the application, but rather the data access layer. In the following code snippet, the SUP synchronization profile is configured and background synchronization is initiated:

```
SUPConnectionProfile* cp = [CustomerApp_CustomerAppDB
getSynchronizationProfile];
[cp setDomainName:@"default"];

[CustomerApp_CustomerAppDB createDatabase];
[CustomerApp_CustomerAppDB startBackgroundSynchronization];

NSInteger status = [SUPMessageClient start];
```

And in order to access the local data, you can use the following SQL-like syntax to make queries:

```
SUPQuery *query = [SUPQuery getInstance];
[query select:@"c.name,c.website,s.phone"];
[query  from:@"Customer":@"c"];
[query  join:@"Address":@"a":@"a.cust_id":@"c.id"];
query.testCriteria =
[SUPAttributeTest match:@"c.name":@"American Express Company"];
SUPQueryResultSet* resultSet = [CustomerApp_CustomerAppDB
executeQuery:query];
if(resultSet == nil)
{
    MBOLog(@"executeQuery failed");
    return;
}
for(SUPDataValueList* result in resultSet)
{
    MBOLog(@"name,website,phone = %@ %@ %@",
    [SUPDataValue  getNullableString:[result item:0]],
    [SUPDataValue getNullableString:[result item:1]],
    [SUPDataValue getNullableString:[result item:2]]);
}
```

Advantages

If you are not interested in building mobile-friendly web services, and would prefer to use middleware to synchronize filtered subsets of existing databases down to the mobile devices, a MEAP like SUP can provide a lot of value as a mobile access gateway and middleware layer.

Also, the code-generation approach of the MEAP can provide code portability and cross-platform support as the code can be generated to support multiple platforms.

Disadvantages

Since the primary purpose of a MEAP like SUP is to provide data-driven middleware and database transactional replication, if RESTful web services are available for lightweight access to data, there is little value provided above a simple RESTful caching and queuing-based approach.

The licensing model of SUP, like most MEAPs, is based on per-client pricing, which may add a significant cost depending on the details of your specific deployment.

Summary

This chapter discussed development approaches for both web and native iPad applications. For web development, the Sencha Touch framework was outlined as an excellent choice for the development of iPad apps with HTML5, CSS3, and JavaScript.

For native development, we discussed several more options, including Objective-C and Cocoa Touch in Xcode, C# .NET with MonoTouch, and Sybase Unwired Platform as an example of a Mobile Enterprise Application Platform.

Now that you've seen the advantages of the various approaches to developing iPad applications, are you clear on the approach that you are going to take for developing apps for your organization?

In the next chapter, we'll discuss how business logic can be shared across applications, through both enterprise libraries and code portability.

Sharing Business Logic between Applications

WHAT'S IN THIS CHAPTER?

- Establishing an enterprise library of reusable components
- Sharing business logic code across architectures
- Planning for portability of app code to other platforms
- Standardizing on JavaScript interfaces for hybrid apps
- Taking advantage of custom URI schemes
- Creating a suite of interconnected iPad applications

The last chapter examined the various languages, development environments, and technology stacks that can be used to create iPad applications.

In this chapter, you're going to examine some of the enterprise iPad app development best practices.

First, you'll cover the design and use of reusable enterprise software libraries and components, to simplify development and to standardize on things like authentication or encryption for security or utilities like logging or analytics.

Then, you'll outline how applications can be designed to allow for flexibility across architectures, as well as future portability to other platforms if that were to become necessary. Establishing standards for hybrid application development will also be covered.

Finally, you'll look at custom URI schemes, and how that can be used to not only provide deep-linking into your iPad applications, but also facilitate the creation of a robust suite of apps.

Using Reusable Components

Independent of the architecture and technology stack that you choose to develop your enterprise iPad apps, it is a good idea to logically design and separate components in such a way that they can be reused as appropriate.

This may involve the creation of an enterprise library or framework to provide standard access to various services, functionality, or utilities that can help jump-start mobile development efforts. It also involves considering how class libraries are structured, as there may be code that is appropriate to be shared by two separate but related apps, but that is not appropriate for inclusion in a shared enterprise library.

Let's take a closer look at these types of reusable software components.

Creating an Enterprise Library

For organizations that are looking to establish a more mature mobile and iPad application development competency, it can be valuable to establish an enterprise library of reusable components, functionality, and services.

In addition to providing application templates and standards around various conventions, an enterprise library should contain the various software components that most iPad applications would require.

For instance, security components are among the most obvious and high-value pieces of reusable functionality that should be standardized. First of all, the organization should establish security standards; by providing a shared library for functionalities like authentication, authorization, encryption, and so forth, consistent security can be ensured. Also, a shared authentication library can allow for a Single Sign-On (SSO) approach where authentication tokens can be securely stored in the iOS keychain and shared between in-house applications. This will be discussed in more detail in Chapter 16.

Additionally, device and hardware access abstraction layers, like barcode scanning, can provide the ability to support multiple barcode scanners and swap out hardware as necessary. Another good example would be utilities like application configuration, logging, analytics, or alerting via push notifications. Standardizing on basic utilities like this can provide significant value to developers, who can focus on the apps they need to create, and not reinvent these common utilities. You can see an example of a collection of enterprise utilities in Figure 14-1.

Organizing Class Libraries

It can also be valuable to separate logic and classes into separate class libraries. As discussed in previous chapters, iPad applications should be inherently focused on a single task and purpose, which often requires existing desktop or web-based applications to be converted into multiple iOS apps. Since many of those same applications may share similar business logic and data structures, it is often appropriate to create class libraries that are shared among two or more applications within a suite, but are not necessarily appropriate for putting in a shared enterprise library of functionality or utilities.

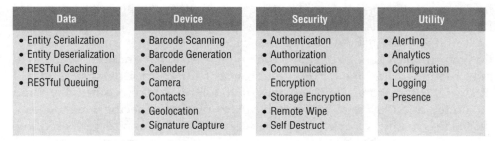

Data	Device	Security	Utility
• Entity Serialization	• Barcode Scanning	• Authentication	• Alerting
• Entity Deserialization	• Barcode Generation	• Authorization	• Analytics
• RESTful Caching	• Calender	• Communication	• Configuration
• RESTful Queuing	• Camera	Encryption	• Logging
	• Contacts	• Storage Encryption	• Presence
	• Geolocation	• Remote Wipe	
	• Signature Capture	• Self Destruct	

Figure 14-1: A library of commonly used enterprise mobile software components can provide significant value and help jump-start mobile development efforts.

Sharing across Architectures

In the last chapter, we looked at developing web-based as well as native applications. Since a web application can be hosted on a server running C# .NET, both the native MonoTouch client and the HTML5 application can share the same business logic and data integration layers, as shown in Figure 14-2.

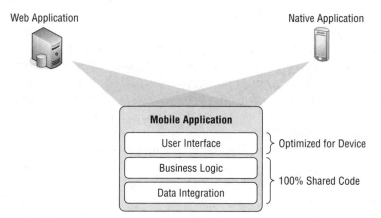

Figure 14-2: Business logic and data application tiers can be shared across both native and web apps.

What's the value of cleanly separating your layers?

Developing your applications in this manner can provide a number of benefits. First of all, you could choose to deploy your applications as web, native, or hybrid apps that all share the same business logic. Or maybe you're developing a web application, and after it is initially deployed your users request a new feature or capability that requires the application to be a native app. You would only have to develop a native user interface to offer the same app as a native iPad app. Or the opposite could be true; you might start with a native app and for some reason need to make it a web app.

Even if you are just developing web apps, implementing this clean separation can still provide a lot of value. You might want to have multiple web-based presentation layers: one for desktop browsers, another for the iPad, and still others for smartphone devices. Finally, if you develop your business logic and data integration layers so as not to have any platform-specific dependencies, that code is highly portable, not just between native apps and server-based web apps, but also to other Windows, Unix, and Linux-based operating systems.

Shared Business Logic and Data Code

In order to understand how code sharing can work, let's take a look at just one of the many ways that this approach can be implemented.

The open-source MonoCross framework illustrates this concept very well, so let's examine how the same customer app example from the previous chapter could be developed in MonoCross.

MonoCross provides a Model View Controller (MVC) framework where the Model and the Controller can be shared across architectures, but the View is tailored to the implementation.

In this example, we'll have a shared Application, Models, and Controllers. These are shared across both the native and web-based architectures, but they have separate implementations of each View for both architectures. For the web-based architecture, the Views are ASP.NET implementations where the generated HTML is sent back to the web client in an AJAX response. For the native MonoTouch application, each View is implemented as a UITableViewController.

One of the first things you might notice about the shared application is that it uses URI-based navigation. This is important, as it provides a unified approach to navigation whether the application is native or web-based. While there are potentially many ways that navigation can be facilitated in native apps, web apps are based on a URI navigation paradigm, and by taking the same approach for native apps, this allows for more complete sharing of application logic. The "{id}" in the URI navigation map relates to a parameter that is passed through when navigation occurs.

The following code shows the implementation of the shared application.

```
public class App : MXApplication
{
    public override void OnAppLoad()
    {
        // Set the application title
        Title = "Customers";

        // Add navigation mappings
        NavigationMap.Add("", new CustomerListController());
        NavigationMap.Add("{id}", new CustomerController());

        // Set default navigation URI
        NavigateOnLoad = "";
    }
}
```

In this example, the base Model is a class called Company, which can contain the data to describe any given customer:

```
public class Company
{
    public string ID { get; set; }
    public string Name { get; set; }
    public string Website { get; set; }
    public string PrimaryPhone { get; set; }
    public Address PrimaryAddress { get; set; }
    public List<Address> Addresses { get; set; }
    public List<Contact> Contacts { get; set; }
}
```

For the list of customers, rather than creating a new class to use as the Model, we simply use a List of type Company:

```
List<Company>
```

So here is the Controller for the list of customers, where the Model is a List of type Company. The Controller makes a web services call and sets the Model as appropriate:

```
public class CustomerListController : MXController<List<Company>>
{
    public override void Load(Dictionary<string, string> parameters)
    {
        Model = new List<Company>();

        try
        {
            XmlSerializer serializer = new
```

```
XmlSerializer(typeof(List<Company>));


            // web request
            string urlCustomers =
"http://dev.acmecorp.com/services/customers.xml";
            HttpWebRequest request =
(HttpWebRequest)HttpWebRequest.Create(urlCustomers);
            using (StreamReader reader =
                    new StreamReader(request.GetResponse()
.GetResponseStream(), true))
            {
                Model = (List<Company>)serializer.Deserialize(reader);
            }
        }
        catch (Exception ex)
        {
            Debug.WriteLine(ex.Message);
            Debug.WriteLine(ex.StackTrace.ToString());
        }
    }
}
```

Here is a second controller to show the details of a specific customer. Notice in this example how the "id" of the customer comes in on the parameters dictionary, and the key on the dictionary points to the dynamic parameter value added to the navigation map:

```
public class CustomerController : MXController<Company>
{
    public override void Load(Dictionary<string, string> parameters)
    {
        Model = new Company();

        try
        {
            XmlSerializer serializer = new XmlSerializer(typeof(Company));

            string urlCustomers = string.Format(
"http://dev.acmecorp.com/services/customers/{0}.xml", parameters["id"]);



            // web request
            HttpWebRequest request =
(HttpWebRequest)HttpWebRequest.Create(urlCustomers);
            using (StreamReader reader =
                new StreamReader(request.GetResponse().GetResponseStream(),
true))
            {
                Model = (Company)serializer.Deserialize(reader);
```

```
        }
    }
    catch (Exception ex)
    {
        Debug.WriteLine(ex.Message);
        Debug.WriteLine(ex.StackTrace.ToString());
    }


}
```

By not encumbering these shared classes with any platform-specific dependencies, the identical code can be used by either platform or architecture without any changes.

Server-Side HTML5 Application

Again, while the base Application as well as Models and Controllers are shared, the Views must be implemented for each platform and/or architecture. To create the HTML5-based web app, we will use ASP.NET running on a server. Since the shared application business logic uses the URI-based navigation paradigm that is standard for web applications, incoming requests are mapped to the appropriate Controller, which then passes the Model to the correct View for rendering. In this example, the client web application makes an AJAX request to the server-based app to request a view for the list of customers. The View is rendered as HTML code that is placed within the XML response, which the client-side JavaScript subsequently injects into the Document Object Model (DOM) for display:

```
public class CustomerListView : MXView<List<Company>>
{
    public override void Render()
    {
        HtmlGenericControl div = new HtmlGenericControl("div");
        div.Attributes.Add("class", "iMenu");

        HtmlGenericControl ul = new HtmlGenericControl("ul");
        ul.Attributes.Add("class", "iArrow");

        foreach (Company customer in Model)
        {
            HtmlGenericControl li = new HtmlGenericControl("li");
            HtmlGenericControl a = new HtmlGenericControl("a");
            a.Attributes.Add("href",
                    HttpUtility.UrlPathEncode(string.Format("{0}",
                    customer.ID)));
            a.Attributes.Add("rev", "async");
            HtmlGenericControl em = new HtmlGenericControl("em");
```

```
            em.InnerText = customer.Name;
            HtmlGenericControl small = new HtmlGenericControl("small");
            small.InnerText = string.Format("{0}<br>{1}, {2}  {3}",
                        customer.PrimaryAddress.Street1,
                        customer.PrimaryAddress.City,
                        customer.PrimaryAddress.State,
                        customer.PrimaryAddress.Zip);

            a.Controls.Add(em);
            a.Controls.Add(small);
            li.Controls.Add(a);
            ul.Controls.Add(li);
        }
        div.Controls.Add(ul);
        MXWebkitContainer.WriteControlToResponse("CustomerList",
                                        "Customers", div);
    }
}
```

As you can see in this example, while the Model and Controllers have no encumbrances with platform-specific dependencies, the View, of course, does. This is necessary; while the business logic and data integration layers of an application can be shared, the presentation layer requires the use of platform-specific technologies.

Client-Side Native Application

For the native version of this example, we will again use the same base Application class as well as the Models and Controllers. In order to create the native iPad user experience, we'll use MonoTouch to access the CocoaTouch application programming interface (API) from C#. The same View that we just showed using HTML, we'll create for the native app using a UITableViewController. We'll use a UITableViewDelegate to trigger the appropriate navigation when an item is selected, and a UITableViewDataSource to actually bind the Model to the native user interface by overriding the GetCell method and returning an appropriately rendered UITableViewCell:

```
[MXTouchViewType(ViewType.Master)]
public class CustomerListView : MXTouchTableViewController<List<Company>>
{
    public CustomerListView()
    {
    }

    public override void Render ()
    {
        Title = "Customers";
```

```csharp
        TableView.Delegate = new TableViewDelegate(Model);
        TableView.DataSource = new TableViewDataSource(Model);
        TableView.ReloadData();
    }

    private class TableViewDelegate : UITableViewDelegate
    {
        private List<Company> list;
        public TableViewDelegate(List<Company> list)
        {
            this.list = list;
        }
        public override void RowSelected (UITableView tableView, NSIndexPath
            indexPath)
        {
            string uri = list[indexPath.Row];
            MXTouchContainer.Navigate(uri);
        }
    }

    private class TableViewDataSource : UITableViewDataSource
    {
        static NSString kCellIdentifier = new NSString ("CustomerCell");
        private List<Company> list;

        public TableViewDataSource (List<Company> list)
        {
            this.list = list;
        }

        public override int RowsInSection (UITableView tableview,
                                           int section)
        {
            return list.Count;
        }

        public override UITableViewCell GetCell (UITableView tableView,
            NSIndexPath indexPath)
        {
            UITableViewCell cell = tableView.DequeueReusableCell
(kCellIdentifier);
            if (cell == null)
            {
                cell = new UITableViewCell
                        (UITableViewCellStyle.Subtitle, kCellIdentifier);
                cell.Accessory =
                        UITableViewCellAccessory.DisclosureIndicator;
            }
            cell.TextLabel.Text = list[indexPath.Row].Name;
```

```
        cell.DetailTextLabel.Text = list[indexPath.Row].Website;
        return cell;
    }
    public override string TitleForHeader (UITableView tableView,
                                           int section)
    {
        return "Customers";
    }
    public override int NumberOfSections (UITableView tableView)
    {
        return 1;
    }
    }
}
```

Any platform-specific code to take advantage of the APIs provided by Apple in the iOS software development kit should be isolated to the presentation layer. By taking this approach, the underlying business logic and data integration tiers of the application are not locked into the platform and can take advantage of architectural flexibility, as shown in this example.

Sharing across Platforms

There are several ways to share the application investments across multiple platforms, whether this is an immediate requirement or simply part of planning for the future of the mobile landscape. Of course, web applications have a certain level of portability, and although cascading style sheets (CSS) and JavaScript support can vary across platforms, a significant amount of reuse is possible. We've touched on this previously, but there are also ways to maximize the portability of your native and hybrid applications.

Portable Source Code

One significant benefit of the standardized nature of C# .NET through Mono is that if you choose to develop your iPad apps on this stack, your code is quite portable to other platforms.

In fact, the above example using MonoCross could easily support other platforms through Windows WPF, Windows Phone 7 Silverlight, or Mono for Android. To implement this example for those other platforms, you would simply create a container project, reference the shared application class library, and create platform-specific presentation layers by implementing each View as appropriate for the platform.

Hybrid JavaScript Interfaces

As mentioned in Chapter 6, one advantage of hybrid applications is that native device functionality can be accessed from web apps through JavaScript interfaces. While the native APIs for things like camera, accelerometer, contacts, or even barcode scanning through third-party hardware accessories or SDKs will be different by platform, the hybrid application can provide a standardized abstraction layer so that hybrid apps can also be portable across multiple platforms (Figure 14-3).

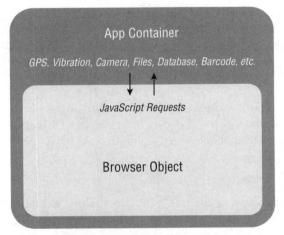

Figure 14-3: JavaScript interfaces for accessing native functionality from hybrid applications can be the same across multiple platforms.

The open-source PhoneGap project provides an excellent example of this architectural approach. PhoneGap exposes standardized JavaScript APIs for native functionality, including accelerometer, camera, compass, contacts, device, events, filesystem, geolocation, media playback, network, notification, and storage. Where applicable, PhoneGap follows the W3C API specifications, so that specific features can be available for more platforms even if the particular platform vendor did not add support for a specific capability. By exposing a standardized JavaScript interface, hybrid apps can take advantage of this abstraction layer for support of a wide variety of platforms.

For example, the PhoneGap API exposes JavaScript helper methods like this:

```
navigator.notification.beep(3);
```

Behind the scenes, this takes advantage of custom URI schemes to pass information back and forth between the web app and the native wrapper. PhoneGap uses the following custom URI scheme to know when the web app navigation should be intercepted:

```
phonegap://
```

The JavaScript in the web application is able to communicate with the native application by using helper methods that convert the methods and parameters into a custom URI, like this:

```
phonegap://notification/beep/3
```

And while PhoneGap uses that particular syntax, you can develop your own hybrid wrappers, if you prefer, by taking a similar approach. Your native wrapper application can implement a UIWebView that intercepts navigation attempts to a particular custom URI, as in this case with your own custom "acmecorpsales":

```
acmecorpsales://notification/beep/3
```

Again, PhoneGap provides significant value out of the box, but if you have requirements like triggering a laser-based barcode scanner from within the application, you could either extend PhoneGap or implement your own capability, as follows:

```
acmecorpsales://barcodescanner/startscan
```

Ultimately, if you are developing hybrid applications, it can be very valuable for the long-term portability of your code to use standard conventions like those implemented by PhoneGap, whether you choose to use the PhoneGap project or not.

Using Custom URI Schemes

One of the most powerful capabilities of iOS is the ability to define custom URI schemes for your applications. This provides the ability to launch your apps from other apps, or even by simply clicking on a link in an e-mail or a web browser. For instance, you can use a mail-to link to launch the user's e-mail app and create a new e-mail message, like this:

```
mailto://
```

In the same way, you can define a custom URI scheme in the info.plist of your application to register a particular scheme with your application, like this:

```
acmecorpsales://
```

Once you register the custom URI scheme, anytime the device navigates to a URL with that custom scheme, your application will launch, and the entire URL will be passed to the application. You can access this on the UIApplicationDelegate of your app.

In Objective-C:

```
- (BOOL)application:(UIApplication *)application openURL:(NSURL *)url
    sourceApplication:(NSString *)sourceApplication annotation:(id)annotation
{
    // validate and navigate within the app as appropriate
}
```

Or in C#:

```
public override void OpenUrl (UIApplication application,
MonoTouch.Foundation.NSUrl url,
    string sourceApplication, MonoTouch.Foundation.NSObject annotation)
{
    // validate and navigate within the app as appropriate
}
```

This is the core mechanism for facilitating the launch of the application, confirming the source application, and passing information into the app upon launch.

Using URIs for Navigation

While a URI-style navigation was discussed earlier in this chapter with regard to the portability of code between native and web-based architectures, there are some other advantages of taking a URI-based approach for navigation, whether you are building your app in Objective-C or C#.

For instance, you could design your application so that the user navigates to:

```
acmecorpsales://customer/12345
```

The user would then be able to view the details of a customer by the specified identifier. If the entire application is designed in this way, it not only can simplify the act of in-app navigation logic, but it can also provide other benefits if you develop more than one in-house iOS application.

Creating a Suite of Applications

Let's imagine that the first in-house iPad application that your organization develops and deploys is for sales force automation. After the first app is developed and deployed, a need emerges to create a second business intelligence or executive dashboard application. Once that second application is deployed, a custom URI scheme is defined to launch that application as well:

```
acmecorpdashboard://
```

This is in addition to the first:

```
acmecorpsales://
```

As a result, the applications can link to each other. By navigating to a particular address from within the dashboard application, the sales app will launch and vice-versa; by navigating to the custom URI of the dashboard app, the dashboard app can launch.

This allows a suite of in-house applications to be created that are separate and stand-alone but can interact with each other by passing execution from one app to another.

Deep-Linking across Applications

So how can that capability for one app to launch other apps be used to enhance the user experience and take full advantage of the suite of in-house applications?

One of the most powerful ways this can be accomplished is by deep-linking applications using the custom URI schemes. For instance, a link like the following could be used to launch a product catalog app and open up to a specific product detail view:

```
acmecorproducts://sku/abc123
```

This product catalog app could be linked to both a sales application and a dashboard application. In the sales app, the user may be looking at the products contained within historical orders and might want to view more information about the product. Rather than adding that capability into the sales app to display product information, the sales app could simply link to the product app. But why create a separate product app instead of just adding that functionality into the sales app? Let's imagine that the executive dashboard app shows sales figures by product. If the product app is available as a stand-alone app, both the sales app and the dashboard app can take advantage of the deep-linking capabilities to share functionality.

Leveraging a Callback Design

Linking to other custom in-house apps is great, but what if the user needs to go back quickly and easily to an initial application?

In this example, the deep-linking into an application includes a callback to the original application:

```
acmecorproducts://sku/abc123?callback=acmecorpsales://customer/12345
```

This allows the second application to return to the original application when the user completes a particular workflow, taps a back button, or closes a modal View. This way, stand-alone applications can provide simple and clearly focused functionality to fulfill their core purposes, and more sophisticated applications and workflow can be implemented that take advantage of the other applications in the suite.

Establishing Enterprise Standards

When using custom URI schemes, it's important to define and establish enterprise standards for their use. A custom URI scheme should be unique both for applications in the App Store and for in-house applications. Your organization should define a prefix and convention to be used for in-house custom URI scheme naming.

This approach has many security ramifications. For instance, you probably don't want to require the user to log in when switching between apps, so authentication should use a shared Single Sign-On mechanism by storing credentials or a session token in a shared group keychain item. Also, you should design your custom URI scheme implementations to securely authenticate and authorize the source, as well as ensure that transactions cannot be accidentally or maliciously performed without the user's intent. It is important to design these mechanisms to be secure. These concepts, which ensure custom URI deep-link security and facilitate Single Sign-On, will be discussed in more detail in Chapter 16.

Summary

In this chapter, you looked at how iPad applications can be designed and developed to maximize code reuse — between multiple applications on the same platform, between applications using different architectures like native and web, and between different versions of the same application for different platforms. You also looked at how standardized abstract JavaScript interfaces can be used to develop consistent hybrid applications. Finally, you learned how custom URI schemes can be used to create a suite of applications that can securely facilitate deep-linking and callbacks for user workflows that can span multiple apps.

In the next chapter, you'll look at the best practices involving server-side development of mobile friendly web services.

CHAPTER 15

Developing Mobile-Friendly Web Services

The last few chapters have discussed the development of iPad applications using a number of different architectures and approaches.

In this chapter, you'll take a look at server-side web services development. As discussed previously in Chapter 8, SOAP-based services generally have a lot more overhead and are heavier than RESTful services, so this chapter will focus on the creation of mobile-friendly RESTful services. Dozens of languages and technology stacks can be used to create RESTful web services, but in the enterprise world two languages and technologies are the most popular: Java and .NET. You'll examine the basics of RESTful service creation using both of these technology stacks. Additionally, you'll touch on how data classes can be shared between the client and the server if C# .NET is used for both the client development and the service development.

You'll look at some of the best practices of mobile-friendly RESTful web service design, including the resource-oriented nature of REST, the importance of keeping everything as lightweight as possible, and RESTful service end-point naming conventions.

Finally, you'll take a look at the creation of an example RESTful web service.

Selecting a Technology Stack

When it comes to selecting a technology stack for your server-side mobile web service development, the decision is usually pretty easy. Most large enterprise IT organizations use Java and/or .NET for application and web services development, and when creating a mobile-friendly web services layer, there usually is not much of a reason to change.

As discussed in the last couple of chapters, there are many different client technology options, most of which will likely be new to an enterprise IT organization. For the server-side technology, though, there really isn't a need to deviate from the enterprise standard.

The most important issue in creating mobile-friendly web services to be consumed by your iPad applications is to design them appropriately so that they can be consumed by mobile apps over wireless connections. The actual language and technology stack used to develop the services usually don't matter that much, so it's generally best to simply use whatever is your enterprise standard for web service development. That being said, if you do choose to develop the client in C# .NET, there can be some benefits to developing the web services in the same language, since the data classes representing the resources and business objects can be shared between client and server.

Java

There are a number of ways to create RESTful web services in Java, but the most common is probably through the use of JAX-RS, which is a Java application programming interface (API) specifically designed for creating RESTful web services. JAX-RS is officially a part of Java EE.

JAX-RS allows a Java class to be mapped to a RESTful end point through the use of annotations. Here is an example of a very simple web service created with JAX-RS:

```
@UriTemplate("/customers.xml")

public class Service {

    @HttpContext UriInfo uriInfo;
    @PersistenceUnit(unitName = "CustomersPU")

    public List<Company> getCustomers() {
        return getCompanies();
    }

}
```

The annotations include @GET, @PUT, @POST, and @DELETE to specify the HTTP verbs for a specific resource request, as well as @Path to describe the relative path for a resource class.

The various implementations of JAX-RS, with vendor in parentheses, include RESTEasy (JBoss); CXF (Apache); and Jersey (Sun/Oracle).

.NET

There are also many ways to create RESTful web services using C# .NET, but the most common way is to use Windows Communication Foundation (WCF). Starting with .NET 3.5 SP1, WCF includes a number of attributes to simplify the creation of RESTful web services.

These attributes allow specific resource end points and HTTP verbs to be mapped to C# classes, which are automatically serialized to send over the wire. Here is an example of a simple C# .NET RESTful service created with WCF:

```
public class Service
{
    [WebGet(UriTemplate = "customers.xml")]
    public List<Company> GetCustomers()
    {
        return GetCompanies();
    }
}
```

The WCF attributes include WebGet, which maps classes to the HTTP GET verb of a specific resource end point, as well as WebInvoke, which maps the HTTP POST, PUT, and DELETE verbs to a resource end point. Additionally, while WCF defaults to XML serialization, it supports JSON serialization as well.

Sharing Code between Client and Server

As mentioned previously, if you have been doing your iPad app development in C# you will see one additional benefit of using C# .NET to create RESTful web services. You will be able to share your data classes between the iPad app and the web service. For example, take a look at the following class:

```
public class Company
{
    public string ID { get; set; }
    public string Name { get; set; }
    public string Website { get; set; }
    public string PrimaryPhone { get; set; }
    public Address PrimaryAddress { get; set; }
    public List<Address> Addresses { get; set; }
    public List<Contact> Contacts { get; set; }
}
```

The code file that contains this class can be used as part of the WCF web service project compiled and running on the server, but the same code file can also be used as part of a C# MonoTouch project compiled as a native iPad app.

Additionally, since WCF automatically serializes the classes to send the data over the wire, the same classes can be used to deserialize the data into objects on the client. For example, the following code could be used to consume the RESTful web service from the iPad app using MonoTouch and sharing the same data class for Company that the WCF web service is using on the server:

```
string urlCustomers =
    "http://dev.acmecorp.com/mobile/services/customers.xml";
HttpWebRequest request = (HttpWebRequest)HttpWebRequest.Create(urlCustomers);
using (StreamReader reader =
    new StreamReader(request.GetResponse().GetResponseStream(), true))
{
    List<Company> companies = serializer.Deserialize(reader);
}
```

Again, this is an added benefit of a unified C# .NET technology stack between the client and the server. However, if the enterprise standard for web services development is Java, and that is the technology stack that the developers on the team have experience with, then this benefit is probably not worth the pain of deviating from the standard.

Development of a RESTful Service

In many ways, RESTful services can be quite simple and straightforward to develop. The biggest challenge is usually the paradigm shift necessary to rethink the approach to web services.

As discussed in Chapter 8, most web service development within the enterprise over the last decade has revolved around Remote Procedure Call (RPC) or SOAP-style services that are generally quite heavy with overhead and metadata. Generally that isn't a problem for the average enterprise application, since everything is consumed on a local network, and service integration often occurs even within the same data center. With mobile software, though, there are significantly more constraints around connectivity, including bandwidth and latency.

As a result, most existing enterprise web services are not ideally consumed from iPad applications, and a more lightweight, user-centric, mobile-friendly RESTful web service is preferred.

Think Resource, Not Procedure

The first thing to recognize when starting RESTful service development is that your services should be focused on "resources" and not "procedures." With REST, you leverage the foundational HTTP verbs — GET, POST, PUT, and DELETE — to interact with those resources, as opposed to a more RPC-style where the verbs are defined in the procedure along with the resource.

When first starting with the development of RESTful services, this can require a certain level of discipline; with both JAX-RS in Java and WCF in C# .NET, it is up to the developer to map a resource end point to a method that returns a specific class. It is the developer's responsibility to map GET, POST, PUT, and DELETE to the appropriate CRUD functions. The four functions keyed to the acronym CRUD are Create maps to POST, Read maps to GET, Update maps to PUT, and Delete (self-explanatory).

Because many existing web services may be procedure-oriented, it can often be difficult to mentally reframe the service in the context of CRUD upon a resource. This just means that the RESTful services should be designed with mobile application consumption in mind.

Remember that when you're developing web services for consumption by an iPad application, you should think about the resource from the perspective of the user. In the case of these various examples, the resource is the customer. The customer resource should be a representation of what is necessary, and only what is necessary, to create the mobile application.

Keeping It Lightweight

While I've mentioned it before, this is so important that I want to mention it at least one more time: keep the services as lightweight as possible. Optimize the service and the data for mobile and wireless consumption on the iPad.

If you start from the outside looking in, by designing the service in the way the mobile application needs to consume it, then this is usually not an issue. But if you start from the inside looking out, your data will often be much more complex and heavy than it needs to be. Remember, the resource exposed by the RESTful service does not need to contain everything that the back-end system knows about the resource. Nor does it even structure the resource in the same way that it may be stored in the back-end data model. The resource can be dramatically simplified and contain pre-calculated, flattened, and denormalized data to allow for much easier and more straightforward consumption of these mobile services.

Resource End-Point Naming Conventions

One of the most important things to consider as you develop your RESTful web services is your end-point naming conventions. These conventions should be logically organized and structured, so that consuming developers can clearly understand what the resource is and how it can be accessed.

Ensuring both simplicity and consistency in these naming conventions is important, and not just within an application, but across the organization as well. As mobile apps become more and more common, a shared mobile services platform for commonly accessed data and resources can facilitate what was described in previous chapters as a "platform for innovation." It's important, though, that web services across this "platform" use consistent end-point naming conventions.

There are, of course, some common practices in the naming of resource end points, but there is a certain level of discretion and variation across the industry. For this example, we'll examine some of the widely used principles in naming conventions.

To start with, let's imagine that we have a resource called "customer." We probably would want to be able to view a list of customers, so let's name that end point:

```
customers.xml
```

While that list of customers might be just a lightly loaded list, indexed appropriately, for searching or displaying a list of customers, you would probably want the ability to view the full detail of a specific customer:

```
customers/{company}.xml
```

And if you wanted to view the addresses for that specific customer:

```
customers/{company}/addresses.xml
```

Or the different contacts for that customer:

```
customers/{company}/contacts.xml
```

That list of contacts could return a lightly-loaded index of customers. You could then specify a new end point for the full details of a particular contact at a specific company, passing in the index:

```
customers/{company}/contacts/{contact}.xml
```

Up to this point, we've been assuming that XML is the preferred format for data responses. You could also provide the identical functionality as the above-mentioned services using JSON:

```
customers.json
customers/{company}.json
customers/{company}/addresses.json
```

```
customers/{company}/contacts.json
customers/{company}/contacts/{contact}.json
```

And while that's logical for the HTTP GET verb, what would be the preferred end point to POST a new customer? There are several ways this could be done. For instance, you could do a POST to either

```
customers.xml
```

or

```
customers/{company}.xml
```

This would create a new customer resource. For PUT and DELETE, you probably wouldn't want to use the plural version, just the singular.

Ultimately, a lot of the naming decisions come down to preference, but once you begin to establish resource end-point conventions, you should make sure that you are consistent in enforcing those conventions.

Other Considerations

In addition to these basic concepts for the development of RESTful services, there are several other ideas that should be considered as you develop your RESTful web services.

End-Point Versioning

To not only simplify the application version management process, but also to help facilitate the need for multiple applications to access the same service, the RESTful service should be managed as if it were a product, with versioning to support innovation without breaking dependent apps.

For example, incorporating end-point versioning into the relative URI might look something like this:

```
mobile/services/v1.0/customers.xml
```

Even if you don't plan on using the web services to support more than one application, it would still be a recommended best practice to incorporate web service versioning into the end point.

Flexible Responses

Since mobile applications are especially sensitive to data bandwidth concerns, it's very valuable to give developers the ability to specify what and how much data they want in their response objects.

For example, you might want to allow an optional parameter on the query string to filter the contents of the response to contain simply the data elements that the consuming application requires. That could look something like this:

```
customers.xml?show=id,name,website
```

This is one way to strategically manage the complexity of RESTful web services if you are planning on supporting multiple mobile applications from a single RESTful web services layer, and you believe that some applications may need more data than others.

Pagination

Again, because mobile applications are especially sensitive to data bandwidth concerns, it can be important to give developers the ability to filter extensive data lists and allow for pagination.

For example, you might choose to implement pagination using query string parameters like:

```
customers.xml?count=10&offset=30
```

This way, applications can request just the information they are looking for, and even lazy-load lists of content. While not necessary for every type of RESTful web service, this can be quite valuable for extensive lists of resources.

Searching

RESTful services are focused on resources, not remote procedure calls. As a result, searching is one of the most common things that developers new to REST have trouble with. Since ultimately a search for a specific type of resource will still return just a list of those resources, a concept like search can easily be implemented like this:

```
customers.xml?term=acme
```

This is certainly not the only way that searching can be facilitated within RESTful conventions, but it is a common example of how a "procedure" can be properly implemented in a resource-centric way.

API Key Management

As more applications use shared services, it's important to keep track of the utilization of the service by application, and the API key can be used to facilitate this.

You might choose to implement this using a query string parameter like:

```
customers.xml?apikey=d8ad3be01d98001865e96e
```

This is a standard practice for external-facing web services, and it is growing increasingly common for web services designed to be consumed internally within an enterprise across multiple internal applications.

Resource Caching

Remember that one of the most significant benefits of REST over SOAP involves that fact that REST uses the HTTP GET verb to access information (as opposed to SOAP, which uses a POST for everything, including when you're just requesting data). Because of this, the response with REST can be easily cached, using off-the-shelf capabilities on both the client and the server.

Authentication

Because RESTful web services are inherently stateless and based on standard HTTP protocols, authentication is commonly facilitated through SSL/TLS and Basic Authentication.

The implementation can be slightly complicated for organizations that utilize Single Sign-On (SSO) solutions to provide authentication for external-facing web applications (either directly or through federated solutions as with OpenID or SAML). The complication is that those solutions generally utilize a cookie to store session state, and since a RESTful service is being consumed by code and not a browser, the cookie support is not provided out of the box. The solution is generally to provide a separate RESTful service to perform authentication, and then take the session token that would have been stored in the cookie, and simply use it in the application client to inject in the header of all HTTP requests.

Example

Now that we've discussed many of the considerations in creating RESTful web services, let's take a close look at what the development of a RESTful web service would actually look like.

As shown earlier in this chapter, here is an example in WCF C# .NET of a simple service that responds with a list of customers:

```
[WebGet(UriTemplate = "customers.xml")]
public List<Company> GetCustomers()
{
    return GetCompanies();
}
```

To view the details of a specific customer, you could create a service that looks something like this:

```
[WebGet(UriTemplate = "customers/{company}.xml")]
public Company GetCompany(string company)
{
     Company retval = GetCompanies()
     .Where(obj => obj.ID == company).FirstOrDefault();
     retval.PrimaryAddress = retval.Addresses.FirstOrDefault();
     retval.Addresses.Clear();
     retval.Contacts.Clear();
     return retval;
}
```

Using an HTTP POST verb to create a new instance of a customer could look like this:

```
[WebInvoke(UriTemplate = "customers.xml", Method = "POST")]
public Company CreateCompany(Company instance)
{
     List<Company> companies = GetCompanies();
     companies.Add(instance);
     SaveCompanies(companies);
     return instance;
}
```

And if we wanted to use JSON instead of the default XML, we could write something like this:

```
[WebGet(UriTemplate = "customers.json", ResponseFormat =
WebMessageFormat.Json)]
public List<Company> GetCustomersJson()
{
     return GetCompanies();
}
```

To show more holistically what an entire set of RESTful web services would look like, here is a complete example in C# .NET WCF. The iPad app examples in the previous chapters were coded against these RESTful web services:

```
using System;
using System.Collections.Generic;
using System.IO;
using System.Linq;
using System.ServiceModel;
using System.ServiceModel.Activation;
using System.ServiceModel.Web;
using System.Text;
using System.Xml.Serialization;
using System.Web;

using CustomerManagement.Shared.Model;
```

```
namespace CustomerManagement.REST
{
    [ServiceContract]
    [AspNetCompatibilityRequirements(RequirementsMode =
        AspNetCompatibilityRequirementsMode.Allowed)]
    [ServiceBehavior(InstanceContextMode = InstanceContextMode.PerCall)]
    public class Service
    {
        [WebGet(UriTemplate = "customers.xml")]
        public List<Company> GetCustomers()
        {
            return GetCompanies();
        }


        [WebGet(UriTemplate = "customers.json",
            ResponseFormat = WebMessageFormat.Json)]
        public List<Company> GetCustomersJson()
        {
            HttpContext.Current.Response.Headers.Add("newValue", "hello!");
            return GetCompanies();
        }


        [WebGet(UriTemplate = "customers/{company}.xml")]
        public Company GetCompany(string company)
        {
            Company retval = GetCompanies()
                .Where(obj => obj.ID == company).FirstOrDefault();
            retval.PrimaryAddress = retval.Addresses.FirstOrDefault();
            retval.Addresses.Clear();
            retval.Contacts.Clear();
            return retval;
        }


        [WebGet(UriTemplate = "customers/{company}.json",
            ResponseFormat = WebMessageFormat.Json)]
        public Company GetCompanyJson(string company)
        {
            Company retval = GetCompanies()
                .Where(obj => obj.ID == company).FirstOrDefault();
            retval.PrimaryAddress = retval.Addresses.FirstOrDefault();
            retval.Addresses.Clear();
            retval.Contacts.Clear();
            return retval;
        }


        [WebInvoke(UriTemplate = "company.xml", Method = "POST")]
        public Company CreateCompany(Company instance)
        {
            List<Company> companies = GetCompanies();
            companies.Add(instance);
            SaveCompanies(companies);
```

```
        return instance;
}


[WebInvoke(UriTemplate = "company.json", Method = "POST",
    RequestFormat=WebMessageFormat.Json,
    ResponseFormat=WebMessageFormat.Json)]
public Company CreateCompanyJson(Company instance)
{
    List<Company> companies = GetCompanies();
    companies.Add(instance);
    SaveCompanies(companies);
    return instance;
}


[WebInvoke(UriTemplate = "customers/{company}.xml", Method = "PUT")]
public Company UpdateCompany(string company, Company instance)
{
    List<Company> companies = GetCompanies();
    companies.Remove(companies.Find(obj => obj.ID == instance.ID));
    companies.Add(instance);
    SaveCompanies(companies);
    return instance;
}


[WebInvoke(UriTemplate = "customers/{company}.json", Method = "PUT",
    RequestFormat = WebMessageFormat.Json,
    ResponseFormat = WebMessageFormat.Json)]
public Company UpdateCompanyJson(string company, Company instance)
{
    List<Company> companies = GetCompanies();
    companies.Remove(companies.Find(obj => obj.ID == instance.ID));
    companies.Add(instance);
    SaveCompanies(companies);
    return instance;
}


[WebInvoke(UriTemplate = "customers/{company}", Method = "DELETE")]
public void DeleteCompany(string company)
{
    List<Company> companies = GetCompanies();
    companies.Remove(companies.Find(obj => obj.ID == company));
    SaveCompanies(companies);
}


[WebGet(UriTemplate = "customers/{company}/contacts")]
public List<Contact> GetContacts(string company)
{
    return GetCompanies()
        .Where(obj => obj.ID == company)
        .FirstOrDefault().Contacts;
}
```

```
[WebGet(UriTemplate = "customers/{company}/{contact}")]
public Contact GetContact(string company, string contact)
{
    return GetContacts(company)
    .Where(obj => obj.ID == contact).FirstOrDefault();
}

[WebInvoke(UriTemplate = "customers/{company}/contacts",
    Method = "POST")]
public Contact CreateContact(string company, Contact instance)
{
    List<Contact> contacts = GetContacts(company);
    contacts.Add(instance);
    SaveContacts(company, contacts);
    return instance;
}

[WebInvoke(UriTemplate = "customers/{company}/{contact}",
    Method = "PUT")]
public Contact UpdateContact(string company, string contact,
    Contact instance)
{
    List<Contact> contacts = GetContacts(company);
    contacts.Remove(contacts.Find(obj => obj.ID == instance.ID));
    contacts.Add(instance);
    SaveContacts(company, contacts);
    return instance;
}

[WebInvoke(UriTemplate = "customers/{company}/{contact}",
    Method = "DELETE")]
public void DeleteContact(string company, string contact)
{
    List<Contact> contacts = GetContacts(company);
    contacts.Remove(contacts.Find(obj => obj.ID == contact));
    SaveContacts(company, contacts);
}

private List<Company> GetCompanies()
{
    using (StreamReader reader = new
StreamReader(HttpContext.Current.Server.MapPath("~/App_Data/Customers.xml")))
    {
        return (List<Company>)new
XmlSerializer(typeof(List<Company>)).Deserialize(reader);
    }
}

private void SaveCompanies(List<Company> companies)
{
    using (StreamWriter writer = new
StreamWriter(HttpContext.Current.Server.MapPath("~/App_Data/Customers.xml")))
```

```
            {
                new XmlSerializer(typeof(List<Company>))
                    .Serialize(writer, companies);
            }
        }
        private void SaveContacts(string company, List<Contact> contacts)
        {
            Company instance = GetCompany(company);
            instance.Contacts = contacts;
            UpdateCompany(company, instance);
        }
    }
}
```

And here is a code file that contains the data classes that can be shared between both the client and the server:

```
using System;
using System.Collections.Generic;
using System.Linq;
using System.Text;

namespace CustomerManagement.Shared.Model
{
    public class Company
    {
        public string ID { get; set; }
        public string Name { get; set; }
        public string Website { get; set; }
        public string PrimaryPhone { get; set; }
        public Address PrimaryAddress { get; set; }
        public List<Address> Addresses { get; set; }
        public List<Contact> Contacts { get; set; }
    }
    public class Address
    {
        public string ID { get; set; }
        public string Description { get; set; }
        public string Street1 { get; set; }
        public string Street2 { get; set; }
        public string City { get; set; }
        public string State { get; set; }
        public string Zip { get; set; }
    }
    public class Contact
    {
        public string ID { get; set; }
        public string FirstName { get; set; }
        public string MiddleName { get; set; }
        public string LastName { get; set; }
        public string Title { get; set; }
```

```
        public string Email { get; set; }
        public string OfficePhone { get; set; }
        public string MobilePhone { get; set; }
    }
}
```

This in fact is the same set of data classes that was used in the previous chapter in the examples to consume the web services implemented here.

Summary

In this chapter, you dug into the details of creating RESTful web services. You started with the discussion of selecting the best technology stack for your environment, examining both Java and .NET.

This chapter covered the resource-oriented nature of REST as opposed to the procedure focus of RPC-style SOAP. Also covered was the importance of keeping the services and the data lightweight, best practices in the naming conventions of RESTful service resource end points, and other considerations and best practices.

Finally, this chapter provided some examples of RESTful web services that were consumed by the iPad app examples in Chapters 13 and 14.

In the next chapter, you'll examine the importance of security in developing iPad applications, including iOS attack vectors, and best practices to ensure consistent security of your enterprise applications.

CHAPTER 16

Ensuring Application and Data Security

- Securing the iOS application sandbox
- Protecting data when in transit and at rest
- Identifying potential security "gotchas"
- Established industry best practices
- How to audit both in-house and commercial iOS applications
- Creating corporate standards for iOS application security

Now that you have a good understanding of how to develop applications for the iPad, it's important to understand how to secure your applications, including the data and functionality contained within them. Although iOS is a relatively new platform for most enterprise IT and security groups, it has emerged and matured quite a bit over the last several versions and iterations. As a result, there are many sophisticated techniques for significantly enhancing application-level security above and beyond any security applied on the device level. It is vital for those with development and security responsibilities to understand these concepts.

In this chapter, we'll discuss the idea of the sandbox security model and how to maximize security by embracing the sandbox concept, as opposed to relying solely on traditional device-level security ideas. We'll discuss how to implement authentication and authorization on the application level, communicate securely with back-end data sources, and establish formal processes for auditing your applications prior to deployment.

Understanding the Sandbox Security Model

There are two ways to think about mobile security. You can think about security on the device level or on the application level. While a lot of traditional enterprise mobility has focused on the security of the device itself, that's not where all today's security efforts should be focused. Of course, this is not to say that you shouldn't attempt to implement security on the device level, but keep in mind that this is not always possible. If you need to develop secure applications for use by your customers or business partners, you will need to make sure that all the appropriate security is implemented on the application level because you will have no control over device-level security.

Additionally, now that iOS has become so popular, there is a growing focus among hackers on targeting the platform. Combine this with many of the known exploits related to *jailbreaking* the device and gaining full access to any unencrypted data on the filesystem of the device, and the challenge of securing the entire iOS device becomes almost overwhelming.

> **NOTE** Jailbreaking is a process where iOS devices are unlocked to gain full access to the operating system and to bypass Apple's restrictions on the platform.

By taking the approach of securing the application sandbox, though, your data and functionality remain protected even if the device is compromised. This reduces some of the pressure to keep the device itself totally secure, because in many ways those potential exploits are completely outside your control. However, the application sandbox is totally within your control to implement as many layers of security as possible.

Securing the Sandbox

When it comes to securing the application sandbox, three overarching areas must be addressed: authentication and authorization centered on providing access to the sandbox, the communication security of data in transit back and forth between the device and the server, and the storage security of any data that is physically persisted on the device itself.

Access and Authorization

If your application contains any proprietary content, data, or functionality, you should always secure your apps. Of course, if your application contains publicly available marketing content or maybe the daily cafeteria menu, then there may not be a need to secure the application, but for the most part the vast majority of enterprise applications should implement an authentication mechanism.

Many developers accustomed to creating enterprise applications in a corporate Windows-centric environment may not be used to having to implement these authentication mechanisms, since Active Directory is often used to automatically authenticate users who are logged onto the domain from their PCs. But there is no out-of-the-box functionality like that for implementing application-level authentication on iOS. Developers are responsible for implementing their own authentication mechanisms.

In Chapter 14, we discussed the concept of a shared enterprise library for various utilities and services. An authentication mechanism is an excellent example of something that can and should be shared across multiple applications. Additionally, a shared authentication library can be used to create a Single Sign-On (SSO) mechanism so that as users navigate between various in-house enterprise apps, they are not prompted to authenticate every single time. In addition to improving the user experience, this can help simplify development of in-house iOS applications across distributed development groups, so that they don't all have to repeatedly implement the same authentication mechanism.

This can be facilitated using a concept called *keychain access groups*, where multiple applications created and signed by the same developer account can share access to keychain items. An authentication mechanism can initially prompt the user for a username and password that can be validated against a back-end Active Directory, Lightweight Directory Access Protocol (LDAP), or other mechanism and return a token that can be stored in the shared keychain item. As the user switches between applications, each app will initially validate the token with the back-end authentication provider. First, it's important to know if the token is still valid (you could, for instance, configure the authentication provider to have a 30-second, 30-minute, 3-hour, 3-day, or even 30-day timeout depending on your corporate policies and the sensitivity of your data). If the token is valid, the application is already authenticated and will provide a seamless experience to the user. If the token has expired, though, the user will be prompted to save the username and password.

From a security perspective, there is often a desire to authenticate with a set of alternative credentials, not just the user's primary network credentials. As a result, mobile authentication can also be provided either through mobile-specific user credentials, or through the federation with external authentication providers using a protocol like Security Assertion Markup Language (SAML) or OpenID.

From a usability perspective, entering an alphanumeric username and password is not always an ideal situation, so if the security sensitivity of the situation lends itself to alternative login mechanisms, a numeric PIN or even mechanisms for randomized graphical pattern recognition can be used as alternatives. Additionally, if there is a desire to add an additional layer of authentication between the application itself and the back-end server beyond the user-supplied credentials, RSA offers a SecurID software development kit (SDK) for iOS that allows soft-token generation from within the application.

Communication Security

Once the user is authenticated and authorized to use the application, it's important to ensure that any data being transmitted over the network is securely encrypted. The easiest and most common way to accomplish this is to use HTTPS and Secure Socket Layer (SSL) for all communications to back-end data sources. By relying on a certificate issued from a trusted root certification authority, you can ensure that the application is securely communicating directly with the server and that nothing is intercepting the data in the middle.

Unfortunately, the protection provided by HTTPS and SSL is often unknowingly eliminated when developers override the certificate validation checks in the code. Development and staging server environments are often initially created with self-signed certificates before the production environment receives a certificate from a trusted root certification authority. Thus developers may receive an error in their application, and in order to get around the problem they may simply override the validation check. If this override is not removed before the application goes into production, the application will be susceptible to a man-in-the-middle attack, even if it is now communicating to a production server that has a certificate signed by a trusted root certification authority.

A man-in-the-middle attack occurs when an attacker can intercept HTTPS traffic and proxy the communication so that the victims believe they are still communicating with each other, when in reality the communication security has been breached. A man-in-the-middle proxy will then provide a self-signed certificate to the mobile application client, and if the validation check has been overridden in the application code, the app will continue with the handshake and transmission and put all transferred data at risk.

This should be addressed by ensuring that developing and testing environments are also secured with SSL certificates signed by trusted root certification authorities, and application code should be audited to ensure that SSL validation overrides are not implemented. When following best practices, SSL and HTTPS can be very secure, but it is crucial that your applications do not override these built-in security mechanisms.

As an alternative to HTTPS and SSL, a Virtual Private Network (VPN) can also be used to secure communications to back-end systems through support for IPSec, L2TP, or PPTP. Additionally, there are SSL-based VPN clients available from Juniper, Cisco, and F5 in the App Store.

One valuable VPN-related feature of iOS is VPN on Demand. When using a configuration with certificate-based authentication, iOS will automatically connect to the VPN when an app attempts to access predefined domains. This helps to dramatically improve the usability of a VPN-based communication channel for iOS apps, so that the users are not responsible for connecting and disconnecting the VPNs as appropriate.

Using a VPN, though, does add performance overhead, and it also may expose some security weaknesses. A VPN provides access to whatever network resources are exposed on that private network, and third-party apps will be able to communicate over the VPN connection as well. So it is important to properly segment your network to allow only appropriate traffic over the VPN.

If additional communication security is desired or required, it is also possible to create a "double envelope" of security where you can use HTTPS and SSL within a VPN and/or the manual encryption of the communicated data within the HTTPS request/response using an algorithm such as AES256.

Securing Data at Rest

Once you've ensured that the user is authenticated and that all data in motion is being securely transferred, the final aspect of sandbox security is to ensure that any data at rest is properly encrypted when physically stored.

Apple provides two very powerful features: the keychain and iOS Data Protection. The keychain is a secure and encrypted store for digital identities, usernames, passwords, tokens, and other sensitive items. Keychain items are partitioned so that they are only accessible from the app where they were created, but as mentioned when discussing the Single Sign-On (SSO) mechanism, applications signed with the same developer account can share keychain items. These shared keychain items are the only editable persistent store that can be accessed across applications within an enterprise in-house suite, since the file system is fully isolated within each application sandbox.

The Data Protection APIs utilize the user's unique device passcode in coordination with the device-level hardware encryption to generate a very strong encryption key. As a result, the application can only access files or keychain items under Data Protection when the user has unlocked the device. If the device is either auto-locked or locked by the user, then the application loses access to that data.

If you wish to provide an additional layer of security on top of the Data Protection APIs, you can always encrypt any data using a software-based encryption algorithm. There are many different libraries available for both Objective-C and C# .NET. Since MonoTouch also exposes .NET Crypto libraries, data encryption code developed in C# .NET can also be extremely portable to other platforms.

Following Security Best Practices

It's important to be aware of the various iOS-related best practices regarding application security. In this section, you'll look at some of the details of recommended best practices as well as potential "gotchas" that you should be on the lookout for.

Taking Advantage of the Keychain

First, you should use the keychain whenever you need to store any sensitive information like a username, password, token, or other identity-related information and credentials. It's also important to remember that the keychain is the only mechanism to allow the sharing of data between a suite of applications. For example, a development group in Apple might have the ID:

```
951A5313EF25.com.acmecorp
```

The application identifiers of their two applications might be:

```
951A5313EF25.com.acmecorp.sales
951A5313EF25.com.acmecorp.service
```

Both applications can add a keychain-access-groups entitlement with one value in the array of access groups:

```
951A5313EF25.com.acmecorp.sso
```

Then both applications will be able to create and access keychain items within a shared space.

This can be done in Objective-C:

```
OSStatus status = SecKeychainAddGenericPassword(NULL,
                        strlen([serviceName UTF8String]),
                        [serviceName UTF8String],
                        strlen([username UTF8String]),
                        [username UTF8String],
                        strlen([password UTF8String]),
                        [password UTF8String],
                        NULL);
```

It can also be done in C#:

```
SecStatusCode status = SecKeyChain.Add ( new SecRecord (
        SecKind.GenericPassword ) {
                        Service = serviceName,
                        Account = username,
                        Generic = NSData.FromString(password,
                        NSStringEncoding.UTF8,
        Accessible = SecAccessible.WhenUnlocked )
} );
```

More information about the keychain and sharing items across applications is available in Apple's Keychain Services Programming Guide.

Using iOS Data Protection

As discussed above, the iOS Data Protection APIs should be used when saving data to persistent storage. You can use the Data Protection APIs both to save data directly to the file system with file protection enabled and to modify a file already on the file system to add or remove the Data Protection attribute.

To save an NSData object to a file with protection enabled, here is code in Objective-C:

```
[secureData writeToFile:file options:NSDataWritingFileProtectionComplete
        error: &error];
```

Here is the code in C#:

```
secureData.Save(file, NSDataWritingOptions.FileProtectionComplete, out error)
```

To enable Data Protection for a file already in the file system using Objective-C:

```
NSDictionary *fileAttributes =
  [NSDictionary dictionaryWithObject:NSFileProtectionComplete
forKey:NSFileProtectionKey];
[[NSFileManager defaultManager] setAttributes:fileAttributes
ofItemAtPath:filePath error:&error];
```

To enable Data Protection for a file already in the file system using C#:

```
NSDictionary fileAttributes = new NSDictionary();
fileAttributes.SetObject ("NSFileProtectionComplete", "NSFileProtectionKey");
NSFileManager.DefaultManager.SetAttributes (filePath, fileAttributes, out
error);
```

A data-protected file is accessible only when the device is unlocked. Apps running data-protected code need to handle the scenario where the device becomes locked while the app is still running. As such, you probably want to know when you are about to lose access to the files, as well as when you are able to access them again.

To receive these notifications in Objective-C:

```
- (void)applicationProtectedDataWillBecomeUnavailable:(UIApplication
*)application
{
    // release any references to protected files
}


- (void)applicationProtectedDataDidBecomeAvailable:(UIApplication *)application
{
```

```
    // you can now save anything that you need to be protected
    // you can now query anything you need under protection
}
```

To receive notifications in C#:

```
public override void ProtectedDataWillBecomeUnavailable (UIApplication
application)
{
    // release any references to protected files
}


public override void ProtectedDataDidBecomeAvailable (UIApplication
application)
{
    // you can now save anything that you need to be protected
    // you can now query anything you need under protection
}
```

If your application attempts to access a file under Data Protection while locked, it will receive an exception.

Securely Designing Custom URI Schemes

In Chapter 14, we discussed how custom URI schemes can be used to create a suite of applications that allow deep-linking across apps. These custom URI schemes can be easily discovered through static file analysis of the application binary, so you should design your custom URI navigation schemes on the assumption that they can be publicly known. In other words, don't try to hide deep-linking functionality, because it will very likely be discovered. As a result, while deep-linking works very well for navigation and workflow, it should not be used for transaction processing, like the updating of data or deleting records, at least not without clear and straightforward messaging for the user along with a request for authorization from the user. Third-party attackers could use knowledge about your custom URI navigation schemes to perform sophisticated phishing attacks, or even embed a link to a custom URI scheme into an `<iframe>` tag of a web page being viewed by a user in Safari that will automatically launch the application and navigate to the URI.

As a result, you should not design URI schemes that can perform actions like these:

```
acmesales://customer/delete/12345
acmeservice://updateworkorder/status=complete
acmehealth://patient/6789/setdiagnosiscode=abc123
acmeoperations://equipment/shutdown/device=456
```

One should consider what might happen if an attacker has the ability to update or delete data simply by linking to an application, either if the application is pre-authenticated using a Single Sign-On mechanism or if the user is prompted to authenticate. The user may very well proceed and successfully authenticate, because this user is viewing the actual application that he or she is supposed to authenticate. What the user doesn't know is what will happen after authentication. If an attacker has the ability to update or delete data simply by linking to an application, without any user input, then the application is at risk, whether the application is pre-authenticated using a Single Sign-On mechanism, or even if the user is prompted to authenticate. In this scenario, without user confirmation, the user could be unaware of any potential risk, and might incorrectly assume that being authenticated meant the application was secure.

You should make sure that you carefully parse any incoming URI requests, and prompt the user before acknowledging any actions. Additionally, with iOS 4.2, Apple deprecated the previous method for receiving incoming URIs and added a new method with a Source Application and Annotation:

```
- (BOOL)application:(UIApplication *)application openURL:(NSURL *)url
    sourceApplication:(NSString *)sourceApplication annotation:(id)annotation
{
    // is the sourceApplication an acceptable and secure source?
    // if so, parse the url and validate
    // if transactional, ask the user for authorization
    // if authorized, navigate appropriately
}
```

Here it is in C#:

```
public override void OpenUrl (UIApplication application,
MonoTouch.Foundation.NSUrl url,
    string sourceApplication, MonoTouch.Foundation.NSObject annotation)
{
    // is the sourceApplication an acceptable and secure source?
    // if so, parse the url and validate
    // if transactional, ask the user for authorization
    // if authorized, navigate appropriately
}
```

Remember, though, that some apps that don't perform proper validation may just attempt to navigate to the relative URL after their customer URI scheme. It may trigger a cascading navigation, "double linking," where an attacker could use a redirection through some other app (that you may allow linking from) to ultimately navigate to your app via the approved app. Here's an example of cascading navigation:

```
otherapp://acmecorpapp://do/something
```

As a result, it's important to audit all applications from which you allow incoming connections to ensure that they do not allow this sort of dynamic redirection, which could be potentially exploited by attackers. If you find this in third-party applications that you would like to use to navigate into your own in-house applications, you should communicate with the third-party developers about these issues so that they can be resolved before implementing them within your environment.

Do Not Override HTTPS Certificate Validation

As discussed earlier in this chapter, HTTPS and SSL provide extremely secure communication channels, but unfortunately it is common for developers to override the certificate validation checks during development and testing. If those overrides are not removed before deployment and production use, then the applications are susceptible to man-in-the-middle attacks where data can be intercepted and security compromised, including the capture of user authentication credentials.

The code snippets below are examples of these overrides. **You do not want to use these code snippets in your applications.** They are listed here only so that you can review your code to audit your application development efforts to ensure that your HTTPS and SSL communication channels remain secure.

You should **not** use code that looks like this Objective-C:

```
- (BOOL)connection:(NSURLConnection *)connection
canAuthenticateAgainstProtectionSpace:(NSURLProtectionSpace *)protectionSpace
{
    return [protectionSpace.authenticationMethod
        isEqualToString:NSURLAuthenticationMethodServerTrust];
}

- (void)connection:(NSURLConnection *)connection
didReceiveAuthenticationChallenge:(NSURLAuthenticationChallenge *)challenge
{
    [challenge.sender useCredential:[NSURLCredential
        credentialForTrust:challenge.protectionSpace.serverTrust]
        forAuthenticationChallenge:challenge];
}
```

You should **not** use code that looks like this C#:

```
public override void CanAuthenticateAgainstProtectionSpace (NSUrlConnection
connection,
    NSUrlProtectionSpace protectionSpace)
{
    return protectionSpace.AuthenticationMethod ==
        protectionSpace.ServerTrust;
}


public override void ReceivedAuthenticationChallenge (NSUrlConnection
connection,
```

```
    NSUrlAuthenticationChallenge challenge)
{
    challenge.Sender.UseCredentials(challenge.ProtectionSpace.ServerTrust,
            challenge);
}
```

The following method is an Apple private API. While Apple would not allow applications using this method to make it to the App Store, developers creating in-house enterprise apps may be tempted to use it.

You do **not** want to use this Objective-C Private API method call:

```
setAllowsAnyHTTPSCertificate:forHost:
```

Since MonoTouch does not provide C# bindings to Apple's private APIs, the above call is only an issue with Objective-C code. On the other hand, if the development is being done in C# .NET, especially if the code is being developed with portability in mind, network access will probably be done using the .NET System.Net namespace with classes like the HttpWebRequest class instead of Apple's NSURLConnection. In that case, the SSL override for the .NET stack can be accomplished with the following code.

You do **not** want to use this C#:

```
ServicePointManager.ServerCertificateValidationCallback =
    delegate(Object obj, X509Certificate certificate, X509Chain chain,
        SslPolicyErrors errors) { return true; };
```

Finally, since there may be other ways for developers to override certificate validation checks, it's always a good idea to attempt a man-in-the-middle attack as part of application testing to ensure that the application responds appropriately and does not allow communication to occur over potentially compromised channels.

Push Notifications Are Not Secure

Apple's Push Notification Service (APNs) provides a centralized and shared mechanism for application developers to trigger alerts to users that can automatically launch and deep-link into a custom application upon acknowledgement.

However, push notifications are not secure. Not only are they visibly displayed on the device even when locked, but since all push notifications are relayed through Apple's APNs infrastructure, Apple has the ability to view these messages in clear text, and depending on the type of sensitive data, there may be legal ramifications to disclosing this type of information to third parties.

Additionally, the delivery of push notifications is not guaranteed. Push notifications are displayed on Apple documents with the caution that the delivery of such notifications occurs on a "best effort" basis.

As a result, push notifications should only be used as an enhancement to a workflow, and never as a critical part of workflow. And if there is a need to provide a notification concerning a type of secure data, the push notification should simply contain a generic message that there is an alert. Once users acknowledge and launch the applications, they can view the messages delivered within the secure sandboxes of the applications.

Preventing Screenshot Caching

Whenever the user presses the Home button on an iOS device, or clicks on a link which triggers a navigation to a different application, iOS takes a screenshot that is saved in the application's cache folder on the file system. If the device were to be lost or stolen and subsequently jailbroken, the file system can be accessed to view these automatically cached screenshots.

Luckily, there is an extremely simple work-around to prevent critical data from being saved to the cache. Basically, you can set the screen to blank the user interface immediately before the screenshot is taken and animation occurs, and it is subsequently redisplayed after the application is relaunched.

The code looks like this in Objective-C:

```
- (void)applicationDidEnterBackground:(UIApplication *)application {
    window.hidden = YES;
}

- (void) applicationWillEnterForeground:(UIApplication *)application {
    window.hidden = NO;
}
```

And it looks like this in C#:

```
public override void DidEnterBackground (UIApplication application) {
    window.Hidden = true;
}

public override void WillEnterForeground (UIApplication application) {
    window.Hidden = false;
}
```

If you don't like the user experience of an empty screen when closing or switching apps, you can alternatively display a splash screen instead of just blanking out the screen.

Watching Out for In-App Phishing Attacks

If your application uses a UIWebView, you can add security checks and balances to ensure that your users are not especially susceptible to phishing attacks. Since many apps use embedded browsers, either for hybrid application functionality or for actually viewing web content while remaining within the application, it's important to make sure that the user hasn't been intercepted and navigated to a remote website. While a browser like Safari will display an address bar, users should notice if they are viewing something odd, like a form requesting secure information while at an IP address instead of a domain name. But if the application does not display the current URL, then the user can easily be tricked into following a phishing attack.

The secure alternative is to display the URL if the embedded UIWebView is to be used for browsing. If it is to be used simply as a hybrid application, it can be programmatically configured to allow only connections to a predefined domain name so connections cannot be highjacked.

Ensuring Secure Data Is Not Outputted to Log

During extensive testing of the application, you and whoever else in IT is responsible for security should monitor the console log to ensure that secure data is not being logged. Logs can be viewed through either Xcode Organizer or the iPhone Configuration Utility. If you do discover secure information in the logs, make sure that the logging code is removed before the application enters production.

Auditing Your Applications

Now that we've discussed some of the basic concepts of application-level security, industry best practices, and potential "gotchas," it's important to make sure that your applications are secure before deploying them to your users. To achieve this level of security, the IT organization should establish a security audit process for applications prior to deployment. This is important to do for in-house applications as well as third-party applications available either through the App Store or through external developers, which will be rolled out through the Enterprise deployment model.

In-House Applications

For internally developed applications, the audit is a little more straightforward because you have access to the source code. You should review the application functionality as well as the source code to make sure that blatant issues do not exist:

- Make sure that credentials are being stored in the keychain.
- Make sure that secure data is stored using Data Protection.
- Scan code for HTTPS and SSL validation overrides.
- Ensure that custom URI strings are validated and authorized.
- Ensure that sensitive data is blanked before a screenshot is cached.

Commercial Applications

Applications distributed through the App Store are encrypted, but it is well documented online how the applications can be decrypted for analysis. Once decrypted, the application binary and supporting resource files can be viewed, and grep (a command line text search utility) can be used to search the application contents for undocumented custom URI scheme transactions, hardcoded passwords, credentials, URLs, and other types of information.

You should also ensure that any commercial applications from which you plan to allow incoming custom URI navigations into your in-house applications are not susceptible to URI relay and redirection.

All iOS Applications

For all applications, whether they were developed in-house or by a third party, you should include the following techniques in a standardized iOS application security audit:

- Attempt a man-in-the-middle attack and ensure proper behavior.
- Make sure that secure data isn't logged to the console.
- Use grep to search for static strings/credentials/secrets/URLs.
- Ensure that mechanisms to prevent in-app phishing are in place.
- Jailbreak a device running the app and monitor the filesystem.
- Make sure custom URI schemes are properly validated.
- Monitor web traffic via proxy for inappropriate transmissions.

Establishing Enterprise Standards

As iPads continue to grow in popularity, there will undoubtedly be exploding demand for enterprise apps. And even if your organization will have development distributed throughout multiple groups or divisions, it's important to establish standards and procedures for ensuring the security of iOS applications.

Given the tools available to iOS developers, extremely secure applications can be developed, but ensuring this level of security requires a certain level of awareness about the growing sophistication of attacks against the iOS platform. In addition to raising awareness of these security best practices among all iOS developers, your enterprise IT security team should develop an internal capability to be able to understand potential risks and how they can be addressed.

Summary

In this chapter, you looked at the basic concept of application sandbox-level security, including ensuring proper access control through authentication and authorization; ensuring communication security by encrypting data in transit; and ensuring storage security by encrypting any persisted data. We also examined a number of industry best practices and "gotchas," as well as the importance of performing a security audit of your applications before they are deployed.

I'm sure that your organization is sensitive to security-related issues, but are you prepared internally to address these topics? It's critical that enterprise IT develop a competency in iOS security if these devices are going to be deployed within the organization.

This chapter wraps up the section on development. In the next section, we'll look at the process of deployment, starting with a chapter on planning your iPad deployment.

Part

V

Deployment

In This Part

Planning a Deployment

WHAT'S IN THIS CHAPTER?

- Deciding on the best approach for device provisioning
- How to manage the hardware procurement process
- Taking advantage of available hardware accessories
- Preparing for the logistics of the deployment
- Planning for user support and self-service

Even though this book has covered "deployment" in the last few chapters, many organizations will actually be rolling out devices and mobile device management solutions before designing and developing any applications.

As a result, these last four chapters may be the first chapters that need to be digested by many readers who are responsible for supporting an iPad deployment within their enterprises. This chapter will cover the strategies and best practices for planning, and will also include the many issues that should be taken into consideration when preparing for an iPad deployment.

First, we'll examine the different deployment options you can take, with either an individual user self-service approach or a centrally provisioned approach, where the device is handed to the user pre-configured and ready to go. Additionally, we'll examine the ramifications of personally owned devices vs. company-owned hardware.

Then we'll look at accessories, and not just the iPad accessories that are commonly used by consumers, but also powerful mobile business accessories like barcode scanners, magnetic stripe readers, and rugged portable printers. These accessories can enable the iPad to perform tasks and activities to power line-of-business solutions that have been the sole domain of Windows Mobile–based devices for years.

Finally, we'll discuss the various logistical issues that should be taken into consideration in preparation for any deployment, and the different types of user support models. We'll look at industry best practices for both enabling user self-service and preparing the call center to effectively support mobile users in the field.

Deployment Options

When it comes to actually rolling out devices, you can take one or a combination of two primary approaches. On one hand, you can create an environment and a process that allows users to self-service their own deployments. On the other hand, you can create the process for centrally provisioning the devices so that they are pre-configured when the users receive them.

Within your organization, one approach might be more appropriate than the other, or it might be best to use a combination of both approaches. Sometimes different user groups and user profiles are better fits for the different deployment models. Sometimes, it can also work to default to a user self-service model, but offer centralized device provisioning if the user prefers that approach. Again, it's really up to you to determine the best approach for your organization, your IT department, and your users.

Self-Service

In many ways, the enterprise capabilities of iOS were designed with user self-service in mind. As Apple's focus for the design of iOS and the iPad is entirely about maximizing the user experience, many of the traditional methods for provisioning, configuring, and managing mobile deployments were replaced with ones that Apple designed to put the user in control.

For example, Apple has worked hard to create a user base of over 200 million user accounts with credit cards on file. Because Apple uses the same account for the App Store that it uses for iTunes and iBooks, it has carefully designed an experience in which the user can buy apps, music, movies, and books with a single tap. One implication of this is that every iPad user needs to have his or her own Apple ID, and in order to download apps, even free ones, must have an active credit card on file. This process of buying music, movies, etc. also implies the need to sync the iPad with a PC or Mac to back up its content. While this could be done on corporately owned computer equipment, most users will want to blend their personal and professional activities on the same device.

So what is an enterprise IT department to do in this environment? It can be very effective to take a "carrot and stick" approach. If users want access to company e-mail, they must accept security restrictions. If they want to use in-house applications, they might need to accept even more strict security rules, and if they want VPN access, they might need extremely tight rules. With a self-service approach, the user is in control. If users, for whatever reasons, are unwilling to submit to the security policies or restrictions for a given capability, they can either reject the capability or remove it from their devices.

Apple accomplishes this through the use of something called a configuration profile. A configuration profile can contain a collection of both account settings and user restrictions. It's important to remember that a configuration profile must always be accepted as all-or-nothing. If Mail, VPN, or other capability is tied to a specific restriction or policy, the user must accept the restriction as well as the capability. If the user won't accept the restriction, or if the user wants to remove the configuration profile that enforces a given restriction after initially accepting it, then the capability is removed as well. This puts users ultimately in control of their own devices, and many organizations have found that users are more willing to accept restrictions when a "carrot and stick" approach is used, rather than having the restrictions simply forced upon them.

By offering the capabilities (i.e., e-mail, apps, VPN) as "carrots," you can more easily get corporate users to accept the necessary restrictions on their personal devices. The self-service approach allows users to feel they're in control while simultaneously giving IT the ability to enforce policies and restrictions on users. That is likely why this approach is gaining significant popularity throughout the overall trend of consumerization within the enterprise.

Centrally Provisioned

Traditionally, mobile deployments have primarily revolved around centralized provisioning processes, and while Apple has helped to popularize the self-service model, there are still many situations where a centrally provisioned iPad deployment makes a lot of sense.

In situations where the iPad user is a task-oriented worker, or where the iPad might be shared by multiple users, it is likely more appropriate to take a centrally provisioned approach. When an individual user is not in a position to take an "ownership" role over the device, the self-service model does not work very well, and a model where the pre-configured and provisioned device is provided to the user is more appropriate.

This model is also common in situations with high-level executives, where users simply want to be handed a device that is fully configured and ready to use.

Hardware Procurement

Whether a deployment is being managed as a self-service model or through central provisioning and configuration, there will still be discussion about whether the mobile hardware should be owned individually by the user or as a corporate asset by the company. Again, as in the earlier case, it's not always a one-or-the-other situation. Many companies are rolling out company-owned iPads to specific users while simultaneously supporting personally owned iPads for any other user who is willing to accept corporately mandated security policies and restrictions.

Personally Owned Hardware

Within the context of personally owned hardware, organizations can take different approaches. The first model is for users to pay for the devices out of their own pockets. The second model is to give users a stipend so that they can select the exact configuration of the device that they want.

The biggest problem with deployments based entirely on personally owned hardware is that there's no guarantee that all, or even a majority, of users within any given user profile will have iPads. This makes it extremely difficult to justify investment in applications that will truly empower workforce productivity.

This is one of the reasons why, across the industry, we're seeing a lot of companies moving to personally owned smartphone devices, but standardizing on the iPad by purchasing units for entire user groups. This makes it easy to justify line-of-business applications that can provide a dramatic return on investment.

Corporately Owned Devices

With corporately owned devices, the question that I hear the most from IT leaders is whether the iPad can actually serve as a laptop or desktop replacement, or whether it's just another device they have to provide to their users. There's no simple answer to this question, but it's important to note that this is also highly dependent on the type of user. For outside sales teams, service technicians, or workers performing survey capture in the field, the iPad can essentially function as a full PC replacement. Other user groups may still need PCs, but will find they need them much less than they did previously.

In any case, the overall trend in the industry has been toward corporately owned iPad deployments, at least for organizations that are embracing the iPad as a platform for business applications. Ultimately, this is a decision that must be made by each business, based on what's best for its own organization, culture, and environment.

Accessories

When it comes to accessories on the consumer side, these often provide optional enhancements to the performance, capabilities, or user experience of the device. In the world of enterprise mobility, though, accessories can be as important to a mobile deployment as the mobile device itself. If the solution requires barcode scanning, magnetic stripe reading, signature capture, and receipt printing, many accessories beyond the iPad itself will be required to use this solution. In this section, we'll take a look at some types of accessories that can be critical to an enterprise deployment of iPads.

The accessories mentioned in this section are not an exhaustive list of products, or even categories of products, but are just some examples of the types of accessories commonly used as part of an enterprise iPad deployment.

Case

While the iPad 2's smart cover is an amazing piece of industrial design, it simply doesn't provide enough protection for many field environments in which the iPad will be used. Luckily, there is an entire cottage industry in iPad cases, including some that provide a significant amount of protection.

For example, the OtterBox Defender series iPad case, shown in Figure 17-1, offers three layers of protection: a self-adhering clear protective film, a high-impact polycarbonate shell, and a durable silicone skin. Given the iPad's capability for business applications in the field, many other rugged iPad cases will continue to appear on the market.

Figure 17-1: The OtterBox Defender series case provides the iPad with three layers of ruggedized protection.

Keyboard

For certain applications that require a lot of typing, or if the iPad is being used as a PC replacement for certain kinds of users, a hardware keyboard is often a valuable accessory.

The Apple Bluetooth keyboard, shown in Figure 17-2, is a small and lightweight keyboard that makes it easy to enter data or even type complete documents on the iPad. Apple also sells an iPad keyboard dock, which is less mobile than the Bluetooth keyboard but can provide a better user experience for typing if the keyboard dock remains in a consistent location like a desk, lounge, or even a shared workspace. Since the iPad is compatible with any Bluetooth keyboard and any USB keyboard (via the camera kit USB adapter), there are virtually limitless options for keyboards.

Figure 17-2: The Apple Bluetooth keyboard can provide the iPad with a small, yet full-sized external keyboard that can be used for applications where extensive typing is required.

Stylus

While simple handwriting functionality is not often part of business applications, there are many other types of business applications that can make good use of a stylus for the iPad. From sketching layouts to annotating diagrams or capturing signatures, there are many apps where a stylus can provide a lot of value. The Griffin Technology Stylus, pictured in Figure 17-3, is just one of the many styluses that are compatible with the iPad's capacitive touch screen.

Figure 17-3: The Griffin Technology Stylus works with the capacitive touch screen in the iPad and can be used for many types of powerful business capabilities like embedded signature capture in iPad applications.

External Display Adapter

The iPad supports Video Graphics Array (VGA) and High-Definition Multimedia Interface (HDMI) video-out with resolutions up to 1080p. It can display the mirroring introduced with iOS 4.3, which automatically outputs whatever is displayed on the iPad screen without any configuration or application customization. But applications can also override this capability by outputting different content to the external display than what is being shown on the iPad screen. For instance, Keynote allows the presenter to view the next slide, notes, and timers, while only the current slide in the presentation is outputted to external display.

As a result, external display adapters will be must-have accessories for many corporate iPad users and deployments. Apple's Digital AV adapter provides HDMI-out and power pass-through for extended charging while mirroring the iPad's screen.

Barcode Scanner

Once the sole domain of Windows-powered, rugged mobile devices, barcode scanning applications for the iPad and other iOS devices are beginning to chip away at Microsoft's monopoly in this space. From inventory lookup, asset tracking, and retail point-of-sale to order transaction processing, the iPad plus a barcode scanner can provide a modern user experience in a traditional category of line-of-business applications. Because of this, there has been a constant stream of new iOS-based barcode scanning products coming to market.

With the iPad 2's camera, software-based barcode-scanning SDKs like RedLaser can easily embed optical barcode scanning into your applications, but sometimes a laser-based scanner is required to provide a higher level of user experience for repeated, rapid scanning. The Mobilogics iScan device, shown in Figure 17-4, is a dongle that can plug into the connector on the bottom of any iPad, iPhone, or iPod touch to provide laser-based scanning, and it starts at a price of only $99.

Figure 17-4: The Mobilogics iScan is an Apple-certified, laser-based barcode scanner for the iPad that starts at $99 and enables entire categories of powerful iPad-based mobile line-of-business solutions.

For applications where 2D barcode scanning is required, or where it would be more convenient for you to use an external Bluetooth-based scanner, the Socket CHS-7x, shown in Figure 17-5, is a very popular and powerful handheld scanning device.

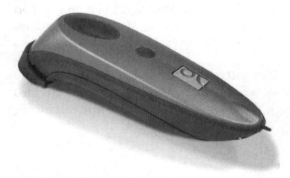

Figure 17-5: The Socket CHS-7x is a Bluetooth-based 1D and 2D barcode scanner that can be used with the iPad to enable rich barcode-scanning functionality within business apps.

For iPad-based scanning applications where it's not always convenient for the user to hold both the scanner and the iPad at the same time, the KoamTac 300i, shown in Figure 17-6, provides a display that gives users feedback about their scans, so that the iPad does not necessarily have to be referred to after each scan.

Magnetic Stripe Reader

A magnetic stripe reader can provide the iPad with a valuable capability for point-of-sale, hospitality, or data capture applications that can read information

from credit cards, driver's licenses, or other types of magnetic stripe cards. The
IDTECH UniMag reader, shown in Figure 17-7, offers this capability by plugging
into the headphone jack of iPad, iPhone, or iPod touch devices.

Figure 17-6: The KoamTac 300i is an Apple-certified
Bluetooth barcode scanner that can be used with an SDK to
provide visual feedback on the handheld scanner unit itself.

Figure 17-7: The IDTECH UniMag mobile magnetic stripe reader uses
the headphone jack on the iPad, and can enable applications to read
credit cards, driver's licenses, and other magnetic stripe cards.

Printer

With OS 4.2, Apple launched the AirPrint capability that gives application developers the ability to print content from their applications to a shared print queue.
In addition to allowing developers to add AirPrint support to their own apps,
Apple added out-of-the-box support to Safari, Mail, Pages, Keynote, Numbers,
and other popular apps.

At the launch, AirPrint supported only a handful of AirPrint-enabled printers,
like the HP Officejet Pro 8500A Premium, shown in Figure 17-8.

Figure 17-8: The HP Officejet Pro 8500A Premium e-All-in-One Printer allows iPad users to print from any AirPrint-compatible application.

Fortunately, there are additional options, like FingerPrint from Collobos Software, that allow any shared printer to be AirPrint-enabled from a Mac or Windows PC. In organizations with extensive iPad deployments, it can often be quite valuable to configure AirPrint-enabled printers for users.

In other situations, though, AirPrint is not the best option for printing. If the user requires a mobile unit for printing receipts or work order confirmations, a portable and rugged printer from Zebra, like the one pictured in Figure 17-9, might be a better fit. Although the Zebra printers are not AirPrint-compatible, Zebra offers an iOS SDK so that developers can embed printing capabilities into their own custom in-house iPad applications.

Figure 17-9: Zebra offers an iOS SDK that gives application developers the ability to embed mobile printing capabilities into their apps.

Managing Deployment Logistics

When it comes to actually rolling out the physical hardware of a deployment, there are bound to be issues, especially when an organization is supporting a new platform or technology like the iPad for the first time. As a result, it's important to extensively pilot-test deployments to identify any issues and work through these so that the solutions are documented for easy reference during a larger-scale deployment. It can be valuable to include users from a wide variety of demographics and technological competencies in the pilot group to help ensure that any potential issues emerge during the pilot. Pilot users are also excellent participants in focus groups to gather feedback on improving the applications as well as the overall deployment process.

After the pilot deployment, when it's time to begin a larger full-scale deployment, it's often a good idea to roll devices to users in waves. This serves two main functions. First, if any critical issues are discovered, it's easier to roll back any single wave than an entire deployment. Secondly, there will be an inevitable volume of calls to the support call center, and by breaking the deployment into waves these calls can be more evenly distributed over time to prevent swamping the call center.

Preparing for User Support

As part of any corporate deployment, you have to be ready when your users have any problems or questions. The iPad is an intuitive device, but users will still have questions from time to time. Across the industry, the biggest trend is to encourage users to support themselves as much as possible and thus cut down on traditional call center IT support. This doesn't mean that you can eliminate the need for call center support, but just that if you enable your users with processes and systems designed to facilitate self-service, your users will feel they have the ability to learn how to use the device and troubleshoot problems on their own.

As you're preparing for mobile deployment, you need to determine if it's appropriate for your organization to provide self-service support options, as well as what level of support will be provided through the call center. For these topics, there is not necessarily any right or wrong approach; it depends entirely on what's best for any given organization.

Allowing User Self-Service

If you're allowing a consumer self-service approach to provisioning and configuration, or if you're allowing personally owned devices to be supported in the enterprise environment, then you'll likely want to create mechanisms for user self-service. As part of the overall industry trend towards consumerization, empowering your users to self-service their own needs helps to both increase user satisfaction and reduce IT support costs. There are many ways this can be done, but let's take a look at two of the most common types of systems and processes for user self-service: wikis and forums.

Wiki

If you go the route of user self-service, it can be valuable to direct all users to a wiki for directions and instructions on how to provide self-service. The advantage of a wiki is that if users have problems, or if something changes (say with an update from iOS), the users will feel empowered to update the information themselves. Of course, this depends on the corporate culture and the user profile.

Again, this is not a one-size-fits-all solution. There are lots of variables in culture and user attitudes, but the key is to determine if this is an appropriate solution for you.

Forums

Forums are especially valuable when the topics are widely varied, such as support for specific business applications. Most effective forums have the same IT support personnel providing answers through the forums. But some problems are common to many users, and a simple search can often provide a user with a solution other users have found to overcome the same issue.

As with the wiki, the success of a forum-based support option depends very much on the corporate culture and the type of user. For instance, senior-level executives are often averse to asking questions in a public forum, but with field sales teams there's often a camaraderie that provides a strong motivation to help each other out.

Preparing the Call Center

With the iPad, the user experience is completely unlike anything else. While support personnel are being trained on new support issues related to the iPad, it's extremely important that they have the chance to touch and play with the iPad to experience it themselves. The iPad is one of those things that's difficult to describe unless you've experienced it firsthand. As a result, call center support personnel will have difficulty explaining and helping troubleshoot issues without first having some understanding of the device themselves.

Summary

When rolling out iPads to users within your organization, it's important to prepare for your deployment. Even if your organization has had experience deploying mobile devices in the past, the iPad is different enough that existing processes will likely need to be re-examined. And beyond that, there are some fundamental decisions every IT organization must make. Will you take a user self-service approach? Or will you go the route of centralized deployment management? And will you allow individually owned devices? Or will you require corporately owned hardware? These are just some of the decisions you must make.

In the next chapter, we'll take a look at what configuration profiles are and how they work. We'll examine how they can be created and managed, as well as how they can be used to implement "carrot and stick" approaches that tie security policies and usage restrictions to specific capabilities like Exchange or VPN access.

Provisioning and Configuring the Devices

WHAT'S IN THIS CHAPTER?

- Understanding the SCEP enrollment process
- What provisioning profiles are and how they work
- How to use configuration profiles for iOS deployments
- Using the iPhone Configuration Utility
- Creating configuration profiles programmatically
- Using third-party vendors for configuration tools

In the last chapter you examined some of the strategic and logistical issues with facilitating an iOS deployment within the enterprise. In this chapter, you're going to dig a little deeper into some of the mechanisms described in the last chapter and see how the technologies and processes for provisioning and configuring iOS devices actually work.

You'll start by digging into the enrollment process through a mechanism called SCEP, or Simple Certificate Enrollment Protocol, which allows the device to uniquely and securely be enrolled into an enterprise environment. Then you'll take a look at exactly what configuration and provisioning profiles are, what they do, and how they differ from each other.

Next you'll examine the different types of configuration "payloads" that can be distributed as part of a configuration profile, and how the iPhone Configuration Utility can be used to quickly and easily create configuration profiles. You'll consider the XML-based contents of a configuration profile and how these can be programmatically generated as part of any type of in-house self-service portal or other custom system. You'll also look at the C# .NET-based API that Apple provides for the iPhone Configuration Utility to help script and automate the generation of dynamic configuration profiles.

Understanding Configuration Profiles

Configuration profiles are the foundation of Apple's enterprise support for iOS. They were first introduced with iPhone OS 2.0, but they were significantly improved with iPhone OS 3.0 and iOS 4.0, and ultimately will be with iOS 5.0. As part of the Mobile Device Management (MDM) capabilities introduced with iOS 4.0, configuration profiles are the fundamental mechanism through which devices are configured and managed, and policies/restrictions enforced. This is not to say that MDM is a prerequisite for using configuration profiles, but simply that configuration profiles are the underlying basis of how MDM actually performs many of its management capabilities. (This will be discussed in greater detail in Chapter 20).

Enrollment

Apple provides several distinct methods that can be used to support device configuration. First, users can configure their own devices manually. This doesn't require any input from IT, but it also doesn't give the enterprise any control over the enforcement of security policies.

Secondly, the enterprise can create and distribute device configuration files that users can install. The configuration files can be sent to the device via e-mail. (If enterprise e-mail hasn't yet been set up on the device, it can be sent to personal e-mail addresses.) You can also have the iPhone user navigate to a special web page via Safari or include a web link to the configuration file in a short-message service (SMS) text message.

The advantages of using configuration files are numerous. Security and usage policies can be linked to specific enterprise resources. In addition, policies can be configured so that they cannot be removed or can only be removed with the approval of the system administrator. (Enterprises should be aware that this may not be legal in certain jurisdictions if the configuration files are being installed on a personally owned device.) A significant downside of using generic configuration files is that they are not tied to a specific user or device and can be shared with and used by unauthorized individuals.

It is always possible for IT to manually install configuration files on each device and customize them for each user. This would ensure that the devices conformed to enterprise policy. However, it's a labor-intensive process that's probably only feasible if there are a limited number of devices involved.

The final option for device configuration, SCEP, was incorporated into iPhone OS 3.0, but wasn't really popularized until Apple also added the new MDM capabilities as part of iOS 4.0. SCEP reduces manual IT-based deployment processes and enhances security by allowing policy enforcement and authentication of users before enrollment and configuration deployment.

The following sections describe the process that needs to be followed by the iPhone user in order to interact with a SCEP service. Keep in mind that because Apple does not provide the actual service — only the specifications of the service — this is something that each enterprise must either create for its own internal use, or implement through a third-party vendor. Most of the iOS MDM vendors support SCEP for enrollment, and MDM will be covered in much greater detail in Chapter 20.

The enrollment process starts with the user navigating to the URL of the profile (configuration) service, using Safari. The user can enter the web address manually or tap on a link embedded in an SMS message sent to his or her device. Once the user connects to the profile service, the user's identity needs to be authenticated. This is another service that is not provided by Apple, so the deploying organization must either create it or use a service provided by a third-party vendor. Any number of authentication mechanisms can be employed, including single-use enrollment tokens, authentication using an existing authentication provider like Active Directory, or something else you would like to use, since the implementation is up to you or a third-party vendor.

Once the user's identity has been authenticated, the service needs to respond with an iPhone configuration profile (.mobileconfig file). This response contains a previously shared key or challenge token, as well as a collection of device attributes that are required to be sent back to the server in the authentication phase of this process. The configuration profile can be set up to request the iPhone OS version, unique device ID (UDID), MAC address, product type (iPad, iPhone, or iPod touch), phone ID (IMEI), and SIM information (ICCID). The process of Phase 1 is outlined in Diagram 18-1.

After the device receives the configuration profile generated during Phase 1, it displays a prompt to the user asking whether the user accepts the installation of the profile. The profile contains a SCEP-initiation payload, and upon acceptance, a response is sent from the iPhone that includes device attributes requested by the payload, along with the challenge token. The response is signed with an Apple-issued certificate using the device's unique identity and is sent as an HTTP POST back up to the server. The process of Phase 2 is shown in Figure 18-2.

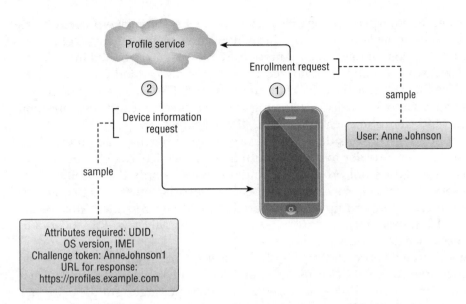

Figure 18-1: In Phase 1, the SCEP enrollment process starts with the device authenticating with a service to request enrollment, to which the service can respond with a request for device attributes.

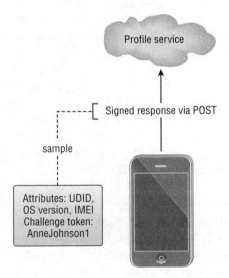

Figure 18-2: In Phase 2, the device generates a response to the service's request for device attributes, signs the response, and posts it back to the service.

The service then responds with a request for the device to generate an RSA 1024 key and return it for certification using SCEP. The SCEP request must be handled in automatic mode, and the challenge in the SCEP packet is used to authenticate the request.

Finally, the certificate authority (CA) provides a unique encryption certificate for the device. This certificate can be used to encrypt data requests and/or responses generated from the device. In addition, it can be used to authenticate the device for a number of enterprise services, including Microsoft Exchange ActiveSync, WPA2 Enterprise wireless networks, corporate on-demand VPNs, and mobile device management. This process is shown in Figure 18-3.

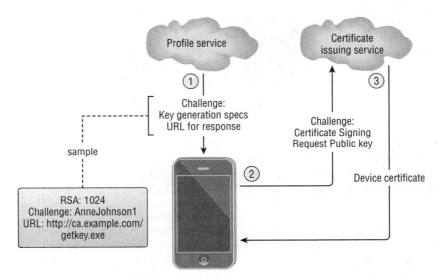

Figure 18-3: In Phase 3, the service responds with a challenge to generate a public/private key pair, post the public key to the certificate authority, and receive a unique device certificate which can be used to uniquely identify that specific iOS device for other various enterprise services.

Now that the device has been issued its own unique encryption certificate from the CA, the device sends back a list of attributes that were originally requested by the service, and signs the reply with the encryption certificate. The profile service responds to the encrypted request with a personalized .mobileconfig file for that particular user and/or device. (It can encrypt that configuration response using its own server-side SSL certificate.) This configuration profile can contain configuration payloads for services like Exchange, Wi-Fi, and VPNs, as well as enterprise security policies. Alternatively, and most commonly, this configuration profile may contain just MDM configuration through which any additional configuration profiles may be added or removed on demand through the mobile device management service.

This configuration profile should also be locked to prevent the user from removing it from the device. The profile can contain additional requests for SCEP-based identity enrollment, which are automatically executed in the background as the initial profile is installed. This is illustrated in Figure 18-4.

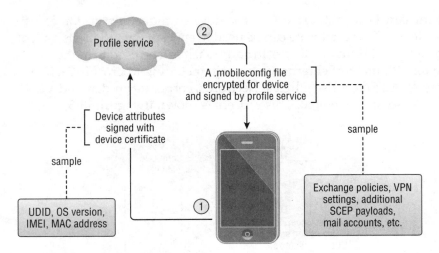

Figure 18-4: In Phase 4, to complete SCEP enrollment, the device attributes are re-signed using the device's new unique certificate, re-posted to the service in response to the challenge, and ultimately receive a configuration profile which is automatically installed onto the iOS device.

Again, because SCEP is a process that Apple supports only from a device-side iOS perspective (it doesn't offer a server-side implementation), it is up to each enterprise to implement its own SCEP service. There are a number of open-source SCEP implementations, as well as many third-party mobile device management vendors that offer their own flavors. As a result, this SCEP enrollment process is somewhat flexible, and the exact steps depend significantly on the details of each particular implementation.

Provisioning

In the context of iOS, the term "provisioning" often carries different connotations, and sometimes has completely different meanings when it is used within other IT-related contexts. In iOS, a provisioning profile is a file with a .mobileprovision extension that is used to sign and authenticate iOS applications. This process will be described in more detail in the next chapter.

It is important to understand, though, that with the exception of apps distributed through the App Store, any apps distributed through ad hoc or enterprise distribution models require that the iOS device have the same provisioning profile installed on the device that was used to sign the application. Over-the-air installation bundles can be configured as single packages, with the provisioning profile embedded in the package along with the application itself. But it can often be valuable for enterprise deployments to split this into two steps, which can add something of an additional layer of security for in-house applications;

for instance, provisioning profiles can be allowed to be distributed and installed only by an MDM server.

Configuration

In addition to the initial configuration profile that can initiate the SCEP enroll-ment process described above, and the MDM configuration details which will be described in more detail in Chapter 20, there are many different types of "payloads" that can be included in an iOS configuration profile. These include account settings like:

- Exchange ActiveSync
- IMAP/POP email
- VPN
- Wi-Fi
- LDAP
- CalDAV
- CardDAV
- Subscribed calendars

They also include security policies like:

- Passcode requirement
- Allow simple value
- Requirement of alphanumeric value
- Passcode length
- Number of complex characters
- Maximum passcode age
- Time before auto-lock
- Number of unique passcodes before reuse
- Grace period for device lock
- Number of failed attempts before wipe
- Control Configuration Profile removal by user

Also included are device restrictions like:

- App installation
- Screen capture
- Automatic sync of mail accounts while roaming

- Voice dialing when locked
- In-application purchasing
- Requirement for encrypted backups to iTunes
- Explicit music and podcasts in iTunes
- Allowed content ratings for movies, TV shows, apps
- YouTube
- iTunes Store
- App Store
- Safari
- Safari security preferences

Other settings include:

- Certificates and identities
- Web Clips
- APN settings

Options for Creating Configuration Profiles

Configuration profiles can be created primarily in four ways: through the iPhone Configuration Utility; dynamically through generating custom XML; programmatically through C# .NET scripting via iPhone Configuration Utility; and through third-party tools. Let's dig into these different options.

iPhone Configuration Utility

The iPhone Configuration Utility (iPCU), shown in Figure 18-5, is a free application from Apple with versions for both Windows and Mac OS X. Whether or not the iPCU is used as a primary tool for creating and managing configuration profiles, it is an invaluable utility that is a must-have for an IT administrator, application developer, or enterprise architect responsible for iOS-related issues. It can be used to view console logs on devices, install or uninstall apps onto devices, and add or remove provisioning profiles. It also has an easy visual interface for creating and managing configuration profiles. Again, even if you don't plan on using this tool for creating or managing configuration profiles in production, it's still the easiest way to play around with the configuration and management capabilities of the iOS platform and quickly learn what kinds of policies can or cannot be used. It also helps in learning how carrot-and-stick scenarios can be strategically crafted.

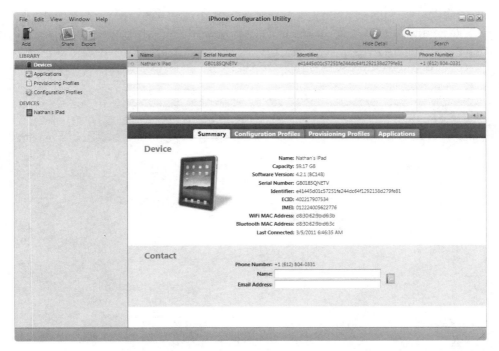

Figure 18-5: The iPhone Configuration Utility (iPCU) provides a visual interface to manage devices, applications, provisioning profiles, and configuration profiles.

As shown in Figure 18-6, by selecting Configuration Profiles from the tab on the left side of the iPhone Configuration Utility, and selecting the New button from the tab bar on the top-left of the screen, you can easily create a new configuration profile.

The list of "payloads" in the lower center column of the screen contains all the different types of configurations that can be included in a configuration profile.

The General payload, which focuses on the name, description, and identity of the configuration profile, is the only required payload, as all of the other types of payloads are optional. The Name is what will be visually shown on the device, so it should be self-descriptive and not too cryptic. The Identifier is unique to each configuration profile, so the naming conventions should be standardized for your organization based on the structure and management approach you'd like to take. The provisioning profile Identifier field should be in the format of "com.company.profile" and is flexible to allow naming structures as deep as necessary. If you install a different profile of the same identifier on top of an existing one, it will replace the existing one (which, incidentally, is the only way to remove profiles that are configured so as not to allow removal). The Organization is the name of your company, and the Description should describe in simple language what is included in this particular profile. This is what will be displayed to users when they are prompted to accept it. Finally, the Security value allows the profile to be configured so it can always be removed by the user, never be removed by the user, or removed only with administrator approval through the use of a password.

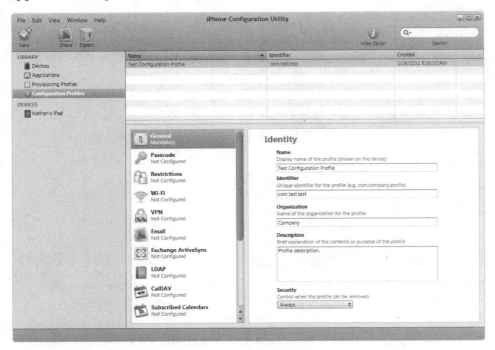

Figure 18-6: The iPCU allows users to easily and rapidly create configuration profiles through its graphical interface.

The Passcode payload (Figure 18-7) allows the various iOS-supported passcode-related security policies to be configured as part of a configuration profile. In addition to the various types of restrictions offered as part of the Restriction bundle, this is how carrot-and-stick profiles can be crafted by tying specific security policies or restrictions to specific enterprise capabilities (like VPN or Wi-Fi).

The Exchange ActiveSync payload (as shown in the iPCU in Figure 18-8) allows organizations to configure mail, calendar, and contacts for iOS synchronization with Exchange. These configuration profiles can be generated in such a way that they are user-specific, with embedded active directory domain, username, and password, or the user-specific security spaces can be left blank with the user prompted for that information. It's also important to remember that configuration profiles can be distributed in a signed or unsigned form, and while it is always a good general rule to ensure security by signing and encrypting the configuration profile, it's an absolute must if security credentials are being embedded in the profile.

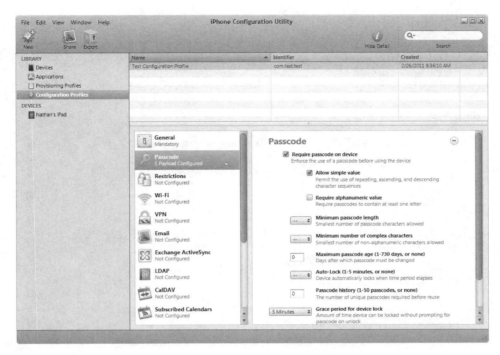

Figure 18-7: The Passcode payload can be strategically used to implement carrot-and-stick policies for various enterprise services.

One very powerful but often misunderstood capability of iOS configuration profiles is the ability to deploy Web Clip payloads (shown in the iPCU in Figure 18-9). A Web Clip is essentially an icon that provides a link to a web application. For most users, if properly designed, this web app will appear to be no different from any other app installed on the user's device. The Web Clip can be configured in full-screen mode so that the user doesn't see the address bar at the top of the Safari screen or the toolbar at the bottom with back and forward buttons.

It's also valuable to note that Web Clips can point to other URI schemes besides the common http:// and https:// used by Safari. For instance, if your organization has developed an in-house app that has registered a custom URI scheme with the iOS device called acme://, then the Web Clip can point to acme://, which will launch the custom application. The real power of this approach, though, can be to "deep-link" into your custom apps with links along the lines of acme://sales/reports or acme://accounts, having multiple icons via Web Clips that can point to different types of functionality within a single native iOS application. This is also powerful in that Web Clips can be pushed onto devices without user involvement via MDM, while in-house apps deployed over the air require user involvement.

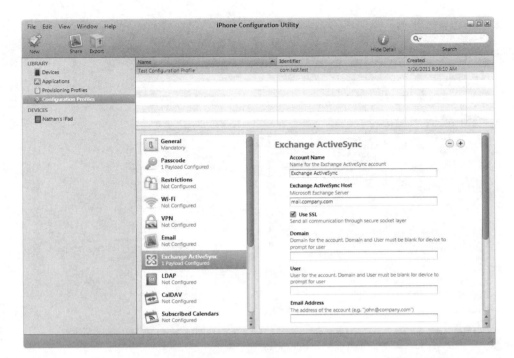

Figure 18-8: The Exchange ActiveSync payload can provide fully configured connections with domain, username, and password, or these items can be left blank for the user to be prompted.

Building XML Files

As a configuration profile is simply an XML file that follows the Apple PLIST format with the .mobileconfig file extension, it is relatively easy to write your own custom applications to generate provisioning profiles. This could be used, for instance, in a user self-service portal where a user could log in, authenticate with Active Directory, select whatever capabilities are wanted, acknowledge the security policies and restrictions that will apply, and then let the service generate the appropriate configuration profile and link to it for installation on the device.

This could also be used as part of an automated mobile device management solution, since some MDM vendors offer custom APIs to integrate with their platforms. You could write code to generate specific configuration profiles and push them programmatically to the appropriate devices through the MDM solution.

Additionally, this could also be used as part of a centrally managed deployment or hardware depot facility, for instance one where barcoded asset tags can be physically applied to devices, scanned, and plugged into a desktop computer, with a configuration profile dynamically generated and deployed to the iOS device.

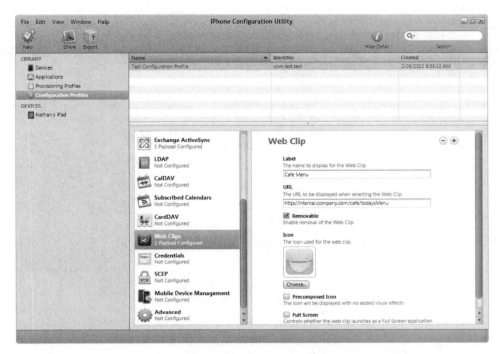

Figure 18-9: Web Clips place an icon on the user's device that points to a specific URL.

Configuration profiles are simply XML files that can be programmatically generated as part of virtually any corporate workflow or automated system. Thus, it's up to each organization to engineer the appropriate processes for its specific requirements. Below is an example of the XML format of a configuration profile. It's easy to create template configuration profiles in iPCU in which you can programmatically substitute whatever values you need to without having to create the entire XML document from scratch.

```
<?xml version="1.0" encoding="UTF-8"?>
<!DOCTYPE plist PUBLIC "-//Apple Inc//DTD PLIST 1.0//EN"
"http://www.apple.com/DTDs/PropertyList-1.0.dtd">
<plist version="1.0">
    <dict>
        <key>PayloadVersion</key>
        <integer>1</integer>
        <key>PayloadUUID</key>
        <string>Ignored</string>
        <key>PayloadType</key>
        <string>Configuration</string>
        <key>PayloadIdentifier</key>
        <string>Ignored</string>
        <key>PayloadContent</key>
        <array>
            <dict>
```

```
                    <key>PayloadContent</key>
                    <dict>
                            <key>URL</key>
                            <string>https://scep.acmecorp.com/scep</string>
                            <key>Name</key>
                            <string>EnrollmentCAInstance</string>
                            <key>Subject</key>
                            <array>
                                    <array>
                                            <array>
                                                    <string>O</string>
                                                    <string>Acme Corp</string>
                                            </array>
                                    </array>
                                    <array>
                                            <array>
                                                    <string>CN</string>
                                                    <string>User Device Cert</string>
                                            </array>
                                    </array>
                            </array>
                            <key>Challenge</key>
                            <string>...</string>
                            <key>Keysize</key>
                            <integer>1024</integer>
                            <key>Key Type</key>
                            <string>RSA</string>
                            <key>Key Usage</key>
                            <integer>5</integer>
                    </dict>
                    <key>PayloadDescription</key>
                    <string>Provides device encryption identity</string>
                    <key>PayloadUUID</key>
                    <string>fd8a6b9e-0fed-406f-9571-8ec98722b713</string>
                    <key>PayloadType</key>
                    <string>com.acmecorp.security.scep</string>
                    <key>PayloadDisplayName</key>
                    <string>Acme Encryption Identity</string>
                    <key>PayloadVersion</key>
                    <integer>1</integer>
                    <key>PayloadOrganization</key>
                    <string>Acme Corp</string>
                <key>PayloadIdentifier</key>

                    <string>com.acmecorp.profile.scep</string>
                </dict>
            </array>
        </dict>
    </plist>
```

Programmatically via iPCU

The iPhone Configuration Utility provides programmatic access to the API with the iPCUScripting.dll. To simplify development through access to IntelliSense code autocompletion, this DLL (located in the iPhone Configuration Utility folder under Program Files on Windows) can be added as a reference to a project in Visual Studio. But in order to use the scripting capabilities, the .cs file containing a class that inherits from the IScript interface (as shown in the following code snippet) must be executed by passing the .cs file into the iPhone Configuration Utility as a command line parameter upon launch of the application.

```
using System;
using Com.Apple.iPCUScripting;

public class TestScript : IScript
{
      private IApplication _host;
      public TestScript()
      {
      }
      public void main(IApplication inHost)
      {
        _host = inHost;
        string message = string.Format("Config profile Count : {0}",
        host.ConfigurationProfiles.Count);
        Console.WriteLine(message);
        IConfigurationProfile profile = _host.AddConfigurationProfile();
        profile.Name = "Acme Corp Scripted Profile";
        profile.Identifier = "com.acmecorp.config";
        profile.Organization = "Acme Corp";
        profile.Description = "Acme Corp Configuration Profile";
        // Passcode Payload
        IPasscodePayload passcodePayload = profile.AddPasscodePayload();
        passcodePayload.PasscodeRequired = true;
        passcodePayload.AllowSimple = true;
        // Restrictions Payload
        IRestrictionsPayload restrictionsPayload =
        profile.AddRestrictionsPayload();
        restrictionsPayload.AllowYouTube = false;
        // Wi-Fi Payload
        IWiFiPayload wifiPayload = profile.AddWiFiPayload();
        wifiPayload.ServiceSetIdentifier = "WPA Wi-Fi";
        wifiPayload.EncryptionType = WirelessEncryptionType.WPA;
        wifiPayload.Password = "WPAWiFiPassword";
        wifiPayload = profile.AddWiFiPayload();
        profile.RemoveWiFiPayload(wifiPayload);
        // VPN Payload
```

```
        IVPNPayload vpnPayload = profile.AddVPNPayload();
        vpnPayload.ConnectionName = "Acme Corp VPN";
        vpnPayload = profile.AddVPNPayload();
        profile.RemoveVPNPayload(vpnPayload);
        // Exchange Payload
        IExchangePayload exchangePayload = profile.AddExchangePayload();
        exchangePayload.AccountName = "AcmeExchangeAccount";
        // Webclip Payload
        IWebClipPayload wcPayload = profile.AddWebClipPayload();
        wcPayload.Label = "Acme Corp App Catalog Web Clip ";
        wcPayload = profile.AddWebClipPayload();
        wcPayload.Label = "Acme Corp Default Web Clip";
    }
}
```

NOTE The C# .NET code included in these iPCU scripts is not compiled ahead of time, but rather is compiled at run time using Reflection.Emit.

Using a Third-Party Solution

In addition to creating configuration profiles manually with the iPhone Configuration Utility, or programmatically by generating the XML or integrating with the iPCU APIs, there are also a wide variety of third-party tools that provide administration consoles to assist with and simplify the process of creating configuration profiles. For the most part, these tools are part of a larger MDM solution, which is covered in Chapter 20, where more than a dozen third-party vendors are identified. Since one of the primary purposes of an MDM solution is to deploy configurations and enforce security policies, the ability to generate iOS configuration profiles from within the MDM administration console is a feature that should be taken into consideration as part of any MDM evaluation and selection.

Summary

In this chapter, you examined the process of configuring and provisioning iOS devices as part of an enterprise deployment. The enrollment process can be done manually, or automated through a process called SCEP. Configuration profiles are the basis for configuring iOS devices and enforcing security policies or usage restrictions, and can be strategically used as part of a carrot-and-stick approach towards enterprise mobility. Configuration profiles can also be created through the iPhone Configuration Utility, XML generation, C# .NET scripting, or third-party tools.

In the next chapter, you'll look at the options for deploying applications, managing updates, and facilitating over-the-air deployment of in-house applications.

Deploying Applications Over the Air

WHAT'S IN THIS CHAPTER?

- Using App Store vs. Ad Hoc vs. Enterprise distribution
- Creating an in-house catalog for internal apps
- Facilitating over-the-air app installation
- Updating management for internal apps
- Using a third-party solution for creating an app catalog

Now that you've determined the best hardware deployment approach and properly secured and provisioned the devices, it's time to deploy software to the mobile hardware.

First, you'll look at the three deployment models for distributing applications publicly through the App Store, privately for testing through Ad Hoc deployments, and internally to an organization for enterprise applications.

Then you'll look at the mechanics of actually deploying native applications over the air by using a special Apple-provided custom URI scheme, along with an XML-based application manifest file, the binary, and any resources or metadata.

You'll also examine the different approaches for creating an internal app catalog and deploying it, either through a Web Clip or as a native application. After the applications are deployed, you'll look at the different ways the applications can be kept up to date.

And while this is a capability that can be built internally, there is also the option of using a third-party vendor to obtain these features off the shelf.

Selecting the Deployment Model

When it comes to deploying iOS applications, three different deployment models can be used: App Store, Ad Hoc, and Enterprise. There is not a right or wrong deployment model; they're all different, and in fact most enterprises will use a combination of all three. It's important to understand each model and how it works so that the appropriate deployment model can be used for any given situation.

App Store

If your application is targeting external customers or business partners, then it's likely that an App Store deployment model is most appropriate for your application. In order to distribute an application through the App Store, you must have a standard iOS developer account. This account costs $99 a year and can be obtained as either an individual or an organizational account.

Applications can be distributed through the App Store either free of charge or for a predetermined price. If it is a paid app, Apple will retain 30 percent of the revenue and the developer will receive 70 percent as payment. For free apps, there is no charge to the developer beyond the $99 annual fee.

Just because an application is distributed through the public App Store does not mean that the functionality and data within the application are public. Companies can require a login account to use the application and can restrict access to those with login credentials, for instance customers, business partners, or employees. Of course, in order to receive approval from Apple to be distributed through the App Store, the app must be submitted to Apple for evaluation, and a user account must be provided to Apple in order to test it. In addition to this, another popular approach is to create an application that contains public functionality and additional features and capabilities that can be unlocked when used by authorized users like customers, business partners, and employees.

Ad Hoc

If your deployment is limited to 100 devices or fewer, then Ad Hoc deployment may be appropriate for your application. Generally speaking, Ad Hoc deployments are best used for testing and possibly even piloting applications to a relatively small number of users. If you're preparing to deploy to the App Store, but you want to deploy the app for testing before submitting it to Apple for approval, Ad Hoc is the way to go.

Otherwise, if you're looking to deploy internal applications, the Enterprise deployment model is probably a better option. It used to be more difficult to get an iOS enterprise developer account, so Ad Hoc deployment was used by many smaller organizations for internal applications. As Apple loosened the restrictions around enterprise accounts, the need to jump through the additional hoops of registering each device for Ad Hoc app deployment became unnecessary for most organizations looking to facilitate deployment of internal apps.

In addition to the 100-device restriction, the biggest pain about the Ad Hoc deployment model is that the Unique Device IDentifier (UDID) must be registered with Apple through the developer portal in order to generate the provisioning profile that is used to "sign" the application bundle. This means that anytime you want to deploy an application to a new device through the Ad Hoc deployment model, you have to retrieve the device's UDID, submit it to Apple via the developer portal, and generate a new provisioning profile. This can add a lot of overhead to what is otherwise a very simple app deployment process.

Enterprise

For in-house applications, the Enterprise deployment model is likely the way to go. In order to do this, you must have an iOS enterprise developer account. (Organizations can and often do have an enterprise developer account in addition to a standard iOS developer account.) This account costs $399 a year and requires a legal contact with whom Apple can communicate. When dealing with the legal departments of many large organizations, this process can take weeks or even months, so don't procrastinate in starting the procurement process of your enterprise development account from Apple.

Up until late 2010, Apple had a restriction for enterprise accounts that required the organization to have a minimum of 500 employees. Since the only other alternative for companies with fewer than 500 employees was to use Ad Hoc deployment, which was limited to 100 devices, there were significant barriers to iOS in-house app development and adoption for many mid-sized organizations. In late 2010, though, Apple quietly lifted this restriction for 500 employees and now allows companies of all sizes to get an enterprise developer account.

Unlike the Ad Hoc deployment model, the Enterprise deployment model does not require that each device be registered with Apple, as the provisioning profile can be used by devices across the organization and is not linked to specific devices. This was one of the reasons Apple previously had so many restrictions on getting an enterprise developer account; it didn't want non-enterprise developers using it as a way to bypass Apple's approval process for the App Store.

As a precaution, Apple created a mechanism whereby the distribution certificate is automatically validated with an Apple server (`ocsp.apple.com`) the first time the application is run. This response is cached for a few days, but is regularly queried over time so that if Apple determines that the iOS enterprise developer account is being abused and the terms of service breached, it can remotely kill all apps built and deployed using the account.

Building an App Catalog

When it comes to building an application catalog, many different approaches can be taken. Of course, a catalog is not required in order to deploy an app, but as most enterprises begin to mature in their mobility strategies, their portfolios of applications will almost certainly contain more than one app, whether available publicly through the App Store or privately deployed over the air as in-house enterprise applications.

Your app catalog can be a combination of links to over-the-air installation packages of enterprise apps as well as to the iTunes App Store. This is important to recognize, since most enterprises will have a combination of internal and off-the-shelf applications (as discussed in Chapter 5). The app catalog can provide a similar experience to Apple's App Store, but can also provide a company-branded experience to both custom in-house apps and listings of company-approved or recommended apps. Also, as described in Chapter 5, there is currently no way for companies to buy bulk versions of paid applications, but as a workaround most enterprise software vendors are taking the approach of making the client iPad application free through the App Store, with the server or cloud-based service licensed separately.

In any case, app catalogs can either be Web Clips (which can be deployed over the air via configuration profiles and pushed via mobile device management (MDM), providing icons that link to HTML-based web apps, or they can be native enterprise apps. If the app catalog is delivered as a native app (as shown in Figure 19-1), the user must install it by clicking on a link (in e-mail, short-message service (SMS), or a web page) and accept the installation when prompted, as opposed to the Web Clip approach that can be "pushed" to the device via configuration profiles and MDM in the background, without requiring any user involvement.

Using Over-the-Air Deployment

While Apple's documentation focuses on the fact that over-the-air deployment works with the Enterprise deployment model, this same process works exactly the same way with the Ad Hoc deployment model.

This process is facilitated through a custom URI scheme called "itms-services," which stands for the iTunes Music Store Protocol. Under this custom URI scheme, the user navigates to a URL with a query string parameter of "action" that is set to "download-manifest" and another query string property of "url" that is set to the fully qualified URL of the application's PLIST-formatted XML manifest. The user will be prompted with a screen requesting permission to install the application.

Figure 19-1: Your in-house app catalog can either be a mobile website that can be deployed as a Web Clip or a native iOS app, shown here.

This `itms-services://` URL can be sent in an e-mail or a text message, or simply linked to from a website or from within a native application. Here is an example of how the URL can be embedded in an HTML link:

```
<a href="itms-services://?action=download-manifest&url=http://example.com/
manifest.plist">Install App</a>
```

The manifest file must be an XML file that follows Apple's PropertyList (PLIST) syntax in order to describe the various properties, attributes, and metadata of the application that is to be deployed over the air. This information is used to provide the device with all the information necessary to facilitate the installation of the application, as well as the appropriate metadata that is displayed to users as part of a prompt to request permission. This XML file can be a static file that resides on a web server, or it can be dynamically generated with PHP, Java, ASP.NET, or any other web server language or technology. Here is an example manifest file:

```
<!DOCTYPE plist PUBLIC "-//Apple//DTD PLIST 1.0//EN"
"http://www.apple.com/DTDs/PropertyList-1.0.dtd">
<plist version="1.0">
<dict>
    <!-- array of downloads if multiple apps are to be bundled -->
    <key>items</key>
```

```xml
<array>
    <dict>
        <!-- an array of assets to download -->
        <key>assets</key>
        <array>
        <!-- software-package: the ipa to install. -->
        <dict>
        <!-- required. the kind of asset. -->
        <key>kind</key>
        <string>software-package</string>
        <!-- optional. md5 every n bytes. will restart a chunk if
        md5 fails. -->
        <key>md5-size</key>
        <integer>10485760</integer>
        <!-- optional. array of md5 hashes for each "md5-size"
        Sized chunk. -->
        <key>md5s</key>
        <array>
        <string>41fa64bb7a7cae5a46bfb45821ac8bba</string>
        <string>51fa64bb7a7cae5a46bfb45821ac8bba</string>
        </array>
        <!-- required. the URL of the file to download. -->
        <key>url</key>
        <string>http://www.acmecorp.com/apps/sales.ipa</string>
        </dict>
        <!-- display-image: the icon to display during
            download.-->
        <dict>
            <key>kind</key>
            <string>display-image</string>
            <!-- optional. indicates if icon needs shine
effect applied.-->
            <key>needs-shine</key>
            <true/>
            <key>url</key>
            <string>http://www.
acmecorp.com/salesicon.57x57.png</string>
        </dict>
        <!-- full-size-image: the large 512x512 icon used by
            iTunes. -->
        <dict>
            <key>kind</key>
            <string>full-size-image</string>
            <!-- optional. one md5 hash for the entire file. -->
            <key>md5</key>
            <string>61fa64bb7a7cae5a46bfb45821ac8bba</string>
            <key>needs-shine</key>
            <true/>
            <key>url</key><string>http://www.
acmecorp.com/salesimage.512x512.jpg</string>
```

```
                    </dict>
                    </array><key>metadata</key>
                    <dict>
                          <!-- required -->
                          <key>bundle-identifier</key>
                          <string>com. acmecorp.sales</string>
                          <!-- optional (software only) -->
                          <key>bundle-version</key>
                          <string>1.0</string>
                          <!-- required. download kind of download. -->
                          <key>kind</key>
                          <string>software</string>
                          <!-- optional. displayed during download; typically
company name
-->
                          <key>subtitle</key>
                          <string>Acme Corp</string>
                          <!-- required. the title to display during the
download. -->
                          <key>title</key>
                         <string>Acme Sales</string>
                    </dict>
             </dict>
        </array>
    </dict>
    </plist>
```

Managing Application Updates

Unlike Apple's App Store, which automatically facilitates the updating process, an internal Enterprise app deployment is responsible for managing its own updating. Since each application is signed with an enterprise certificate that is valid for only a year, there will be a need to update applications over time. Additionally, changes in iOS may require updates to the app in order to take advantage of new features and capabilities.

As a result, both the in-house app catalog and the in-house apps themselves should keep track of application versioning and manage updates accordingly. For instance, every in-house app can be programmed to check for an updated version, and if it finds one, prompt the user to install it. It can be done in such a way that the user has a choice whether to upgrade or not, or the application can prevent itself from being used until the updated version is installed.

It's important for several reasons when updating applications that the updated app uses the same application bundle identifier (com.example.app). If it's different, both apps will remain on the device and it may be difficult for the user to determine which app is which. Additionally, any data stored within the application sandbox is tied to the bundle identifier. If an application update is installed on top of an existing app with the same bundle identifier, all the application and user data contained within the sandbox will remain untouched. If the user removes the app first, before installing the updated version, then all data will be lost. It's important to communicate this clearly to your users.

While this can be done through custom code, there are a variety of third-party vendors that provide both the logic in the pre-built app catalog template as well as a software development kit (SDK) that can be embedded within custom in-house apps to automatically detect and manage updates. For example, Apperian's app catalog, as shown in Figure 19-2, provides easy access to updates within its template app catalog as well as an SDK for the update capability to be easily included in custom apps.

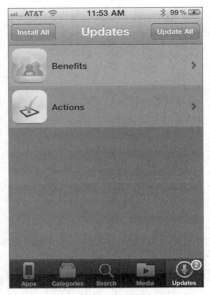

Figure 19-2: Managing application updates is the responsibility of each enterprise, so you can either build that capability internally or use a third-party solution.

Using a Third-Party Solution

In addition to the option of building an app catalog yourself, there is also the option of using a solution from a third-party vendor. There are a number of vendors with enterprise app catalog products. Most of those vendors offer the app catalog as part of an overall mobile device management (MDM) product, but there are also stand-alone products. The MDM vendors will be discussed in more detail in the next chapter, but for the stand-alone app catalog vendors, let's take a deeper look at a leading product from a company called Apperian, already mentioned in this chapter.

Apperian's offering (Figure 19-3) consists of a cloud-based app server that provides a web-based administration portal as well as private database and Active Directory proxy that can authenticate users for access to internal apps and facilitate Single Sign-On (SSO) capabilities within the custom apps themselves. Apperian also includes an iOS app template that can be customized to include a company's own brand and then dynamically serves up apps and updates as managed by the app server. The Apperian SDK allows in-house app developers to easily manage app versioning and updates, as well as track usage analytics and authenticate centrally through the same app server mechanism.

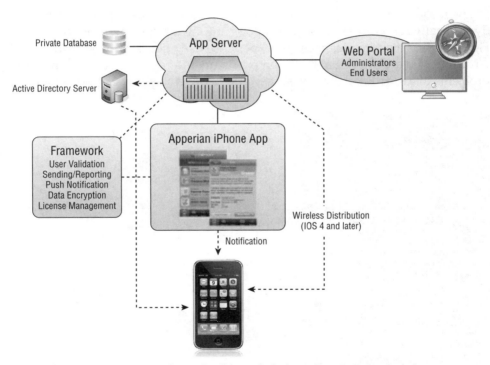

Figure 19-3: Apperian provides a cloud-based platform for managing in-house enterprise iOS app deployments.

The web-based management console (as shown in Figure 19-4) allows enterprise administrators to securely log in, upload, and configure apps, manage users and groups, and view analytics and usage reports.

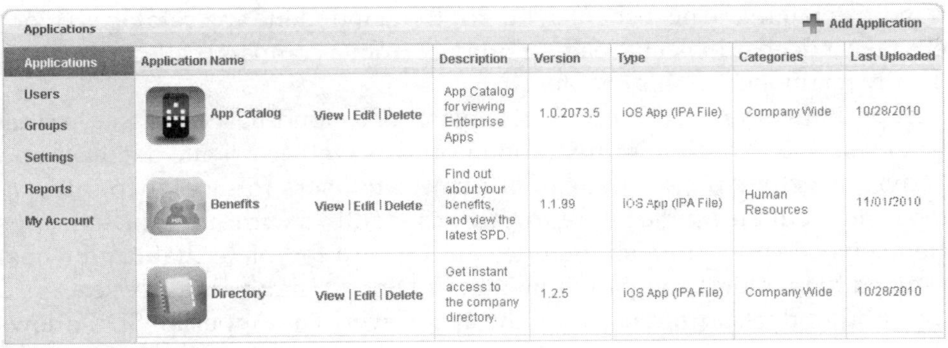
Applications
Add Application
Applications
Users
Groups
Settings
Reports
My Account
Application Name
Description
Version
Type
Categories
Last Uploaded
App Catalog
View | Edit | Delete
App Catalog for viewing Enterprise Apps
1.0.2073.5
iOS App (IPA File)
Company Wide
10/28/2010
Benefits
View | Edit | Delete
Find out about your benefits, and view the latest SPD.
1.1.99
iOS App (IPA File)
Human Resources
11/01/2010
Directory
View | Edit | Delete
Get instant access to the company directory.
1.2.5
iOS App (IPA File)
Company Wide
10/28/2010

Figure 19-4: Apperian's web-based app management console allows system administrators to upload and organize applications.

The information that is inputted to the web-based administration console is dynamically served up to the app catalog running on the iOS device (shown in Figure 19-5). This provides a similar experience to Apple's App Store, except that it is controlled and managed by the enterprise instead of Apple. Users can report problems that are routed directly to the appropriate enterprise support personnel.

AT&T
11:53 AM
99%
Apps
Info
Sales Training
INSTALL
The Sales Study Guide will help you master the information you need on our products and services. This helpful Guide is an exercise-based iPhone version of the company catalog, providing information on all of our products. Each product is provided in multiple formats, including text, graphics and video.
Report Problem
Related Media
Company Apperian, Inc.
Post Date Sep 10, 2010
Version 1.2
Size 345.3 KB
Apps
Categories
Search
Media
Updates

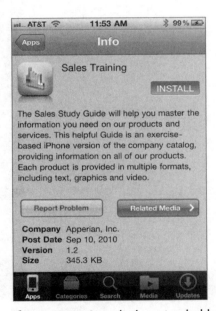

Figure 19-5: Apperian's customizable enterprise app catalog provides a similar user experience to Apple's own App Store.

As with Apple's App Store, internal apps can be grouped into different categories. According to the permissions for the currently authenticated user, Apperian's solution (as shown in Figure 19-6) displays only the categories of applications that the current user has permission to install.

Figure 19-6: Applications can be organized and viewed by categories from within Apperian's app catalog.

One unique feature provided by Apperian's solution is the ability to centrally manage and deploy media files, like images, videos, documents, or files of a custom file format that can be associated with custom in-house applications (illustrated in Figure 19-7). This can help organizations keep content up to date and distribute it to users when and where they need it.

Apperian is just one of many vendors offering functionality that can be relatively simple to develop in-house. Many of the MDM vendors discussed in the next chapter provide very similar functionality and capabilities, but if you go with an MDM approach that doesn't include an app catalog feature, then Apperian is one option to consider.

Figure 19-7: A unique feature provided by Apperian's app catalog is the ability to push media and content to iOS devices for easy consumption by users.

Summary

Once you've developed your in-house enterprise apps and have deployed your hardware, you need to install the software on your users' devices. There are three ways this can be accomplished: the App Store, Ad Hoc, or Enterprise deployment models. Depending on the application and the situation, any of those three models can be appropriate options, and most organizations will utilize a combination of all three. Additionally, since most companies will deploy more than one in-house app, providing your users with an in-house catalog can offer a lot of value and empower users with a self-service capability on a par with Apple's own App Store. Facilitating the deployment of applications and the update of those apps is a relatively straightforward process, but you don't have to reinvent the wheel, since there are a number of third-party vendors that offer pre-built solutions to accomplish this.

In the next chapter, you'll dig into the concepts and vendors involved in mobile device management. Many of those same third parties will also provide the app catalog capabilities discussed in this chapter.

CHAPTER 20

Managing and Securing the Deployment

WHAT'S IN THIS CHAPTER?

- Using Exchange ActiveSync to enforce security policies
- Understanding how Apple's iOS MDM APIs work
- Third-party MDM vendors that support Apple's iOS APIs
- How do the MDM vendors provide differentiation?
- Evaluating MDM vendors based on your specific needs

In the last several chapters, you've examined the process of planning a deployment and selecting the proper approaches. You've looked into the details of provisioning and configuring the devices, as well as the different methods to deploy applications to the mobile device.

Now in this chapter, and to round out the section of the book on deployment, you're going to examine the details about managing and securing a deployment of iOS devices like the iPad.

First, you're going to look at the two primary ways to manage iOS devices by enforcing security policies and performing actions upon them, like remotely wiping the devices when lost or stolen. These basic management capabilities can be provided by both Exchange ActiveSync (EAS) as well as Apple's iOS MDM application programming interfaces (APIs). EAS provides more basic features, while MDM offers more advanced capabilities.

You'll dig into the details of Apple's iOS MDM capabilities and how it actually works, as well as take a look at a list of some of the dozens of third-party vendors that have offerings in this industry. Since the vendors are limited by the APIs that Apple provides them, most of the features of the different products from the various vendors are quite similar, so we'll examine the areas of primary differentiation among the vendors and their various products.

Using Exchange ActiveSync

As discussed earlier in the book, one of the most interesting developments in the mobile industry over the last few years has been the industry-wide standardization on Exchange ActiveSync (EAS) for both server-side and mobile device communication and collaboration data synchronization.

In addition to providing push synchronization of mail, calendar, and contacts to iOS devices, EAS also provides the ability to enforce security policies as well as remotely wipe devices if they are lost or stolen. Although EAS does not offer as many features or capabilities as Apple's MDM APIs, EAS may provide enough features for some organizations to be comfortable with the security of iOS.

Enforcing Policies

When a policy is applied to Exchange ActiveSync, users will be forced to comply with the policy or they will be unable to connect their devices to sync with the Exchange server. In some cases, like requiring a passcode or establishing a specific passcode complexity requirement, users will be prompted to configure their devices accordingly. Other policies, like requiring device encryption, are completely dependent on the device hardware (and in that specific case will allow only iOS devices with hardware-based encryption to connect, which includes all iPads and iPhone 3GS and newer but not older iOS devices).

Exchange ActiveSync (EAS) for Exchange Server 2003 SP2 supports enforcement of several basic policies on iOS devices:

- Enforce passcode on device (DevicePasswordEnabled)
- Minimum passcode length (MinDevicePasswordLength)
- Maximum failed passcode attempts (MaxDevicePasswordFailedAttempts)
- Passcode requires both numbers and letters (AlphanumericPasswordEnabled)
- Inactivity time in minutes (MaxInactivityTimeDeviceLock)

Additionally, Exchange ActiveSync (EAS) for Exchange Server 2007 SP1 and Exchange Server 2010 support the enforcement of many additional policies on iOS devices:

- Enforce passcode on device (DevicePasswordEnabled)
- Prohibit simple passcode (AllowSimpleDevicePassword)
- Passcode expiration in days (DevicePasswordExpiration)

- Passcode history (DevicePasswordHistory)
- Minimum number of complex characters in passcode (MinDevice PasswordComplexCharacters)
- Require manual syncing while roaming (RequireManualSyncWhenRoaming)
- Allow camera (AllowCamera)
- Allow web browser (AllowBrowser)
- Maximum age of e-mail messages synced (MaxEmailAgeFilter)
- Require device encryption (RequireDeviceEncryption)

While EAS supports even more policies than these, the ones listed here are the only EAS policies that are currently supported by iOS.

Remote Wipe

In addition to enforcing security policies, EAS provides a mechanism for remotely wiping a device if it is lost or stolen. Keep in mind that this will wipe the entire device, including all apps, data, pictures, videos, music, and anything else, whether personal or business-related. Due to the potential legal liability associated with deleting personal content and data on personally owned devices, many organizations require that users sign a legal agreement acknowledging that the company has the right to remotely wipe the device, including any personal information.

Using Mobile Device Management

For many organizations, the device management capabilities provided by EAS are not satisfactory to meet security compliance requirements. Apple listened to the enterprise community and with iOS 4.x introduced a number of MDM APIs that provide enterprise IT organizations significantly more control than was previously available. In the process, dozens of third-party MDM vendors have appeared in the marketplace. Since the vendors are limited by the capabilities of the iOS MDM APIs provided by Apple, many organizations have found the MDM landscape confusing in determining exactly what's different among the various MDM solutions and vendors. In order to clear up some of the confusion, let's examine how Apple's MDM capabilities work on iOS.

Understanding MDM

Apple's iOS MDM APIs are based upon a relatively simple architecture. Unlike many prior device management architectures used on other mobile platforms,

Apple decided to piggy-back on the same unified Apple Push Notification Service (APNS). This is the same channel that application developers can use to deliver push notifications to individual users' devices, and it also powers communication initiation for Apple's FaceTime service.

Once a device has been enrolled with an MDM server, the server can apply a configuration policy, make a management change, or query a device attribute by sending a device-specific notification through APNS. When the device receives the push notification, it gets a message that the MDM server requests contact. Rather than displaying a message like other push notifications, this MDM process runs quietly in the background.

When the device gets a request from the MDM server, it then opens a connection to the MDM server and requests whatever the MDM server has waiting for it. This can include a batch of management requests, configuration or provisioning profiles to be applied, or queries to be responded to. This process is shown in Figure 20-1.

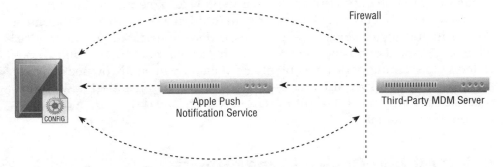

Figure 20-1: In order to save battery life and be more efficient overall, Apple's approach to MDM does not include a stand-alone device management "agent," but rather uses the existing Apple Push Notification Service.

It's important to understand that the configuration profiles, queries, and responses do not go through the Apple Push Notification Service. The APNs only acts as a trigger to let the device know that it needs to contact the MDM server.

Enroll

The MDM enrollment process generally follows the same Simple Certificate Enrollment Protocol (SCEP) that was described in Chapter 18. Rather than deploying specific service configurations like EAS or VPN, though, a configuration profile containing an MDM payload would be delivered. Then, after the device has been enrolled in MDM, the MDM server can push and manage any additional configuration profiles to the device.

Configure

Once an iOS device has been enrolled in MDM, the management server has the ability to configure the devices by adding or removing configuration profiles. The configuration profiles are exactly the same as those discussed in Chapter 18, except that when deployed via MDM the user is not prompted and the configuration profiles can be silently applied and updated in the background transparently to the user.

Query

In addition to managing configuration and provisioning profiles, the iOS MDM APIs also allow the MDM server to query many different attributes of the device hardware, communications information, compliance and security, and application-related data.

Device Information:

- Unique Device Identifier (UDID)
- Device name
- iOS and build version
- Model name and number
- Serial number
- Capacity and space available
- International Mobile Equipment Identity (IMEI)
- Modem firmware

Communication Information:

- Integrated Circuit Card ID (ICCID)
- Bluetooth and Wi-Fi MAC addresses
- Current carrier network
- Subscriber Identity Module (SIM) carrier network
- Carrier settings version
- Phone number
- Data roaming setting (on/off)

Compliance and Security Information:

- Configuration Profiles installed
- Certificates installed with expiration dates

- List of all restrictions enforced
- Hardware encryption capability
- Passcode present

Applications Information:

- Applications installed (app ID, name, version, size, and size of app data)
- Provisioning profiles installed with expiration dates

Manage

Finally, the iOS MDM APIs allow for several important management actions that can be performed on a device: remote wipe, remote lock, and clear passcode, and the ability to apply configuration and provisioning profiles.

Remote Wipe

While most iOS deployments will also use EAS, it's important to note that this remote wipe capability is distinct and independent from the remote wipe capability of EAS. This is significant, because there is often the need for task-based iPad deployments or shared devices where EAS is not appropriate but the ability to remotely wipe the device is critical.

Remote Lock

If a remote device is misplaced, lost, or stolen, and if it does not already contain a passcode, one can be applied remotely to prevent prying eyes from accessing information contained on the device.

Clear Passcode

Users will occasionally forget their passcodes, and if the device is configured to wipe itself after a certain number of failed login attempts, it can be valuable to allow IT to centrally reset passcodes for individual users.

Apply Configuration and Provisioning Profiles

Configuration profiles can be applied to and removed from managed devices silently in the background without prompting the user. As described in Chapter 18, configuration profiles can hold payloads including account settings, security policies, device restrictions, certificates, and Web Clips. Additionally, MDM-enrolled devices can have enterprise provisioning profiles added to and removed from devices — profiles which must be present on a device in order for an in-house enterprise app to execute.

Third-Party Vendors

The Mobile Device Management marketplace has recently seen explosive growth. As a result, there is currently a very rapid pace of development and innovation that will likely continue for the foreseeable future. Until the market matures somewhat and we see some consolidation of the MDM vendors, it can be a full-time job just staying on top of all the developments in the industry. As a result, this is not an exhaustive list of iOS MDM vendors, and it's also very likely that many of the vendors listed here will consolidate as clear leaders emerge and other large software firms decide to get into this space through acquisitions.

As this industry is undergoing such rapid change, the capabilities and features of each vendor's solution will not be covered in the book, as this would be quickly out of date. Each vendor's listing includes a self-description. Following the list of vendors is a collection of criteria that can be used to evaluate and compare vendors to determine the right solution for your organization.

Absolute Manage

"Absolute® Software specializes in software and services for the management and security of computers and mobile devices. Absolute Manage for Mobile Device Management allows you to remotely manage iPhone, iPod Touch, and iPad devices in your deployment."

Afaria by Sybase

"Afaria enables enterprises to manage and secure iPhones and iPads for business use. Afaria enables easy configuration and set-up over the air, ongoing management, and the ability to selectively or fully wipe enterprise data. Overall, Afaria enables personally owned or corporate-owned iOS devices to be confidently secured in the enterprise."

AirWatch

"Designed to secure, monitor, manage, and support all mobile devices deployed across your enterprise, AirWatch reduces the challenges associated with mobility. AirWatch's comprehensive MDM functionality for iOS 4 devices includes over-the-air enrollment, configuration, security policies and restrictions, real-time monitoring of device and network information, encryption, certificates, application, and configuration settings."

BoxTone

"Simplify management of the full mobile lifecycle: self-provision, secure, configure, support, optimize. Automate deployment and enforcement of security and compliance. Publish internal app catalog. Monitor real-time mobile service health and performance with diagnostics for efficient support. Enterprise-grade: proven in Fortune 100, but designed for all. Mobilize your business with BoxTone."

Good for Enterprise

"Good for Enterprise™ is a powerful, easy-to-use mobility suite that supports mobile collaboration with a great end-user experience on popular handhelds like the iPhone and iPad without compromising IT security and control. Because security and compliance are major concerns for businesses, Good for Enterprise is built on a proven security architecture that has been adopted by top Fortune 500 companies and government agencies, including the Department of Defense."

IBELEM

"IBELEM has been an Enterprise Mobile Management Solution since 2001. IBELEM is a mobility software editor and an expert in integrating and managing mobility solutions dedicated to iPhone and iPad. IBELEM brings visibility, security, and facility in mobile fleet management. IBELEM's cutting-edge solutions remotely supervise your users, devices, applications, and mobile infrastructure."

JAMF

"JAMF Software, founded in 2002 and headquartered in Minneapolis, MN, is the creator of the Casper Suite, the only suite of client management software developed exclusively for the Apple platform. Within a single comprehensive console, the Casper Suite features broad management capabilities for iOS devices and Mac OS X computers."

McAfee Enterprise Mobility Management

"McAfee Enterprise Mobility Management (McAfee EMM) is an award-winning solution that enables enterprises to offer employees mobile device choice while delivering secure and easy access to mobile corporate applications. With secure mobile application access, strong authentication, high availability, scalable architecture, and compliance reporting in a seamless system, McAfee EMM brings the same level of control to mobile devices — including employee-owned smartphones — that IT applies to laptops and desktops."

MobileIron

"MobileIron is solving the problems CIOs face as enterprise data moves to the smartphone. The MobileIron Virtual Smartphone Platform is the first solution to give IT and users real-time intelligence and control over smartphone content, activity, and apps in order to secure the enterprise, reduce wireless cost, and improve the mobile user experience."

SOTI

"SOTI Inc. develops industry-leading technology that solves the unique challenges involved in managing, securing, supporting, and tracking remote mobile and desktop computing devices. Today, over 80,000 customers around the world rely on SOTI products to reduce costs by enabling the central management, security, and support of remote mobile field-forces. SOTI's innovative technology now allows Apple iOS 4+ devices to be managed in a brand new multi-platform web console anywhere at any time."

Tangoe

"Tangoe integrates Mobile Device Management with Telecom Expense Management to provide enterprise smartphone users with unparalleled support, increased device and data security, and lower usage costs. Tangoe's MDM solution increases employee productivity and drives down costs by centralizing device visibility, maximizing application control, and ensuring security policy enforcement."

Tarmac by Equinux

"Equinux, with its headquarters in Munich, Germany, and U.S. office located in South San Francisco, CA, develops and distributes market-leading solutions for Mac, iPhone, and iPad for both private and professional use. With TARMAC you can tailor any iPhone or iPad in your enterprise to your specifications. Set up iPhones over the air and remotely administer secure, personalized profiles."

ubitexx by Research in Motion

"ubitexx is a software company specializing in the development of innovative mobile device and security management solutions for smartphones in the enterprise. The company was founded in 2002 with headquarters in Munich, Germany, and now has over 30 employees. Since 2009 IDC and Forrester Research have listed ubitexx among the world's leading providers." In May 2011, Research in Motion (RIM) announced support for the management of iOS services from a unified web-based console for the BlackBerry Enterprise Server via RIM's pending acquisition of ubitexx.

Zenprise

"Zenprise enables large enterprises to configure, manage and deploy employee- and corporate-owned iOS devices. The software is up and running within hours and scales to support 50,000+ users on a single server. Zenprise was founded in 2003 and has received the Gartner Cool Vendor & InfoWorld Technology of the Year awards."

Evaluating the Vendors

Due to the fundamental constraints within the iOS MDM environment, and the fact that there are so many vendors jumping into this industry, it's important to understand some of the primary criteria that can differentiate the different solutions provided by the vendors. I have worked with many customers in the evaluation of iOS MDM vendors, and the industry is emerging so rapidly and is so immature overall that it presents a unique challenge to enterprises looking to make the best decision based upon both short-term capabilities as well as long-term viability and potential for continued research and development and innovation. The following are some of the key criteria that can be used to organize, differentiate, and evaluate MDM vendors:

Approach

First of all, it's important to understand that not all the MDM vendors go about solving the problem of security the same way. There are two primary approaches that are the source of much confusion within the industry.

Apple's iOS MDM APIs

As discussed in the previous section, the majority of MDM vendors use Apple's APIs to enroll, configure, query, and manage devices. The vendors that take this approach are essentially equal in their security and management functions, in that they are limited by Apple in what they can do and its policies are enforced upon the device.

E-mail Replacement Sandbox

Before Apple offered MDM APIs with iOS 4.x, some MDM vendors, Good Technology for example, decided to take the approach of securing and managing a sandbox instead of the entire device. This was because an enterprise sandbox could be entirely controlled, but controlling, securing, and managing the device wasn't as fully possible.

Rather than using the device's built-in mail, calendar, and contacts application, Good Technology's approach is to replace those applications with a separate app sandbox that can provide an additional layer of security.

Again, it's important to remember that this sandbox-based approach used to be the only way to ensure a high level of security for corporate data on iOS, but since Apple has now released MDM APIs there is a lot of debate within the industry about whether this approach is still necessary.

Architecture

One of the biggest differences that will affect the overall flexibility and scalability of MDM solutions from the various vendors is the underlying solution architecture. There are three basic types of architecture: cloud, appliance, or on-premise. Some vendors offer all three architectures, while others offer just one or two. Also, some vendors offer portability of implementations between architectures (i.e., start in the cloud and move to on-premise or start with an appliance and move to the cloud).

Cloud

The cloud-based solutions provide mobile device management capabilities through a Software-as-a-Service (SaaS) model. The solution may be hosted in a data center by the MDM vendors themselves, or on a cloud platform from another vendor like the Amazon Elastic Compute Cloud (EC2), Rackspace Cloud, or Microsoft Azure.

The advantage of the cloud-based approach is very rapid deployment and implementation of an MDM solution, but the disadvantage is that many organizations remain uncomfortable with the security of solutions like this residing on someone else's infrastructure in the cloud.

Appliance

The appliance-based model allows MDM solutions to be sold as hardware that can be simply racked in a data center. Some MDM vendors have leveraged the simplicity of this approach and through Value-Added Resellers (VARs) have rapidly gained market share.

The advantage of the appliance-based approach is that the implementation and deployment are almost as simple as the cloud-based model but can be hosted in your own data center. The downside is that the "canned" solution provides limited flexibility in the potential configuration and implementation, and may not be as scalable as the other architectures.

On Premise

The on-premise hosted model is generally similar to the appliance model in which the server resides in your own data center, but rather than using a pre-configured appliance, the server software is installed and configured on your own server hardware and physical infrastructure. As a result, organizations can maintain higher levels of control and can theoretically scale as well as the cloud-based model (assuming the organization has the appropriate hardware and infrastructure) but can be hosted entirely within the organization's own data center.

The advantage of the on-premise approach is greater control, but the disadvantage can be potentially higher total cost of ownership and greater management overhead.

Management Console

In addition to underlying architecture, one of the biggest differentiators between MDM vendors is the management console, because this is the aspect of the solution that has the most visibility. Most vendors provide a web-based administration console, while other vendors provide plug-ins to existing infrastructure management consoles. Some may even provide iPad apps themselves as management interfaces, like the MobileIron Sentry application shown in Figure 20-2.

Provisioning

While the provisioning process is similar for most MDM vendors, some vendors provide unique capabilities for device provisioning that may be used in a device support depot to support centrally provisioned and configured device deployments. Depending on your organization's needs and approach to deployment provisioning, this may be an important criterion with which to evaluate vendors.

Integration

Some MDM vendors provide an API that can allow programmatic integration into the MDM platform. While this will not be a requirement for many organizations, some companies may find that it's easy to automate much of the administration by integrating with other internal systems or tools. The ability to access the MDM's capabilities programmatically (as by enforcing policies or querying device attributes) can provide significant value in terms of solution integration.

In-House App Sandbox Management

Some MDM vendors provide an SDK for in-house iOS application development to take advantage of pre-built features, like app Single Sign-On, data encryption, app analytics, and additional management of the application itself, above and beyond the device management capabilities that are constrained by Apple's MDM APIs.

In-House App Catalog Management

Some MDM vendors offer the capability to create an in-house app catalog similar to the stand-alone app catalog capabilities of Apperian, discussed in the previous chapter. While it's not necessary for an MDM solution to also provide your in-house app catalog, some organizations prefer to have a single platform for both app and device management.

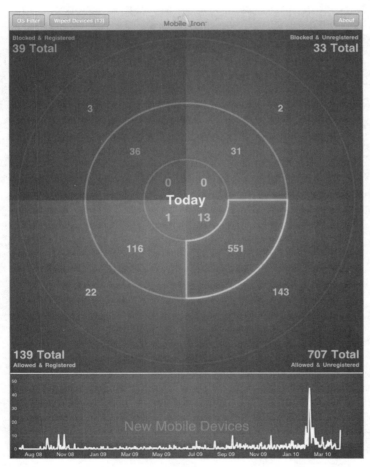

Figure 20-2: In addition to providing a web-based administration console, MobileIron also provides an iPad app called Sentry that gives administrators real-time visibility into their mobile device management infrastructure.

Support for Other Platforms

Because iOS-based MDM vendors are constrained by the APIs and capabilities provided by Apple, one of the widest variations in functionality across MDM vendors is support for other platforms beyond iOS. Some MDM vendors are iOS only, while others support various combinations of other platforms. It's also important to point out, though, that since Apple's approach to MDM is unique, it may be the best decision for your organization to have one MDM solution for iOS and a different MDM solution for other platforms. On the other hand, many organizations would prefer to consolidate their MDM solutions if possible; if they need to support and manage multiple platforms beyond iOS, then support for those platforms becomes critical in the evaluation of MDM solutions and vendors.

Summary

In this chapter, we looked at both EAS and third-party MDM solutions as ways to manage a deployment of iOS devices like the iPad. We looked at what EAS is capable of doing, and contrasted that with the more advanced features and management capabilities of the Apple iOS MDM APIs implemented through various third-party vendors. Since most of the vendors' products do basically the same thing, we also covered the primary areas of differentiation between the different products and vendors.

Index

Index